HOMO LUDENS

HOMO LUDENS

A STUDY OF THE PLAY-ELEMENT IN CULTURE

by

J. HUIZINGA

GYAN

Published by

Gyan Publishing House
5, Ansari Road
Daryaganj, New Delhi-110002
Phone: 011-47034999, 9811692060
E-mail: books@gyanbooks.com

Distribution Network
gyanbooks.com
India, USA, Canada, UK, Australia

ISBN: 978-93-6208-034-9 (HB)
First Published, 1938

2nd Impression 2024

Printed at: Gyan Press, Delhi.

HOMO LUDENS
Author: J. HUIZINGA

HOMO LUDENS

A STUDY OF THE PLAY-ELEMENT IN CULTURE

by

J. HUIZINGA

THE BEACON PRESS BOSTON

TABLE OF CONTENTS

	Translator's Note	vii
	Foreword	ix
I	Nature and Significance of Play as a Cultural Phenomenon	1
II	The Play-Concept as Expressed in Language	28
III	Play and Contest as Civilizing Functions	46
IV	Play and Law	76
V	Play and War	89
VI	Playing and Knowing	105
VII	Play and Poetry	119
VIII	The Elements of Mythopoiesis	136
IX	Play-Forms in Philosophy	146
X	Play-Forms in Art	158
XI	Western Civilization *Sub Specie Ludi*	173
XII	The Play-Element in Contemporary Civilization	195
	Index	214

TRANSLATOR'S NOTE

This edition is prepared from the German edition published in Switzerland, 1944, and also from the author's own English translation of the text, which he made shortly before his death. Comparison of the two texts shows a number of discrepancies and a marked difference in style; the translator hopes that the following version has achieved a reasonable synthesis.

FOREWORD

A HAPPIER age than ours once made bold to call our species by the name of *Homo Sapiens*. In the course of time we have come to realize that we are not so reasonable after all as the Eighteenth Century, with its worship of reason and its naive optimism, thought us; hence modern fashion inclines to designate our species as *Homo Faber:* Man the Maker. But though *faber* may not be quite so dubious as *sapiens* it is, as a name specific of the human being, even less appropriate, seeing that many animals too are makers. There is a third function, however, applicable to both human and animal life, and just as important as reasoning and making—namely, playing. It seems to me that next to *Homo Faber*, and perhaps on the same level as *Homo Sapiens*, Homo Ludens, Man the Player, deserves a place in our nomenclature.

It is ancient wisdom, but it is also a little cheap, to call all human activity "play". Those who are willing to content themselves with a metaphysical conclusion of this kind should not read this book. Nevertheless, we find no reason to abandon the notion of play as a distinct and highly important factor in the world's life and doings. For many years the conviction has grown upon me that civilization arises and unfolds in and as play. Traces of such an opinion are to be found in my writings ever since 1903. I took it as the theme for my annual address as Rector of Leyden University in 1933, and afterwards for lectures in Zürich, Vienna and London, in the last instance under the title: "The Play Element of Culture". Each time my hosts wanted to correct it to "in" Culture, and each time I protested and clung to the genitive,* because it was not my object to define the place of play among all the other manifestations of culture, but rather to ascertain how far culture itself bears the character of play. The aim of the present full-length study is to try to integrate the concept of play into that of culture. Consequently, play is to be understood here not as a biological phenomenon but as a cultural phenomenon. It is approached historically, not scientifically. The reader will find that I have made next to no use of any psycho-

* Logically, of course, Huizinga is correct; but as English prepositions are not governed by logic I have retained the more euphonious ablative in this sub-title.—Trans.

logical interpretations of play however important these may be, and that I have employed anthropological terms and explanations but sparingly, even where I have had to quote ethnological facts. He will find no mention of *mana* and the like, and hardly any of magic. Were I compelled to put my argument tersely in the form of theses, one of them would be that anthropology and its sister sciences have so far laid too little stress on the concept of play and on the supreme importance to civilization of the play-factor.

The reader of these pages should not look for detailed documentation of every word. In treating of the general problems of culture one is constantly obliged to undertake predatory incursions into provinces not sufficiently explored by the raider himself. To fill in all the gaps in my knowledge beforehand was out of the question for me. I had to write now, or not at all. And I wanted to write.

Leyden,

June 1938.

HOMO LUDENS

I

NATURE AND SIGNIFICANCE OF PLAY AS A CULTURAL PHENOMENON

PLAY is older than culture, for culture, however inadequately defined, always presupposes human society, and animals have not waited for man to teach them their playing. We can safely assert, even, that human civilization has added no essential feature to the general idea of play. Animals play just like men. We have only to watch young dogs to see that all the essentials of human play are present in their merry gambols. They invite one another to play by a certain ceremoniousness of attitude and gesture. They keep to the rule that you shall not bite, or not bite hard, your brother's ear. They pretend to get terribly angry. And—what is most important—in all these doings they plainly experience tremendous fun and enjoyment. Such rompings of young dogs are only one of the simpler forms of animal play. There are other, much more highly developed forms: regular contests and beautiful performances before an admiring public.

Here we have at once a very important point: even in its simplest forms on the animal level, play is more than a mere physiological phenomenon or a psychological reflex. It goes beyond the confines of purely physical or purely biological activity. It is a *significant* function—that is to say, there is some sense to it. In play there is something "at play" which transcends the immediate needs of life and imparts meaning to the action. All play means something. If we call the active principle that makes up the essence of play, "instinct", we explain nothing; if we call it "mind" or "will" we say too much. However we may regard it, the very fact that play has a meaning implies a non-materialistic quality in the nature of the thing itself.

Psychology and physiology deal with the observation, description and explanation of the play of animals, children, and grown-ups. They try to determine the nature and significance of play and to assign it its place in the scheme of life. The high importance of this place and the necessity, or at least the utility, of play as a function are generally taken for granted and form the starting-point of all such scientific researches. The numerous attempts to define the biological function of play show a striking variation. By some the origin and fundamentals of play have been described as a discharge of superabundant vital energy, by others as the satisfaction of some "imitative instinct", or again as simply a "need" for relaxation. According to one theory play constitutes a training of the young creature for the serious work that life will demand later on. According to another it serves as an exercise in restraint needful to the individual. Some find the principle of play in an innate urge to exercise a certain faculty, or in the desire to dominate or compete. Yet others regard it as an "abreaction"—an outlet for harmful impulses, as the necessary restorer of energy wasted by one-sided activity, as "wish-fulfilment", as a fiction designed to keep up the feeling of personal value, etc.[1]

All these hypotheses have one thing in common: they all start from the assumption that play must serve something which is *not* play, that it must have some kind of biological purpose. They all enquire into the why and the wherefore of play. The various answers they give tend rather to overlap than to exclude one another. It would be perfectly possible to accept nearly all the explanations without getting into any real confusion of thought—and without coming much nearer to a real understanding of the play-concept. They are all only partial solutions of the problem. If any of them were really decisive it ought either to exclude all the others or comprehend them in a higher unity. Most of them only deal incidentally with the question of what play is *in itself* and what it means for the player. They attack play direct with the quantitative methods of experimental science without first paying attention to its profoundly aesthetic quality. As a rule they leave the primary quality of play as such, virtually untouched. To each and every one of the above "explanations" it might well be objected: "So far so good, but what actually is the *fun* of playing? Why does the baby crow with pleasure? Why does the gambler lose himself in his passion? Why is a huge crowd roused to frenzy by a football match?" This intensity of, and absorption in, play finds no explanation in biological analysis. Yet in this intensity, this absorption, this power of maddening, lies the very

[1]For these theories see H. Zondervan, *Het Spel bij Dieren, Kinderen en Volwassen Menschen* (Amsterdam, 1928), and F. J. J. Buytendijk, *Het Spel van Mensch en Diet als openbaring van levensdriften* (Amsterdam, 1932).

essence, the primordial quality of play. Nature, so our reasoning mind tells us, could just as easily have given her children all those useful functions of discharging superabundant energy, of relaxing after exertion, of training for the demands of life, of compensating for unfulfilled longings, etc., in the form of purely mechanical exercises and reactions. But no, she gave us play, with its tension, its mirth, and its fun.

Now this last-named element, the *fun* of playing, resists all analysis, all logical interpretation. As a concept, it cannot be reduced to any other mental category. No other modern language known to me has the exact equivalent of the English "fun". The Dutch "aardigkeit" perhaps comes nearest to it (derived from "aard" which means the same as "Art" and "Wesen"[1] in German, and thus evidence, perhaps, that the matter cannot be reduced further). We may note in passing that "fun" in its current usage is of rather recent origin. French, oddly enough, has no corresponding term at all; German half makes up for it by "Spass" and "Witz" together. Nevertheless it is precisely this fun-element that characterizes the essence of play. Here we have to do with an absolutely primary category of life, familiar to everybody at a glance right down to the animal level. We may well call play a "totality" in the modern sense of the word, and it is as a totality that we must try to understand and evaluate it.

Since the reality of play extends beyond the sphere of human life it cannot have its foundations in any rational nexus, because this would limit it to mankind. The incidence of play is not associated with any particular stage of civilization or view of the universe. Any thinking person can see at a glance that play is a thing on its own, even if his language possesses no general concept to express it. Play cannot be denied. You can deny, if you like, nearly all abstractions: justice, beauty, truth, goodness, mind, God. You can deny seriousness, but not play.

But in acknowledging play you acknowledge mind, for whatever else play is, it is not matter. Even in the animal world it bursts the bounds of the physically existent. From the point of view of a world wholly determined by the operation of blind forces, play would be altogether superfluous. Play only becomes possible, thinkable and understandable when an influx of *mind* breaks down the absolute determinism of the cosmos. The very existence of play continually confirms the supra-logical nature of the human

[1]Nature, kind, being, essence, etc. Trans.

situation. Animals play, so they must be more than merely mechanical things. We play and know that we play, so we must be more than merely rational beings, for play is irrational.

In tackling the problem of play as a function of culture proper and not as it appears in the life of the animal or the child, we begin where biology and psychology leave off. In culture we find play as a given magnitude existing before culture itself existed, accompanying it and pervading it from the earliest beginnings right up to the phase of civilization we are now living in. We find play present everywhere as a well-defined quality of action which is different from "ordinary" life. We can disregard the question of how far science has succeeded in reducing this quality to quantitative factors. In our opinion it has not. At all events it is precisely this quality, itself so characteristic of the form of life we call "play", which matters. Play as a special form of activity, as a "significant form", as a social function—that is our subject. We shall not look for the natural impulses and habits conditioning play in general, but shall consider play in its manifold concrete forms as itself a social construction. We shall try to take play as the player himself takes it: in its primary significance. If we find that play is based on the manipulation of certain images, on a certain "imagination" of reality (i.e. its conversion into images), then our main concern will be to grasp the value and significance of these images and their "imagination". We shall observe their action in play itself and thus try to understand play as a cultural factor in life.

The great archetypal activities of human society are all permeated with play from the start. Take language, for instance—that first and supreme instrument which man shapes in order to communicate, to teach, to command. Language allows him to distinguish, to establish, to state things; in short, to name them and by naming them to raise them into the domain of the spirit. In the making of speech and language the spirit is continually "sparking" between matter and mind, as it were, playing with this wondrous nominative faculty. Behind every abstract expression there lie the boldest of metaphors, and every metaphor is a play upon words. Thus in giving expression to life man creates a second, poetic world alongside the world of nature.

Or take myth. This, too, is a transformation or an "imagination" of the outer world, only here the process is more elaborate and ornate than is the case with individual words. In myth, primitive man seeks to account for the world of phenomena by grounding it in the Divine. In all the wild imaginings of mythology a fanciful spirit is playing on the border-line between jest and earnest. Or finally, let us take ritual. Primitive society performs its sacred rites, its sacrifices, consecrations and mysteries, all of which serve to guarantee the well-being of the world, in a spirit of pure play truly understood.

Now in myth and ritual the great instinctive forces of civilized life have their origin: law and order, commerce and profit, craft and art, poetry, wisdom and science. All are rooted in the primaeval soil of play.

The object of the present essay is to demonstrate that it is more than a rhetorical comparison to view culture *sub specie ludi*. The thought is not at all new. There was a time when it was generally accepted, though in a limited sense quite different from the one intended here: in the 17th century, the age of world theatre. Drama, in a glittering succession of figures ranging from Shakespeare and Calderon to Racine, then dominated the literature of the West. It was the fashion to liken the world to a stage on which every man plays his part. Does this mean that the play-element in civilization was openly acknowledged? Not at all. On closer examination this fashionable comparison of life to a stage proves to be little more than an echo of the Neo-platonism that was then in vogue, with a markedly moralistic accent. It was a variation on the ancient theme of the vanity of all things. The fact that play and culture are actually interwoven with one another was neither observed nor expressed, whereas for us the whole point is to show that genuine, pure play is one of the main bases of civilisation.

To our way of thinking, play is the direct opposite of seriousness. At first sight this opposition seems as irreducible to other categories as the play-concept itself. Examined more closely, however, the contrast between play and seriousness proves to be neither conclusive nor fixed. We can say: play is non-seriousness. But apart from the fact that this proposition tells us nothing about the positive qualities of play, it is extraordinarily easy to refute. As soon as we proceed from "play is non-seriousness" to "play is not serious", the contrast leaves us in the lurch—for some play can be very serious indeed. Moreover we can immediately name several other fundamental categories that likewise come under the heading "non-seriousness" yet have no correspondence whatever with "play". Laughter, for instance, is in a sense the opposite of seriousness without being absolutely bound up with play. Children's games, football, and chess are played in profound seriousness; the players have not the slightest inclination to laugh. It is worth noting that the purely physiological act of laughing is exclusive to man, whilst the significant function of play is common to both men and animals. The Aristotelian *animal ridens* characterizes man as distinct from the animal almost more absolutely than *homo sapiens*.

What is true of laughter is true also of the comic. The comic comes under the category of non-seriousness and has certain affinities with laughter—it provokes to laughter. But its relation to play is subsidiary. In itself play is not comical either for player or public. The play of young animals or small children may sometimes be ludicrous, but the sight of grown dogs chasing one another hardly moves us to laughter. When we call a farce or a comedy "comic", it is not so much on account of the play-acting as such as on account of the situation or the thoughts expressed. The mimic and laughter-provoking art of the clown is comic as well as ludicrous, but it can scarcely be termed genuine play.

The category of the comic is closely connected with *folly* in the highest and lowest sense of that word. Play, however, is not foolish. It lies outside the antithesis of wisdom and folly. The later Middle Ages tended to express the two cardinal moods of life—play and seriousness—somewhat imperfectly by opposing *folie* to *sense*, until Erasmus in his *Laus Stultitiae* showed the inadequacy of the contrast.

All the terms in this loosely connected group of ideas—play, laughter, folly, wit, jest, joke, the comic, etc.—share the characteristic which we had to attribute to play, namely, that of resisting any attempt to reduce it to other terms. Their rationale and their mutual relationships must lie in a very deep layer of our mental being.

The more we try to mark off the form we call "play" from other forms apparently related to it, the more the absolute independence of the play-concept stands out. And the segregation of play from the domain of the great categorical antitheses does not stop there. Play lies outside the antithesis of wisdom and folly, and equally outside those of truth and falsehood, good and evil. Although it is a non-material activity it has no moral function. The valuations of vice and virtue do not apply here.

If, therefore, play cannot be directly referred to the categories of truth or goodness, can it be included perhaps in the realm of the aesthetic? Here our judgement wavers. For although the attribute of beauty does not attach to play as such, play nevertheless tends to assume marked elements of beauty. Mirth and grace adhere at the outset to the more primitive forms of play. In play the beauty of the human body in motion reaches its zenith. In its more developed forms it is saturated with rhythm and harmony, the noblest gifts of aesthetic perception known to man. Many and close are the links that connect play with beauty. All the same, we cannot say that beauty is inherent in play as such; so we must leave it at that: play is a function of the living, but is not susceptible of exact definition either logically, biologically, or æsthetically. The play-concept must always remain distinct from all the other forms of thought in which we express the structure of mental and social life. Hence we shall have to confine ourselves to describing the main characteristics of play.

Since our theme is the relation of play to culture we need not enter into all the possible forms of play but can restrict ourselves to its social manifestations. These we might call the higher forms of play. They are generally much easier to describe than the more primitive play of infants and young animals, because they are more distinct and articulate in form and their features more various and conspicuous, whereas in interpreting primitive play we immediately come up against that irreducible quality of pure playfulness which is not, in our opinion, amenable to further analysis. We shall have to speak of contests and races, of performances and exhibitions, of dancing and music, pageants, masquerades and tournaments. Some of the characteristics we shall enumerate are proper to play in general, others to social play in particular.

First and foremost, then, all play is a voluntary activity. Play to order is no longer play: it could at best be but a forcible imitation of it. By this quality of freedom alone, play marks itself off from the course of the natural process. It is something added thereto and spread out over it like a flowering, an ornament, a garment. Obviously, freedom must be understood here in the wider sense that leaves untouched the philosophical problem of determinism. It may be objected that this freedom does not exist for the animal and the child; they *must* play because their instinct drives them to it and because it serves to develop their bodily faculties and their powers of selection. The term "instinct", however, introduces an unknown quantity, and to presuppose the utility of play from the start is to be guilty of a *petitio principii*. Child and animal play because they enjoy playing, and therein precisely lies their freedom.

Be that as it may, for the adult and responsible human being play is a function which he could equally well leave alone. Play is superfluous. The need for it is only urgent to the extent that the enjoyment of it makes it a need. Play can be deferred or suspended at any time. It is never imposed by physical necessity or moral duty. It is never a task. It is done at leisure, during "free time". Only when play is a recognized cultural function—a rite, a ceremony—is it bound up with notions of obligation and duty.

Here, then, we have the first main characteristic of play: that it is free, is in fact freedom. A second characteristic is closely connected with this, namely, that play is not "ordinary" or "real" life. It is rather a stepping out of "real" life into a temporary sphere of activity with a disposition all of its own. Every child knows perfectly well that he is "only pretending", or that it was "only for fun". How deep-seated this awareness is in the child's soul is strikingly illustrated by the following story, told to me by the father of the boy in question. He found his four-year-old son sitting at the front of a row of chairs, playing "trains". As he hugged him the boy said: "Don't kiss the engine, Daddy, or the carriages won't think it's real". This "only pretending" quality of play betrays a consciousness of the inferiority of play compared with "seriousness", a feeling that seems to be something as primary as play itself. Nevertheless, as we have already pointed out, the consciousness of play being "only a pretend" does not by any means prevent it from proceeding with the utmost seriousness, with an absorption, a devotion that passes into rapture and, temporarily at least, completely abolishes that troublesome "only" feeling. Any game can at any time wholly run away with the players. The contrast between play and seriousness is always fluid. The inferiority of play is continually being offset by the corresponding superiority of its seriousness. Play turns to seriousness and seriousness to play. Play may rise to heights of beauty and sublimity that leave seriousness far beneath. Tricky questions such as these will come up for discussion when we start examining the relationship between play and ritual.

As regards its formal characteristics, all students lay stress on the *disinterestedness* of play. Not being "ordinary" life it stands outside the immediate satisfaction of wants and appetites, indeed it interrupts the appetitive process. It interpolates itself as a temporary activity satisfying in itself and ending there. Such at least is the way in which play presents itself to us in the first instance: as an intermezzo, an *interlude* in our daily lives. As a regularly recurring relaxation, however, it becomes the accompaniment, the complement, in fact an integral part of life in general. It adorns life, amplifies it and is to that extent a necessity both for the individual—as a life function—and for society by reason of the meaning it contains, its significance, its expressive value, its spiritual and social associations, in short, as a culture function. The expression of it satisfies all kinds of communal ideals. It thus has its place in a sphere superior to the strictly biological processes of nutrition, reproduction and self-preservation. This assertion is apparently contradicted by the fact that play, or rather sexual display, is predominant in animal life precisely at the mating-season. But would it be too absurd to assign a place *outside* the purely physiological, to the singing, cooing and strutting of birds just as we do to human play? In all its higher forms the latter at any rate always belongs to the sphere of festival and ritual—the sacred sphere.

Now, does the fact that play is a necessity, that it subserves culture, or indeed that it actually becomes culture, detract from its disinterested character? No, for the purposes it serves are external to immediate material interests or the individual satisfaction of biological needs. As a sacred activity play naturally contributes to the well-being of the group, but in quite another way and by other means than the acquisition of the necessities of life.

Play is distinct from "ordinary" life both as to locality and duration. This is the third main characteristic of play: its secludedness, its limitedness. It is "played out" within certain limits of time and place. It contains its own course and meaning.

Play begins, and then at a certain moment it is "over". It plays itself to an end. While it is in progress all is movement, change, alternation, succession, association, separation. But immediately connected with its limitation as to time there is a further curious feature of play: it at once assumes fixed form as a cultural phenomenon. Once played, it endures as a new-found creation of the mind, a treasure to be retained by the memory. It is transmitted, it becomes tradition. It can be repeated at any time, whether it be "child's play" or a game of chess, or at fixed intervals like a mystery. In this faculty of repetition lies one of the most essential qualities of play. It holds good not only of play as a whole but also of its inner structure. In nearly all the higher forms of play the elements of repetition and alternation (as in the *refrain*), are like the warp and woof of a fabric.

More striking even than the limitation as to time is the limitation as to space. All play moves and has its being within a play-ground marked off beforehand either materially or ideally, deliberately or as a matter of course. Just as there is no formal difference between play and ritual, so the "consecrated spot" cannot be formally distinguished from the play-ground. The arena, the card-table, the magic circle, the temple, the stage, the screen, the tennis court, the court of justice, etc., are all in form and function play-grounds, i.e. forbidden spots, isolated, hedged round, hallowed, within which special rules obtain. All are temporary worlds within the ordinary world, dedicated to the performance of an act apart.

Inside the play-ground an absolute and peculiar order reigns. Here we come across another, very positive feature of play: it creates order, *is* order. Into an imperfect world and into the confusion of life it brings a temporary, a limited perfection. Play demands order absolute and supreme. The least deviation from it "spoils the game", robs it of its character and makes it worthless. The profound affinity between play and order is perhaps the reason why play, as we noted in passing, seems to lie to such a large extent in the field of aesthetics. Play has a tendency to be beautiful. It may be that this aesthetic factor is identical with the impulse to create orderly form, which animates play in all its aspects. The words we use to denote the elements of play belong for the most part to aesthetics, terms with which we try to describe the effects of beauty: tension, poise, balance, contrast, variation, solution, resolution, etc. Play casts a spell over us; it is "enchanting", "captivating". It is invested with the noblest qualities we are capable of perceiving in things: rhythm and harmony.

The element of tension in play to which we have just referred plays a particularly important part. Tension means uncertainty, chanciness; a striving to decide the issue and so end it. The player wants something to "go", to "come off"; he wants to "succeed" by his own exertions. Baby reaching for a toy, pussy patting a bobbin, a little girl playing ball—all want to achieve something difficult, to succeed, to end a tension. Play is "tense", as we say. It is this element of tension and solution that governs all solitary games of skill and application such as puzzles, jig-saws, mosaic-making, patience, target-shooting, and the more play bears the character of competition the more fervent it will be. In gambling and athletics it is at its height. Though play as such is outside the range of good and bad, the element of tension imparts to it a certain ethical value in so far as it means a testing of the player's prowess: his courage, tenacity, resources and, last but not least, his spiritual powers—his "fairness"; because, despite his ardent desire to win, he must still stick to the rules of the game.

These rules in their turn are a very important factor in the play-concept. All play has its rules. They determine what "holds" in the temporary world circumscribed by play. The rules of a game are absolutely binding and allow no doubt. Paul Valéry once in passing gave expression to a very cogent thought when he said: "No scepticism is possible where the rules of a game are concerned, for the principle underlying them is an unshakable truth. . . ." Indeed, as soon as the rules are transgressed the whole play-world collapses. The game is over. The umpire's whistle breaks the spell and sets "real" life going again.

The player who trespasses against the rules or ignores them is a "spoil-sport". The spoil-sport is not the same as the false player, the cheat; for the latter pretends to be playing the game and, on the face of it, still acknowledges the magic circle. It is curious to note how much more lenient society is to the cheat than to the spoil-sport. This is because the spoil-sport shatters the play-world itself. By withdrawing from the game he reveals the relativity and fragility of the play-world in which he had temporarily shut himself with others. He robs play of its *illusion*—a pregnant word which means literally "in-play" (from *inlusio*, *illudere* or *inludere*). Therefore he must be cast out, for he threatens the existence of the play-community. The figure of the spoil-sport is most apparent in boys' games. The little community does not enquire whether the spoil-sport is guilty of defection because he dares not enter into the game or because he is not allowed to. Rather, it does not recognize "not being allowed" and calls it "not daring". For it, the problem of obedience and conscience is no more than fear of punishment. The spoil-sport breaks the magic world, therefore he is a coward and must be ejected. In the world of high seriousness, too, the cheat and the hypocrite have always had an easier time of it than the spoil-sports, here called apostates, heretics, innovators, prophets, conscientious objectors, etc. It sometimes happens, however, that the spoil-sports in their turn make a new community with rules of its own. The outlaw, the revolutionary, the cabbalist or member of a secret society, indeed heretics of all kinds are of a highly associative if not sociable disposition, and a certain element of play is prominent in all their doings.

A play-community generally tends to become permanent even after the game is over. Of course, not every game of marbles or every bridge-party leads to the founding of a club. But the feeling of being "apart together" in an exceptional situation, of sharing something important, of mutually withdrawing from the rest of the world and rejecting the usual norms, retains its magic beyond the duration of the individual game. The club pertains to play as the hat to the head. It would be rash to explain all the associations which the anthropologist calls "phratria"—e.g. clans, brotherhoods, etc.—simply as play-communities; nevertheless it has been shown again and again how difficult it is to draw the line between, on the one hand, permanent social groupings—particularly in archaic cultures with their extremely important, solemn, indeed sacred customs—and the sphere of play on the other.

The exceptional and special position of play is most tellingly illustrated by the fact that it loves to surround itself with an air of secrecy. Even in early childhood the charm of play is enhanced by making a "secret" out of it. This is for *us*, not for the "others". What the "others" do "outside" is no concern of ours at the moment. Inside the circle of the game the laws and customs of ordinary life no longer count. We are different and do things differently. This temporary abolition of the ordinary world is fully acknowledged in child-life, but it is no less evident in the great ceremonial games of savage societies. During the great feast of initiation when the youths are accepted into the male community, it is not the neophytes only that are exempt from the ordinary laws and regulations: there is a truce to all feuds in the tribe. All retaliatory acts and vendettas are suspended. This temporary suspension of normal social life on account of the sacred play-season has numerous traces in the more advanced civilizations as well. Everything that pertains to saturnalia and carnival customs belongs to it. Even with us a bygone age of robuster private habits than ours, more marked class-privileges and a more complaisant police recognized the orgies of young men of rank under the name of a "rag". The saturnalian licence of young men still survives, in fact, in the ragging at English universities, which the *Oxford English Dictionary* defines as "an extensive display of noisy and disorderly conduct carried out in defiance of authority and discipline".

The "differentness" and secrecy of play are most vividly expressed in "dressing up". Here the "extra-ordinary" nature of play reaches perfection. The disguised or masked individual "plays" another part, another being. He *is* another being. The terrors of childhood, open-hearted gaiety, mystic fantasy and sacred awe are all inextricably entangled in this strange business of masks and disguises.

Summing up the formal characteristics of play we might call it a free activity standing quite consciously outside "ordinary" life as being "not serious", but at the same time absorbing the player intensely and utterly. It is an activity connected with no material interest, and no profit can be gained by it. It proceeds within its own proper boundaries of time and space according to fixed rules and in an orderly manner. It promotes the formation of social groupings which tend to surround themselves with secrecy and to stress their difference from the common world by disguise or other means.

The function of play in the higher forms which concern us here can largely be derived from the two basic aspects under which we meet it: as a contest *for* something or a representation *of* something. These two functions can unite in such a way that the game "represents" a contest, or else becomes a contest for the best representation of something.

Representation means display, and this may simply consist in the exhibition of something naturally given, before an audience. The peacock and the turkey merely display their gorgeous plumage to the females, but the essential feature of it lies in the parading of something out of the ordinary and calculated to arouse admiration. If the bird accompanies this exhibition with dance-steps we have a performance, a *stepping out of* common reality into a higher order. We are ignorant of the bird's sensations while so engaged. We know, however, that in child-life performances of this kind are full of imagination. The child is *making an image* of something different, something more beautiful, or more sublime, or more dangerous than what he usually *is*. One is a Prince, or one is Daddy or a wicked witch or a tiger. The child is quite literally "beside himself" with delight, transported beyond himself to such an extent that he almost believes he actually is such and such a thing, without, however, wholly losing consciousness of "ordinary reality". His representation is not so much a sham-reality as a realization in appearance: "imagination" in the original sense of the word.

Passing now from children's games to the sacred performances in archaic culture we find that there is more of a mental element "at play" in the latter, though it is excessively difficult to define. The sacred performance is more than an actualization in appearance only, a sham reality; it is also more than a symbolical actualization—it is a mystical one. In it, something invisible and inactual takes beautiful, actual, holy form. The participants in the rite are convinced that the action actualizes and effects a definite beatification, brings about an order of things higher than that in which they customarily live. All the same this "actualization by representation" still retains the formal characteristics of play in every respect. It is played or performed within a playground that is literally "staked out", and played moreover as a feast, i.e. in mirth and freedom. A sacred space, a temporarily real world of its own, has been expressly hedged off for it. But with the end of the play its effect is not lost; rather it continues to shed its radiance on the ordinary world outside, a wholesome influence working security, order and prosperity for the whole community until the sacred play-season comes round again.

Examples can be taken from all over the world. According to ancient Chinese lore the purpose of music and the dance is to keep the world in its right course and to force Nature into benevolence towards man. The year's prosperity will depend on the right performance of sacred contests at the seasonal feasts. If these gatherings do not take place the crops will not ripen.[1]

The rite is a *dromenon*, which means "something acted", an act, action. That which is enacted, or the stuff of the action, is a *drama*, which again means act, action represented on a stage. Such action may occur as a performance or a contest. The rite, or "ritual act" represents a cosmic happening, an event in the natural

[1]M. Granet, *Festivals and Songs of Ancient China; Dances and Legends of Ancient China; Chinese Civilization* (Routledge).

process. The word "represents", however, does not cover the exact meaning of the act, at least not in its looser, modern connotation; for here "representation" is really *identification*, the mystic repetition or *re-presentation* of the event. The rite produces the effect which is then not so much *shown figuratively* as *actually reproduced* in the action. The function of the rite, therefore, is far from being merely imitative; it causes the worshippers to participate in the sacred happening itself. As the Greeks would say, "it is *methectic* rather than *mimetic*".[1] It is "a helping-out of the action".[2]

Anthropology is not primarily interested in how psychology will assess the mental attitude displayed in these phenomena. The psychologist may seek to settle the matter by calling such performances an *identification compensatrice*, a kind of substitute, "a representative act undertaken in view of the impossibility of staging real, purposive action".[3] Are the performers mocking, or are they mocked? The business of the anthropologist is to understand the significance of these "imaginations" in the mind of the peoples who practise and believe in them.

We touch here on the very core of comparative religion: the nature and essence of ritual and mystery. The whole of the ancient Vedic sacrificial rites rests on the idea that the ceremony—be it sacrifice, contest or performance—by representing a certain desired cosmic event, compels the gods to effect that event in reality. We could well say, by "playing" it. Leaving the religious issues aside we shall only concern ourselves here with the play-element in archaic ritual.

Ritual is thus in the main a matter of shows, representations, dramatic performances, imaginative actualizations of a vicarious nature. At the great seasonal festivals the community celebrates the grand happenings in the life of nature by staging sacred performances, which represent the change of seasons, the rising and setting of the constellations, the growth and ripening of crops, birth, life and death in man and beast. As Leo Frobenius puts it, archaic man *plays* the order of nature as imprinted on his consciousness.[4] In the remote past, so Frobenius thinks, man first

[1]Jane Harrison, *Themis: A Study of the Social Origins of Greek Religion* (Cambridge, 1912), p. 125.

[2]R. R. Marett, *The Threshold of Religion*, 1912, p. 48.

[3]Buytendijk, *Het Spel van Mensch en Dier als openbaring van levensdriften* (Amsterdam, 1932), pp. 70–71.

[4]*Kulturgeschichte Afrikas, Prolegomena zu einer historischen Gestaltlehre; Schicksalskunde im Sinne des Kulturwerdens* (Leipzig, 1932).

assimilated the phenomena of vegetation and animal life and then conceived an idea of time and space, of months and seasons, of the course of the sun and moon. And now he plays this great processional order of existence in a sacred play, in and through which he actualizes anew, or "recreates", the events represented and thus helps to maintain the cosmic order. Frobenius draws even more far-reaching conclusions from this "playing at nature". He deems it the starting-point of all social order and social institutions, too. Through this ritual play, savage society acquires its rude forms of government. The king is the sun, his kingship the image of the sun's course. All his life the king plays "sun" and in the end he suffers the fate of the sun: he must be killed in ritual forms by his own people.

We can leave aside the question of how far this explanation of ritual regicide and the whole underlying conception can be taken as "proved". The question that interests us here is: what are we to think of this concrete projection of primitive nature-consciousness? What are we to make of a mental process that begins with an unexpressed experience of cosmic phenomena and ends in an imaginative rendering of them in play?

Frobenius is right to discard the facile hypothesis which contents itself with hypothecating an innate "play instinct". The term "instinct", he says, is "a makeshift, an admission of helplessness before the problem of reality".[1] Equally explicitly and for even better reasons he rejects as a vestige of obsolete thinking the tendency to explain every advance in culture in terms of a "special purpose", a "why" and a "wherefore" thrust down the throat of the culture-creating community. "Tyranny of causality at its worst," "antiquated utilitarianism" he calls such a point of view.[2]

The conception Frobenius has of the mental process in question is roughly as follows. In archaic man the experience of life and nature, still unexpressed, takes the form of a "seizure"—being seized on, thrilled, enraptured. "The creative faculty in a people as in the child or every creative person, springs from this state of being seized." "Man is seized by the revelation of fate." "The reality of the natural rhythm of genesis and extinction has seized hold of his consciousness, and this, inevitably and by reflex action, leads him to represent his emotion in an act." So that according

[1] *Kulturgeschichte*, pp. 23, 122.
[2] *Ibid.* p. 21.

to him we are dealing with a necessary mental process of transformation. The thrill, the "being seized" by the phenomena of life and nature is condensed by reflex action, as it were, to poetic expression and art. It is difficult to describe the process of creative imagination in words that are more to the point, though they can hardly be called a true "explanation". The mental road from aesthetic or mystical, or at any rate meta-logical, perception of cosmic order to ritual play remains as dark as before.

While repeatedly using the term "play" for these performances the great anthropologist omits, however, to state what exactly he understands by it. He would even seem to have surreptitiously re-admitted the very thing he so strongly deprecates and which does not altogether fit in with the essential quality of play: the concept of purpose. For, in Frobenius' description of it, play quite explicitly *serves* to represent a cosmic event and thus bring it about. A quasi-rationalistic element irresistibly creeps in. For Frobenius, play and representation have their *raison d'être* after all, in the expression of something else, namely, the "being seized" by a cosmic event. But the very fact that the dramatization is *played* is, apparently, of secondary importance for him. Theoretically at least, the emotion could have been communicated in some other way. In our view, on the contrary, the whole point is the *playing*. Such ritual play is essentially no different from one of the higher forms of common child-play or indeed animal-play. Now in the case of these two latter forms one could hardly suppose their origin to lie in some cosmic emotion struggling for expression. Child-play possesses the play-form in its veriest essence, and most purely.

We might, perhaps, describe the process leading from "seizure" by nature to ritual performance, in terms that would avoid the above-mentioned inadequacy without, however, claiming to lay bare the inscrutable. Archaic society, we would say, plays as the child or animal plays. Such playing contains at the outset all the elements proper to play: order, tension, movement, change, solemnity, rhythm, rapture. Only in a later phase of society is play associated with the idea of something to be expressed in and by it, namely, what we would call "life" or "nature". Then, what was wordless play assumes poetic form. In the form and function of play, itself an independent entity which is senseless and irrational, man's consciousness that he is embedded in a sacred order of things finds its first, highest, and holiest expression.

Gradually the significance of a sacred act permeates the playing. Ritual grafts itself upon it; but the primary thing is and remains play.

We are hovering over spheres of thought barely accessible either to psychology or to philosophy. Such questions as these plumb the depths of our consciousness. Ritual is seriousness at its highest and holiest. Can it nevertheless be play? We began by saying that all play, both of children and of grown-ups, can be performed in the most perfect seriousness. Does this go so far as to imply that play is still bound up with the sacred emotion of the sacramental act? Our conclusions are to some extent impeded by the rigidity of our accepted ideas. We are accustomed to think of play and seriousness as an absolute antithesis. It would seem, however, that this does not go to the heart of the matter.

Let us consider for a moment the following argument. The child plays in complete—we can well say, in sacred—earnest. But it plays and knows that it plays. The sportsman, too, plays with all the fervour of a man enraptured, but he still knows that he is playing. The actor on the stage is wholly absorbed in his playing, but is all the time conscious of "the play". The same holds good of the violinist, though he may soar to realms beyond this world. The play-character, therefore, may attach to the sublimest forms of action. Can we now extend the line to ritual and say that the priest performing the rites of sacrifice is only playing? At first sight it seems preposterous, for if you grant it for one religion you must grant it for all. Hence our ideas of ritual, magic, liturgy, sacrament and mystery would all fall within the play-concept. In dealing with abstractions we must always guard against over-straining their significance. We would merely be playing with words were we to stretch the play-concept unduly. But, all things considered, I do not think we are falling into that error when we characterize ritual as play. The ritual act has all the formal and essential characteristics of play which we enumerated above, particularly in so far as it transports the participants to another world. This identity of ritual and play was unreservedly recognized by Plato as a given fact. He had no hesitation in comprising the *sacra* in the category of play. "I say that a man must be serious with the serious," he says (*Laws*, vii, 803). "God alone is worthy of supreme seriousness, but man is made God's plaything, and that is the best part of him. Therefore every man and woman should live life accordingly, and play the noblest games and be of another mind from what they are at present. . . . For they deem war a serious thing, though in war there is neither play nor culture worthy the name (οὔτ' οὖν παιδιὰ . . . οὔτ' αὖ παιδεία), which are the things *we* deem most serious. Hence all must live in peace as well as they possibly can. What, then, is the right way of living? Life must be lived as play, playing certain games, making sacrifices, singing and dancing, and then a man will be able to propitiate the gods, and defend himself against his enemies, and win in the contest."[1]

The close connections between mystery and play have been touched on most tellingly by Romano Guardini in his book *The Spirit of the Liturgy* (Ecclesia Orans I, Freiburg, 1922), particularly the chapter entitled "Die Liturgie als Spiel". He does not actually cite Plato, but comes as near the above quotation as may be. He ascribes to liturgy more than one of the features we held to be characteristic of play, amongst others the fact that, in its highest examples, liturgy is "zwecklos aber doch sinnvoll"—"pointless but significant".

The Platonic identification of play and holiness does not defile the latter by calling it play, rather it exalts the concept of play to the highest regions of the spirit. We said at the beginning that play was anterior to culture; in a certain sense it is also superior to it or at least detached from it. In play we may move below the level of the serious, as the child does; but we can also move above it—in the realm of the beautiful and the sacred.

From this point of view we can now define the relationship between ritual and play more closely. We are no longer astonished at the substantial similarity of the two forms, and the question as to how far every ritual act falls within the category of play continues to hold our attention.

We found that one of the most important characteristics of play was its spatial separation from ordinary life. A closed space is marked out for it, either materially or ideally, hedged off from the everyday surroundings. Inside this space the play proceeds, inside it the rules obtain. Now, the marking out of some sacred spot is also the primary characteristic of every sacred act. This requirement of isolation for ritual, including magic and law, is much

[1]Cf. *Laws*, vii, 796, where Plato speaks of the sacred dances of the Kouretes of Crete, calling them ἐνόπλια παίγνια.

more than merely spatial and temporal. Nearly all rites of consecration and initiation entail a certain artificial seclusion for the performers and those to be initiated. Whenever it is a question of taking a vow or being received into an Order or confraternity, or of oaths and secret societies, in one way or another there is always such a delimitation of room for play. The magician, the augur, the sacrificer begins his work by circumscribing his sacred space. Sacrament and mystery presuppose a hallowed spot.

Formally speaking, there is no distinction whatever between marking out a space for a sacred purpose and marking it out for purposes of sheer play. The turf, the tennis-court, the chess-board and pavement-hopscotch cannot formally be distinguished from the temple or the magic circle. The striking similarity between sacrificial rites all over the earth shows that such customs must be rooted in a very fundamental, an aboriginal layer of the human mind. As a rule people reduce this over-all congruity of cultural forms to some "reasonable", "logical" cause by explaining the need for isolation and seclusion as an anxiety to protect the consecrated individual from noxious influences—because, in his consecrated state, he is particularly exposed to the malign workings of ghosts, besides being himself a danger to his surroundings. Such an explanation puts intellection and utilitarian purpose at the beginning of the cultural process: the very thing Frobenius warned against. Even if we do not fall back here on the antiquated notion of a priestcraft inventing religion, we are still introducing a rationalistic element better avoided. If, on the other hand, we accept the essential and original identity of play and ritual we simply recognize the hallowed spot as a play-ground, and the misleading question of the "why and the wherefore" does not arise at all.

If ritual proves to be formally indistinguishable from play the question remains whether this resemblance goes further than the purely formal. It is surprising that anthropology and comparative religion have paid so little attention to the problem of how far such sacred activities as proceed within the forms of play also proceed in the attitude and mood of play. Even Frobenius has not, to my knowledge, asked this question.

Needless to say, the mental attitude in which a community performs and experiences its sacred rites is one of high and holy earnest. But let it be emphasized again that genuine and spontaneous play can also be profoundly serious. The player can abandon himself body and soul to the game, and the consciousness of its being "merely" a game can be thrust into the background. The joy inextricably bound up with playing can turn not only into tension, but into elation. Frivolity and ecstasy are the twin poles between which play moves.

The play-mood is *labile* in its very nature. At any moment "ordinary life" may reassert its rights either by an impact from without, which interrupts the game, or by an offence against the rules, or else from within, by a collapse of the play spirit, a sobering, a disenchantment.

What, then, is the attitude and mood prevailing at holy festivals? The sacred act is "celebrated" on a "holiday"—i.e. it forms part of a general feast on the occasion of a holy day. When the people foregather at the sanctuary they gather together for collective rejoicing. Consecrations, sacrifices, sacred dances and contests, performances, mysteries—all are comprehended within the act of celebrating a festival. The rites may be bloody, the probations of the young men awaiting initiation may be cruel, the masks may be terrifying, but the whole thing has a festal nature. Ordinary life is at a standstill. Banquets, junketings and all kinds of wanton revels are going on all the time the feast lasts. Whether we think of the Ancient Greek festivities or of the African religions to-day we can hardly draw any sharp line between the festival mood in general and the holy frenzy surrounding the central mystery.

Almost simultaneously with the appearance of the Dutch edition of this book the Hungarian scholar Karl Kerényi published a treatise on the nature of the festival which has the closest ties with our theme.[1] According to Kerényi, the festival too has that character of primacy and absolute independence which we predicated of play. "Among the psychic realities," he says, "the feast is a thing in itself, not to be confused with anything else in the world." Just as we thought the play-concept somewhat negligently treated by the anthropologist, so in his view is the feast. "The phenomenon of the feast appears to have been completely passed over by the ethnologist." "For all science is concerned it might not exist at all." Neither might play, we would like to add.

In the very nature of things the relationship between feast and

[1] *Vom Wesen des Festes*, Paideuma, Mitteilungen zur Kulturkunde 1, Heft 2 (Dez., 1938), pp. 59–74.

play is very close. Both proclaim a standstill to ordinary life. In both mirth and joy dominate, though not necessarily—for the feast too can be serious; both are limited as to time and place; both combine strict rules with genuine freedom. In short, feast and play have their main characteristics in common. The two seem most intimately related in dancing. According to Kerényi, the Cora Indians inhabiting the Pacific coast of Mexico call their sacred feast of the young corn-cobs and the corn-roasting the "play" of their highest god.

Kerényi's ideas about the feast as an autonomous culture-concept amplify and corroborate those on which this book is built. For all that, however, the establishment of a close connection between the spirit of play and ritual does not explain everything. Genuine play possesses besides its formal characteristics and its joyful mood, at least one further very essential feature, namely, the consciousness, however latent, of "only pretending". The question remains how far such a consciousness is compatible with the ritual act performed in devotion.

If we confine ourselves to the sacred rites in archaic culture it is not impossible to adumbrate the degree of seriousness with which they are performed. As far as I know, ethnologists and anthropologists concur in the opinion that the mental attitude in which the great religious feasts of savages are celebrated and witnessed is not one of complete illusion. There is an underlying consciousness of things "not being real". A vivid picture of this attitude is given by Ad. E. Jensen in his book on the circumcision and puberty ceremonies in savage society.[1] The men seem to have no fear of the ghosts that are hovering about everywhere during the feast and appear to everyone at its height. This is small wonder, seeing that these same men have had the staging of the whole ceremony: they have carved and decorated the masks, wear them themselves and after use conceal them from the women. They make the noises heralding the appearance of the ghosts, they trace their footprints in the sand, they blow the flutes that represent the voices of the ancestors, and brandish the bull-roarers. In short, says Jensen, "their position is much like that of parents playing Santa Claus for their children: they know of the mask, but hide it from them". The men tell the women gruesome tales about the goings-on in the sacred bush. The attitude of the neophytes alternates between ecstasy, feigned madness, flesh-

[1] *Beschneidung und Reifezeremonien bei Naturvölkern* (Stuttgart, 1933).

creeping and boyish swagger. Nor, in the last resort, are the women wholly duped. They know perfectly well who is hiding behind this mask or that. All the same they get fearfully excited when a mask comes up to them with minatory gestures, and fly shrieking in all directions. These expressions of terror, says Jensen, are in part quite genuine and spontaneous, and in part only acting up to a part imposed by tradition. It is "the done thing". The women are, as it were, the chorus to the play and they know that they must not be "spoil-sports".

In all this it is impossible to fix accurately the lower limit where holy earnest reduces itself to mere "fun". With us, a father of somewhat childish disposition might get seriously angry if his children caught him in the act of preparing Christmas presents. A Kwakiutl father in British Columbia killed his daughter who surprised him whilst carving things for a tribal ceremony.[1] The unstable nature of religious feeling among the Loango negroes is described by Pechuel-Loesche in terms similar to those used by Jensen. Their belief in the sanctities is a sort of half-belief, and goes with scoffing and pretended indifference. The really important thing is the *mood*, he concludes by saying.[2] R. R. Marett, in his chapter on "Primitive Credulity" in *The Threshold of Religion*, develops the idea that a certain element of "make-believe" is operative in all primitive religions. Whether one is sorcerer or sorcerized one is always knower and dupe at once. But one chooses to be the dupe. "The savage is a good actor who can be quite absorbed in his role, like a child at play; and, also like a child, a good spectator who can be frightened to death by the roaring of something he knows perfectly well to be no 'real' lion." The native, says Malinowski, feels and fears his belief rather than formulates it clearly to himself.[3] He uses certain terms and expressions, and these we must collect as documents of belief just as they are, without working them up into a consistent theory. The behaviour of those to whom the savage community attributes "supernatural" powers can often be best expressed by "acting up to the part".[4]

Despite this partial consciousness of things "not being real" in magic and supernatural phenomena generally, these authorities

[1] F. Boas, *The Social Organisation and the Secret Societies of the Kwakiutl Indians*, Washington, 1897, p. 435.

[2] *Volkskunde von Loango*, Stuttgart, 1907, p. 345.

[3] *The Argonauts of the Western Pacific*, London, 1922, p. 339.

[4] *Ibid.* p. 240.

still warn against drawing the inference that the whole system of beliefs and practices is only a fraud invented by a group of "unbelievers" with a view to dominating the credulous. It is true that such an interpretation is given not only by many travellers but sometimes even by the traditions of the natives themselves. Yet it cannot be the right one. "The origin of any sacred act can only lie in the credulity of all, and the spurious maintaining of it in the interests of a special group can only be the final phase of a long line of development." As I see it, psychoanalysis tends to fall back on this antiquated interpretation of circumcision and puberty practices, so rightly rejected by Jensen.[1]

From the foregoing it is quite clear, to my mind at least, that where savage ritual is concerned we never lose sight of the play-concept for a single moment. To describe the phenomena we have to use the term "play" over and over again. What is more, the unity and indivisibility of belief and unbelief, the indissoluble connection between sacred earnest and "make-believe" or "fun", are best understood in the concept of play itself. Jensen, though admitting the similarity of the child's world to that of the savage, still tries to distinguish in principle between the mentality of the two. The child, he says, when confronted with the figure of Santa Claus, has to do with a "ready-made concept", in which he "finds his way" with a lucidity and endowment of his own. But "the creative attitude of the savage with regard to the ceremonies here in question is quite another thing. He has to do not with ready-made concepts but with his natural surroundings, which themselves demand interpretation; he grasps their mysterious daemonism and tries to give it in representative form".[2] Here we recognize the views of Frobenius, who was Jensen's teacher. Still, two objections occur. Firstly, when calling the process in the savage mind "quite another thing" from that in the child-mind, he is speaking of the *originators* of the ritual on the one hand and of the child of *to-day* on the other. But we know nothing of these originators. All we can study is a ritualistic community which receives its religious imagery as traditional material just as "ready-made" as the child does, and responds to it similarly. Secondly, even if we ignore this, the process of "interpreting" the natural surroundings, of "grasping" them and "representing" them in a ritual image remains altogether inaccessible to our observation. It is only by fanciful metaphors that Frobenius and Jensen force

[1] Jensen, *op. cit.* p. 152.

[2] *Op. cit.* p. 149 f.

an approach to it. The most we can say of the function that is operative in the process of image-making or imagination is that it is a poetic function; and we define it best of all by calling it a function of play—the *ludic* function, in fact.

So that the apparently quite simple question of what play really is, leads us deep into the problem of the nature and origin of religious concepts. As we all know, one of the most important basic ideas with which every student of comparative religion has to acquaint himself is the following. When a certain form of religion accepts a sacred identity between two things of a different order, say a human being and an animal, this relationship is not adequately expressed by calling it a "symbolical correspondence" as *we* conceive this. The identity, the essential oneness of the two goes far deeper than the correspondence between a substance and its symbolic image. It is a mystic unity. The one has *become* the other. In his magic dance the savage *is* a kangaroo. We must always be on our guard against the deficiencies and differences of our means of expression. In order to form any idea at all of the mental habits of the savage we are forced to give them in our terminology. Whether we will or not we are always transposing the savage's ideas of religion into the strictly logical modes of our own thought. We express the relationship between him and the animal he "identifies" himself with, as a "being" for him but a "playing" for us. He has taken on the "essence" of the kangaroo, says the savage; he is playing the kangaroo, say we. The savage, however, knows nothing of the conceptual distinctions between "being" and "playing"; he knows nothing of "identity", "image" or "symbol". Hence it remains an open question whether we do not come nearest to the mental attitude of the savage performing a ritual act, by adhering to this primary, universally understandable term "play". In play as we conceive it the distinction between belief and make-believe breaks down. The concept of play merges quite naturally with that of holiness. Any Prelude of Bach, any line of tragedy proves it. By considering the whole sphere of so-called primitive culture as a play-sphere we pave the way to a more direct and more general understanding of its peculiarities than any meticulous psychological or sociological analysis would allow.

Primitive, or let us say, archaic ritual is thus sacred play, indispensable for the well-being of the community, fecund of cosmic insight and social development but always play in the sense Plato gave to it—an action accomplishing itself outside and above the necessities and seriousness of everyday life. In this sphere of sacred play the child and the poet are at home with the savage. His aesthetic sensibility has brought the modern man closer to this sphere than the "enlightened" man of the 18th century ever was. Think of the peculiar charm that the mask as an *objet d'art* has for the modern mind. People nowadays try to feel the essence of savage life. This kind of exoticism may sometimes be a little affected, but it goes a good deal deeper than the 18th century *engouement* for Turks, "Chinamen" and Indians. Modern man is very sensitive to the far-off and the strange. Nothing helps him so much in his understanding of savage society as his feeling for masks and disguise. While ethnology has demonstrated their enormous social importance, they arouse in the educated layman and art-lover an immediate aesthetic emotion compounded of beauty, fright, and mystery. Even for the cultured adult of to-day the mask still retains something of its terrifying power, although no religious emotions are attached to it. The sight of the masked figure, as a purely aesthetic experience, carries us beyond "ordinary life" into a world where something other than daylight reigns; it carries us back to the world of the savage, the child and the poet, which is the world of play.

Even if we can legitimately reduce our ideas on the significance of primitive ritual to an irreducible play-concept, one extremely troublesome question still remains. What if we now ascend from the lower religions to the higher? From the rude and outlandish ritual of the African, American or Australian aborigines our vision shifts to Vedic sacrificial lore, already, in the hymns of the *Rig-Veda*, pregnant with the wisdom of the Upanishads, or to the profoundly mystical identifications of god, man, and beast in Egyptian religion, or to the Orphic and Eleusinian mysteries. In form and practice all these are closely allied to the so-called primitive religions even to bizarre and bloody particulars. But the high degree of wisdom and truth we discern, or think we can discern in them, forbids us to speak of them with that air of superiority which, as a matter of fact, is equally out of place in "primitive" cultures. We must ask whether this formal similarity entitles us to extend the qualification "play" to the consciousness of the holy, the faith embodied in these higher creeds. If we accept the Platonic definition of play there is nothing preposterous or irreverent in doing so. Play consecrated to the Deity, the highest goal of man's endeavour—such was Plato's conception of religion. In following him we in no way abandon the holy mystery, or cease to rate it as the highest attainable expression of that which escapes logical understanding. The ritual act, or an important part of it, will always remain within the play category, but in this seeming subordination the recognition of its holiness is not lost.

II

THE PLAY-CONCEPT AS EXPRESSED IN LANGUAGE

When speaking of play as something known to all, and when trying to analyse or define the idea expressed in that word, we must always bear in mind that the idea as we know it is defined and perhaps limited by the word we use for it. Word and idea are not born of scientific or logical thinking but of creative language, which means of innumerable languages—for this act of "conception" has taken place over and over again. Nobody will expect that every language, in forming its idea of and expression for play, could have hit on the same idea or found a single word for it, in the way that every language has one definite word for "hand" or "foot". The matter is not as simple as that.

We can only start from the play-concept that is common to us, i.e. the one covered, with slight variations, by the words corresponding to the English word "play" in most modern European languages. Such a concept, we felt, seemed to be tolerably well defined in the following terms: play is a voluntary activity or occupation executed within certain fixed limits of time and place, according to rules freely accepted but absolutely binding, having its aim in itself and accompanied by a feeling of tension, joy and the consciousness that it is "different" from "ordinary life". Thus defined, the concept seemed capable of embracing everything we call "play" in animals, children and grown-ups: games of strength and skill, inventing games, guessing games, games of chance, exhibitions and performances of all kinds. We ventured to call the category "play" one of the most fundamental in life.

Now it appears at once that a general play-category has not been distinguished with equal definiteness by all languages everywhere, nor expressed in one word. All peoples play, and play remarkably alike; but their languages differ widely in their conception of play, conceiving it neither as distinctly nor as broadly as modern European languages do. From a nominalist point of view we might deny the validity of a general concept and say that for every human group the concept "play" contains just what is expressed in the word—or rather words. For it is arguable that one language has succeeded better than others in getting the various aspects of play into one word. And such indeed appears to be the case. One culture has abstracted a general notion of play much earlier and more completely than another, with the curious result that there are highly developed languages which have retained totally different words for the various play-forms and that this multiplicity of terms has itself impeded the aggregation of all the forms under one head. One is reminded here of the well-known fact that some of the so-called primitive languages have words for the different species of a common genus, as for eel and pike, but none for fish.

Various indications convince us that the abstraction of a general play-concept has been as tardy and secondary in some cultures as the play-function itself is fundamental and primary. In this respect it seems to me highly significant that in none of the mythologies known to me has play been embodied in a divine or daemonic figure,[1] while on the other hand the gods are often represented as playing. The absence of a common Indo-European word for play also points to the late conception of a general play-concept. Even the Germanic group of languages differs widely in the naming of play and divides it into three compartments.

It is probably no accident that the very peoples who have a pronounced and multifarious play-"instinct" have several distinct expressions for the play-activity. I think this is more or less true of Greek, Sanskrit, Chinese and English. Greek possesses a curious and specific expression for children's games in the ending *-inda*. In themselves the syllables do not signify anything; they merely give to any word the connotation of "playing at something". *-inda* is an indeclinable and, linguistically speaking, underivable suffix.[2] Greek children played *sphairinda*—at ball; *helkustinda*—tug o' war; *streptinda*—a throwing game; *basilinda*—king of the castle. The complete grammatical independence of the suffix is a symbol, as it were, of the underivable nature of the play-concept. In contrast to this unique and specific designation of child-play Greek has no less than three different words for play in

[1]Needless to say, Lusus, son or companion of Bacchus and progenitor of the Lusitanians, is a bookish invention of very late date.

[2]At best we may conjecture some affinity with-*ινδος* and hence infer a pre-indogermanic or Aegæan origin. The ending occurs as a verbal suffix in *ἀλίνδω*, *κυλίνδω*, both in the sense of "revolving", variants of *ἀλίω* and *κυλίω*. The idea of "playing" has only a faint echo here.

general. First of all: παιδιά, the most familiar of the three. Its etymology is obvious; it means "of or pertaining to the child", but is immediately distinguished by its accent from παιδία—childishness. The use of παιδιά, however, is not by any means restricted to children's games. With its derivates παίζειν, to play, παῖγμα, παίγνιον, a toy, it serves to denote all kinds of play, even the highest and most sacred, as we have seen from the passage in Plato's *Laws*. A note of light-heartedness and carefree joyfulness seems to be struck in the whole word-group. Compared with παιδιά the other word for play—ἀδύρω, ἄδυρμα—stays very much in the background. It is tinged with the idea of the trifling, the nugatory.

There remains, however, an extensive and very important domain which in our terminology would come under the head of playing but which is not covered in Greek either by παιδιά or ἄδυρμα: to wit, matches and contests. The whole of this sphere, so extremely important in Greek life, is expressed by the word ἀγών. We can well say that an essential part of the play-concept is concealed in the field of operation of the ἀγών. At the same time we must ask whether the Greeks were not right to make a verbal distinction between contest and play. It is true that the element of "non-seriousness", the ludic factor proper, is not as a rule explicitly expressed in the word ἀγών. Moreover, contests of every description played such an enormous part in Greek culture and in the daily life of every Greek that it might seem overbold to class so great a section of Greek civilization with "play". This indeed is the point of view taken by Professor Bolkestein in his criticism of my opinions to the contrary.[1] He reproaches me with having "illegitimately included the Greek contests, which range from those rooted in ritual to the most trifling, in the play-category". He goes on: "When speaking of the Olympic *games* we inadvertently make use of a Latin term which expresses a Roman valuation of the contests so designated, totally different from the valuation of the Greeks themselves". After enumerating a long series of *agonistic* activities showing how the competitive impulse dominated the whole of Greek life, my critic concludes: "All this has nothing to do with *play*—unless one would assert that the whole of life was play for the Greeks!"

In a certain sense such indeed will be the contention of this

[1] *Proceedings of the 17th Congress of Dutch Philologists*, Leyden, 1937, where he refers to my rectoral address on "The Borderline between Play and Seriousness in Culture".

book. Despite my admiration for Professor Bolkestein's lasting and lucid interpretation of Greek culture, and despite the fact that Greek is not alone in linguistically distinguishing between contest and play, I am fervently convinced of their underlying identity. Since we shall have to return again and again to this conceptual distinction I shall confine myself here to one argument only. The *agon* in Greek life, or the contest anywhere else in the world, bears all the formal characteristics of play, and as to its function belongs almost wholly to the sphere of the festival, which is the play-sphere. It is quite impossible to separate the contest as a cultural function from the complex "play-festival-rite". As to why the Greek language makes this remarkable terminological distinction between play and contest, this might, in my opinion, be explained as follows. The conception of a general, all-embracing and logically homogeneous play-concept is, as we have seen, a rather late invention of language. From very early on, however, sacred and profane contests had taken such an enormous place in Greek social life and gained so momentous a value that people were no longer aware of their play-character. The contest, in all things and on every occasion, had become so intense a cultural function that the Greeks felt it as quite "ordinary", something existing in its own right. For this reason the Greeks, possessing as they did two distinct words for play and contest, failed to perceive the essential play-element in the latter very clearly, with the result that the conceptual, and hence the linguistic, union never took place.[1]

As we shall see, Greek terminology does not stand alone in the matter of play. Sanskrit too has at least four verbal roots for the play-concept. The most general word for playing is *krīdati*, denoting the play of animals, children and grown-ups. Like the word "play" in the Germanic languages it also serves for the movement of wind or waves. It can mean hopping, skipping, or dancing in general without being expressly related to playing in particular. In these latter connotations it approximates to the root *nrt*, which covers the whole field of the dance and dramatic performances. Next there is *divyati*, meaning primarily gambling, dicing, but also playing in the sense of joking, jesting, trifling, making mock of. The original meaning appears to be throwing,

[1]This argument does not occur in the German edition of Huizinga's book, and the presentation of it in his own English version is somewhat obscure. It is hoped that the drift of his argument has been re-constructed without undue distortion. Trans.

casting; but there is a further connection with shining and radiance.[1] Then, the root *las* (whence *vilāsa*) combines the meanings of shining, sudden appearance, sudden noise, blazing up, moving to and fro, playing and "pursuing" an occupation (as in the German "etwas treiben"). Lastly, the noun *līlā*, with its denominative verb *līlayati* (the primary sense of which is probably rocking, swinging), expresses all the light, aerial, frivolous, effortless and insignificant sides of playing. Over and above this, however, *līlā* is used in the sense of "as if", to denote "seeming", "imitation", the "appearance" of things, as in the English "like", "likeness" or German "gleich", "Gleichnis". Thus *gajalīlayā* (literally: "with elephant play") means "like an elephant"; *gājendralīla* (literally: "elephant-play-man") means a man representing an elephant or playing the elephant. In all these denominations of play the semantic starting-point seems to be the idea of rapid movement—a connection found in many other languages. This is not to say, of course, that in the beginning the words denoted rapid movement exclusively and were only later applied to play. To my knowledge, the contest as such is not expressed by any of the play-words in Sanskrit; oddly enough there is no specific word for it, although contests of the most various kinds were common in Ancient India.

Professor Duyvendak's friendly help allows me to say something about the Chinese expressions for the play-function. Here too there can be no grouping of all the activities we are wont to regard as play, under one head. Most important is the word *wan*, in which ideas of children's games predominate, but extending its semantic range to the following special meanings: to be busy, to enjoy something, to trifle, to romp, to jest, to crack jokes, to make mock of. It also means to finger, to feel, to examine, to sniff at, to twiddle little ornaments, and finally to enjoy the moonlight. Hence the semantic starting-point would seem to be "handling something with playful attention", or "to be lightly engrossed". The word is not used for games of skill, contests, gambling or theatrical performances. For this, for orderly dramatic play, Chinese has words which belong to the conceptual field of "position", "situation", "arrangement". Anything to do with contests is expressed by the special word *cheng*, the perfect equivalent of the Greek *agon*; apart from which *sai* denotes an organized contest for a prize.

[1]We must leave to one side a possible connection with *dyu*—the clear sky.

To Professor Uhlenbeck, my former colleague at Leyden, I am indebted for examples showing how the play-concept is expressed in one of the so-called primitive languages—Blackfoot, one of the Algonkin group. The verbal stem *koani* serves for all children's games. It is not connected with the name of any particular game; it means child's-play in general. As soon as it is a question of the games of grown-ups or half-grown-ups, however, they no longer speak of them as *koani*, even if it is the same games that children play. On the other hand, *koani* now comes back again, curiously enough, in the erotic sense and especially for illicit relationships—as we would say, "dallying". Organized play according to rules is called *kachtsi*, and this also applies to games of chance as well as to games of skill and strength. Here the semantic element is "winning" and "competing". The relationship between *koani* and *kachtsi*, therefore, resembles that between παιδιά and ἀγών in Greek, except that the Blackfoot terms are verbs, not nouns, and that games of chance, which in Greek would come under παίζω, in Blackfoot come in the category of the agonistic. Everything that belongs to the sphere of magic and religion, i.e. dances and ceremonial, is expressed neither by *koani* nor *kachtsi*. Blackfoot has two separate words for "winning": *amots* for winning a contest, a race, or a game, but also for winning in battle—in this case in the sense of "playing havoc" or "running amok"; and *skets* or *skits*, used exclusively for winning games and sports. To all appearances the play-sphere proper and the agonistic sphere are completely merged in the latter word. There is, further, a special word for betting: *apska*. A very singular feature is the possibility of giving any verb a secondary meaning of "for fun", "not seriously" by adding the prefix *kip*-, literally "merely so", or "only". Thus, for instance, *aniu* means "he says"; *kipaniu*, "he says for a joke", or "he only says".

All in all, the conception and expression of play in Blackfoot would seem to be akin to, though not identical with, Greek.

So we have already found three languages in which the words for contest are distinct from those for play, namely Greek, Sanskrit and Chinese, while Blackfoot draws the line slightly differently. Should we therefore incline after all to Professor Bolkestein's opinion that this linguistic division corresponds to a deep-seated sociological, psychological and biological difference between play and contest? Not only does the whole of the anthropological material to be expounded hereafter, militate against such a conclusion, but so does the linguistic counter-evidence. Over against the languages we have just named we can set a whole series of others, equally discrete, which may be shown to present a wider conception of play. Apart from most of the modern European languages this holds good of Latin, Japanese and at least one of the Semitic tongues.

As to Japanese, Professor Rahder's kind help has enabled me to offer a few remarks. In contrast to Chinese and very like the modern languages of the West, it has a single, very definite word for the play-function and, in conjunction with this, an antonym denoting seriousness. The substantive *asobi* and the verb *asobu* mean: play in general, recreation, relaxation, amusement, passing the time or pastime, a trip or jaunt, dissipation, gambling, idling, lying idle, being unemployed. They also serve for: playing at something (e.g. the fool), representing something, imitation. Noteworthy too is "play" used in the sense of the limited mobility of a wheel, tool or any other structure, just as in Dutch, German and English.[1] *Asobu*, again, means to study under a teacher or at a university, which is reminiscent of the Latin word *ludus* in the sense of school. It can also mean jugglery, i.e. a sham-fight, but not the contest as such: here again there is another if slightly different demarcation between contest and play. Lastly, *asobu* is the word used for those Japanese aesthetic tea-parties where ceramics are passed admiringly from hand to hand amid utterances of approbation. Associations with rapid movement, shining and jesting seem to be lacking here.

A closer investigation of the Japanese conception of play would lead us more deeply into the study of Japanese culture than space allows. The following must suffice. The extraordinary earnestness and profound gravity of the Japanese ideal of life is masked by the fashionable fiction that everything is only play. Like the *chevalerie* of the Christian Middle Ages, Japanese *bushido* took shape almost entirely in the play-sphere and was enacted in play-forms. The language still preserves this conception in the *asobase-kotoba* (literally play-language) or polite speech, the mode of address used in conversation with persons of higher rank. The convention is that the higher classes are merely playing at all they do. The polite form for "you arrive in Tokio" is, literally, "you play arrival in Tokio"; and for "I hear that your father is dead", "I

[1] I could not discover whether there was any influence here of the English technical term.

hear that your father has played dying". In other words, the revered person is imagined as living in an elevated sphere where only pleasure or condescension moves to action.

As against this masking of the aristocratic life behind play, Japanese has a very outspoken idea of seriousness or non-play. The word *majime* is variously rendered by seriousness, sobriety, gravity, honesty, solemnity, stateliness; also quietness, decency, "good form". It is related to the word which we render by "face" in the well-known Chinese expression "to lose face". As an question remains how far such a consciousness is compatible with the ritual act performed in devotion.

In Semitic languages the semantic field of play, as my late friend Professor Wensinck informed me, is dominated by the root *la'ab*, obviously cognate with *la'at*. Here, however, apart from meaning play in its proper sense, the word also means laughing and mocking. The Arabic *la'iba* covers playing in general, making mock of, and teasing. In Aramaic *la'ab* means laughing and mocking. Besides this, in Arabic and Syriac the same root serves for the dribbling and drooling of a baby (to be understood, perhaps, from its habit of blowing bubbles with spit, which can confidently be taken as a form of play). The Hebrew *sahaq* also associates laughing and playing. Lastly, it is worth noting that *la'iba* in Arabic is used for the "playing" of a musical instrument, as in some modern European languages. In Semitic languages, therefore, the play-concept would seem to be of a somewhat vaguer and looser character than in the ones we have examined so far. As we shall see, Hebrew affords striking evidence of the identity between the agonistic and the play principle.

In remarkable contrast to Greek with its changing and heterogeneous terms for the play-function, Latin has really only one word to cover the whole field of play: *ludus*, from *ludere*, of which *lusus* is a direct derivative. We should observe that *jocus*, *jocari* in the special sense of joking and jesting does not mean play proper in classical Latin. Though *ludere* may be used for the leaping of fishes, the fluttering of birds and the plashing of water, its etymology does not appear to lie in the sphere of rapid movement, flashing, etc., but in that of non-seriousness, and particularly of "semblance" or "deception". *Ludus* covers children's games, recreation, contests, liturgical and theatrical representations, and games of chance. In the expression *lares ludentes* it means "dancing". The idea of "feigning" or "taking on the semblance of" seems to be uppermost. The compounds *alludo*, *colludo*, *illudo* all point in the direction of the unreal, the illusory. This semantic base is barely visible in *ludi* as denoting the great public games which occupied so important a place in Roman life, or in *ludi* in the sense of "schools". The semantic starting-point in the first instance is the contest, in the second—probably—it is "practice".

It is remarkable that *ludus*, as the general term for play, has not only not passed into the Romance languages but has left hardly any traces there, so far as I can see. In all of them—and this necessarily means at a quite early period—*ludus* has been supplanted by a derivative of *jocus*, which extended its specific sense of joking and jesting to "play" in general. Thus French has *jeu*, *jouer*; Italian *gioco*, *giocare*; Spanish *juego*, *jugar*; Portuguese *jogo*, *jogar*; Rumanian *joc*, *juca*; while similar words occur in Catalan, Provençal and Rhaeto-Romanic. We must leave to one side the question whether the disappearance of *ludus* and *ludere* is due to phonetic or to semantic causes.

In modern European languages the word "play" covers a very wide field. As we saw, in both the Romance and the Germanic languages we find it spread out over various groups of concepts dealing with movement or action which have nothing to do with play in the strict or formal sense of the term. Thus, for instance, "play" as applied to the limited mobility of the parts of a mechanism is common to French, Italian, English, Spanish, German and Dutch; also, as we noted above, to Japanese. The play-concept would seem to be covering an ever wider field much larger than that of παίζειν or even of *ludere*; a field in which the specific idea of play is completely submerged in one of light activity and movement. This is particularly observable in the Germanic languages.

These, as we have said above, possess no common word for play. We must take it, therefore, that in the hypothetical archaic Germanic period play had not yet been conceived as a general idea. But as soon as each individual branch of the Germanic languages threw up a word for play, these words all developed semantically in exactly the same way, or rather, this extensive and seemingly heterogeneous group of ideas was understood under the heading of "play".

In the very fragmentary Old Gothic texts that have come down to us—comprising little more than a part of the New Testament—there is no word for play; but from the translation of Mark x, 34:

καὶ ἐμπαίζουσιν αὐτῷ ("and they will mock him") by the words *jah bīlaikand ina*, it is tolerably certain that Gothic expressed play by the same *laikan* which has fathered the ordinary word for play in the Scandinavian languages, and which also appears in this sense in Old English and in High and Low German. In the Gothic texts themselves *laikan* only occurs in the sense of "leaping". As we have seen before, rapid movement must be regarded as the concrete starting-point of many play-words. We recall Plato's conjecture that the origin of play lies in the need of all young creatures, animal and human, to leap (*Laws*, ii, 653). Thus in Grimm's German Dictionary the original meaning of the High German substantive *leich* is given as "a lively rhythmical movement", its further significations lying wholly in the play-sphere; while the Anglo-Saxon *lâcan* is given in the concrete sense of "to swing, to wave about" like a ship on the waves, or to "flutter" like birds, or "flicker" like flames. Further, *lâc* and *lâcan*, as with the Old Norse *leikr*, *leika*,[1] serve to describe all kinds of playing, dancing and bodily exercises. In the younger Scandinavian languages *lege*, *leka* is almost exclusively restricted to playing.

The luxurious outcrop of words from the root *spil*, *spel* in the Germanic languages is brought to light in the very detailed articles on Play and Playing by M. Heyne and others in the *Deutsches Wörterbuch* (x, 1, 1905). The points that matter here are the following. First of all, the connection of the verb with its predicate. Though you can "ein Spiel treiben" in German and "een Spiel doen" in Dutch and "pursue a game" in English, the proper verb is "play" itself. You "play a game", or "spielen ein Spiel". To some extent this is lost in English by the doublet *play* and *game*. Nevertheless the fact remains that in order to express the nature of the activity the idea contained in the noun must be repeated in the verb. Does not this mean that the act of playing is of such a peculiar and independent nature as to lie outside the ordinary categories of action? Playing is no "doing" in the ordinary sense; you do not "do" a game as you "do" or "go" fishing, or hunting, or Morris-dancing, or woodwork—you "play" it.

Another significant point is this. No matter what language we think in we have a constant tendency to tone down the idea of play to a merely general activity connected with play proper only by one of its various attributes, such as lightness, tension and uncertainty as to the outcome, orderly alternation, free choice, etc.

[1]See below.

This tendency can be seen very early on as in the Old Norse *leika*, which has an extraordinarily wide range of meaning, including "to move freely", "to lay hold of", "to cause or effect", "to handle", "to occupy oneself", "to pass the time", "to practise". We have discussed before the use of "play" in the sense of limited mobility or freedom of movement. In this connection the President of the Netherlands Bank said on the occasion of the devaluation of the guilder, quite without any intention of being either poetic or witty, that "in so restricted an area as is now left for it, the Gold Standard cannot play". Expressions like "to have free play", or "to be played out", show that the play-concept is becoming attenuated. This is not so much due to a metaphorical transfer of the idea to concepts other than that of the play-activity proper, as to a spontaneous dissolving of the idea in unconscious irony. It is probably no accident that in Middle High German play (*spil*) and its compounds were much favoured in the language of the mystics; for certain domains of thought have a special demand for these hazy play-terms. Compare Kant's evident predilection for expressions like "the play of imagination", "the play of ideas", "the whole dialectical play of cosmological ideas".

Before we come to the third root of the play-concept in the Germanic languages, i.e. *play* itself, we may note in passing that apart from *lâc* and *plega* Old English or Anglo-Saxon also knew the word *spelian*, but exclusively in the specific sense of "to represent somebody else" or "to take another's place", *vicem gerere*. It is used for instance of the ram which was offered up in the place of Isaac. This connotation, though proper also to "play" in the sense of "playing a part", is not the primary one. We must leave aside the question of how far *spelian* is grammatically connected with the German "spielen", and abstain from discussing the relationship between "Spiel" and the English "spell", "gospel". The ending *-spiel* as in the German "Beispiel" or "Kirchspiel" and the Dutch *kerspel*, *dingspel* (an old judiciary district) is usually derived from the same root as the above English words, and not from "Spiel" (*spel*).

The English "play", "to play" is very remarkable from a semantic point of view. Etymologically the word comes from the Anglo-Saxon *plega*, *plegan* meaning primarily "play" or "to play", but also rapid movement, a gesture, a grasp of the hands, clapping, playing on a musical instrument and all kinds of bodily activity.

Later English still preserves much of this wider significance, e.g. in Shakespeare's Richard the Third, Act IV:

> "Ah, Buckingham, now do I play the touch,
> To try if thou be current gold indeed".

Now, the formal correspondence between the Old English *plegan* and the (continental) Old Saxon *plegan*, the Old High German *pflegan* and the Old Frisian *plega* is complete and beyond doubt. All these words, from which the modern German *pflegen* and the Dutch *plegen* are directly derived, have, however, an abstract sense which is not that of play. The oldest meaning is "to vouch or stand guarantee for, to take a risk, to expose oneself to danger for someone or something".[1] Next comes "to bind or engage oneself (*sich verpflichten*), to attend to, take care of (*verpflegen*)". The German *pflegen* is also used in connection with the performance of a sacred act, the giving of advice, the administration of justice (*Rechtspflege*), and in other Germanic languages you can "pflegen" homage, thanks, oaths, mourning, work, love, sorcery and—lastly but rarely—even "play".[2] Hence the word is mainly at home in the sphere of religion, law, and ethics. Hitherto, on account of the manifest difference of meaning, it has generally been accepted that "to play" and *pflegen* (or its other Germanic equivalents) are etymologically homonymous: deriving from roots alike in sound but different in origin. Our preceding observations allow us to hold a contrary opinion. The difference lies rather in the fact that "play" moves and develops along the line of the concrete while *pflegen* does so along the line of the abstract; both, however, being semantically akin to the play-sphere. We might call it the sphere of ceremonial. Among the oldest significations of *pflegen* occurs the "celebrating of festivals" and "the exhibition of wealth"—whence the Dutch *plechtig*: "ceremonious", "solemn". In form, the German *Pflicht* and the Dutch *Plicht* correspond to the Anglo-Saxon *pliht* (whence the

[1] Cf. J. Franck, *Etymologisch Woordenboek der Nederlandsche taal*, edited by N. van Wijk (Haag, 1912); *Woordenboek der Nederlandsche taal*, xii, 1, edited by G. J. Boekenoogen and J. H. van Lessen (Haag-Leiden, 1931).

[2] In one of the songs of Hadewych, nun of Brabant (13th century) there is the following verse:

> Der minnen ghebruken, dat es een spel,
> Dat niemand wel ghetoenen en mach,
> Ende al mocht dies pleget iet toenen wel,
> Hine const verstaen, dies noijt en plach.

Liedeven van Hadewijch, ed. Johanna Snellen (Amsterdam, 1907).
Plegen can here be understood unhesitatingly as play.

English *plight*).[1] While the Dutch and German words mean "duty" and hardly anything else, *pliht* means primarily "peril", secondarily "offence", "fault", "blame", and finally "pledge", "engagement". The verb *plihtan* has the sense of "exposing oneself to danger", "to compromise", "to oblige". As to *pledge*, Mediaeval Latin formed the word *plegium* from the Germanic *plegan*; and *plegium* in its turn became the Old French *pleige*—whence the English *pledge*. The oldest meaning of this is "surety", "warrant", "hostage", hence "gage" in the sense of a challenge or a "wager" ("wage" being a doublet of "gage"), and finally the ceremony of taking on the "engagement", and so "the drinking" of a pledge or of someone's health, a promise or a vow.[2]

Who can deny that in all these concepts—challenge, danger, contest, etc.—we are very close to the play-sphere? Play and danger, risk, chance, feat—it is all a single field of action where something is at stake. One is tempted to conclude that the words *play* and *pflegen* together with their derivatives are not only formally but semantically identical.

This brings us back to the relationship between play and contest, and contest and strife in the more general sense. In all Germanic languages and in many others besides, play-terms are regularly applied to armed strife as well. Anglo-Saxon poetry—to limit ourselves to but one example—is full of such terms and phrases. Armed strife, or battle, is called *heado-lac* or *beadu-lac*, literally "battle-play"; or *asc-plega*, "spear-play". In these compounds we are dealing without a doubt with poetic metaphors, a fully conscious transfer of the play-concept to the battle-concept. The same is true, if less obviously, of the line "Spilodun ther Vrankon" ("there played the Franks") in the Old High German song called the "Ludwigslied", celebrating the victory of the king of West Francia, Ludwig III, over the Norsemen at Saucourt in 881. All the same it would be rash to assert that every use of the word "play" in connection with serious strife is nothing but poetic licence. We have to feel our way into the archaic sphere of thought, where serious combat with weapons and all kinds of contests ranging from the most trifling games to bloody and mortal strife were comprised, together with play proper, in the single

[1]Presumably "plight" in the sense of "pledge", since "plight" meaning "predicament" is held to be an erroneous spelling. Huizinga's own note in this place runs: Cf. *pleoh*, Old Frisian *plê*=danger [Trans.].

[2]With *pledge* in these senses compare the Anglo-Saxon *beadoweg*, *baedeweg*=*poculum certaminis*, *certamen*.

fundamental idea of a struggle with fate limited by certain rules. Seen in this way, the application of the word "play" to battle can hardly be called a conscious metaphor. Play is battle and battle is play.

No illustration of the essential identity of play and battle in archaic culture could be more striking than the one offered in the Old Testament. In the Second Book of Samuel (ii, 14), Abner says to Joab: "Let the young men now arise and play before us" (Vulgate: "Surgant pueri et ludant coram nobis"). "And there came twelve from each side, and they caught every one his fellow by the head and thrust his sword into his fellow's side, so that they fell down together. And the place where they fell was henceforth called the Field of the Strong." The point for us is not whether the tale has any historical foundation or is simply an etymological legend invented to explain the name of a certain locality. The only point that matters is that this action is called play and that there is no mention of its not being play. The rendering of the Vulgate *ludant* is faultless: "let them play". The Hebrew text has here a form of the verb *sahaq*, meaning primarily "to laugh", next "to do something jestingly", and also "to dance". In the Septuagint the wording is as follows: ἀναστήτωσαν δὴ τὰ παιδάρια καὶ παιζάτωσαν ἐνώπιον ἡμῶν. It is clear that there can be no question of poetic licence; the plain fact is that play may be deadly yet still remain play—which is all the more reason for not separating play and contest as concepts.[1] A further conclusion emerges from this. Given the indivisibility of play and battle in the archaic mind, the assimilation of hunting to play naturally follows. We find it everywhere in language and literature and there is no need to dwell upon it here.

When treating of the root of the word "play" (*pflegen*) we discovered that the play-term can occur in the sphere of ceremonial. This is particularly the case with the common Dutch word for marriage—*huwelijk*—which still reflects the Middle Low Dutch *huweleec* or *huweleic* (literally "wedding-play"). Compare also *feestelic* (feast, festival), *vechtelic* (fighting: Old Frisian *fyuchtleek*). All these words are compounds of the root *leik* already discussed, which has yielded the ordinary word for play in the Scandinavian languages. In its Anglo-Saxon form *lác*, *lácan* it means, apart from play, leaping, rhythmical movement, also sacrifice, offering, gift,

[1]We may remark in passing that the strange contests between Thor and Loki are called *leika* in the *Gylfaginning*.

favour, even liberality, bounty. The starting-point of this rather curious semantic development is held to lie in such words as *ecgalâc* and *sveorda-lâc*, sword-dance; hence, according to Grimm, in the concept of a solemn, sacrificial dance.[1]

Before concluding our linguistic survey of the play-concept we must discuss some special applications of the word "play", particularly the use of it in the handling of musical instruments. We mentioned earlier that the Arabic *la'iba* bears this sense in common with a number of European languages, namely the Germanic (and some of the Slavonic) which, as far back as their mediaeval phase, designate instrumental skill by the word "play".[2] Of the Romance languages it appears that only French has *jeu* and *jouer* in this sense, which might be taken as an indication of Germanic influence; while Italian uses *sonare*, and Spanish *tocar*. Neither Greek nor Latin has it at all. The fact that "Spielmann" in German ("Speelman" in Dutch) has taken on the connotation "musician" need not be directly connected with the playing of an instrument: "Spielmann" corresponds exactly to *joculator*, *jongleur*, the original wide meaning of which (a performing artist of any kind) was narrowed down on the one hand to the poetic singer and on the other to the musician, and finally to anybody who did tricks with knives or balls.

It is quite natural that we should tend to conceive music as lying within the sphere of play, even apart from these special linguistic instances. Making music bears at the outset all the formal characteristics of play proper: the activity begins and ends within strict limits of time and place, is repeatable, consists essentially in order, rhythm, alternation, transports audience and performers alike out of "ordinary" life into a sphere of gladness and serenity, which makes even sad music a lofty pleasure. In other words, it "enchants" and "enraptures" them. In itself it would be perfectly understandable, therefore, to comprise all music under the heading of play. Yet we know that play is something different, standing on its own. Further, bearing in mind that the term "playing" is never applied to singing, and to music-making only in certain languages, it seems probable that the connecting link between play and instrumental skill is to be sought in the nimble and orderly movements of the fingers.

[1]Grimm, *Deutsche Mythologie*, ed. E. H. Meyer, I (Göttingen, 1875).

[2]Modern Frisian distinguishes between *boartsje* (children's games) and *spylje* (the playing of instruments). The latter has probably been taken over from Dutch.

There is yet another use of the word "play" which is just as widespread and just as fundamental as the equation of play with serious strife, namely, in relation to the erotic. The Germanic languages abound in erotic applications of the word, and it is hardly necessary to cite many examples. German has "Spielkind" (Dutch "speelkind") for a child born out of wedlock; compare also the Dutch "aanspelen" for the mating of dogs, "minnespel" for the act of copulation. In the German words "Laich" and "laichen" ("spawn" and "spawning" of fish), in the Swedish *leka* (coupling of birds), and in the English "lechery" the old Germanic root *leik, leikan* still persists. Similar applications hold good in Sanskrit, where *krīdati* (play) is frequently used in the erotic sense: e.g. *krīdaratnam* ("the jewel of games") means copulation. Professor Buytendijk therefore calls love-play the most perfect example of all play, exhibiting the essential features of play in the clearest form.[1] But we must be more particular. If we stick to the formal and functional characteristics of play as summed up earlier it is evident that few of them are really illustrative of the sexual act. It is not the act as such that the spirit of language tends to conceive as play; rather the road thereto, the preparation for and introduction to "love", which is often made enticing by all sorts of playing. This is particularly true when one of the sexes has to rouse or win the other over to copulating. The dynamic elements of play mentioned by Buytendijk, such as the deliberate creation of obstacles, adornment, surprise, pretence, tension, etc., all belong to the process of flirting and wooing. Nevertheless none of these functions can be called play in the strict sense. Only in the dance-steps, the preening and strutting of birds does the real play-element show itself. Caresses as such do not bear the character of play, though they may do on occasion; but it would be erroneous to incorporate the sexual act itself, as love-play, in the play category. The biological process of pairing does not answer to the formal characteristics of play as we postulated them. Language also normally distinguishes between love-play and copulation. The term "play" is specially or even exclusively reserved for erotic relationships falling outside the social norm. As we saw in Blackfoot, the same word *koani* is used for the ordinary playing of children and for illicit sexual intercourse. All in all, therefore, and in marked contrast to the deep-seated affinity between playing and fighting, we feel compelled to regard the

[1] *Op. cit.*, p. 95.

erotic use of the play-term, universally accepted and obvious though it be, as a typical and conscious metaphor.

The conceptual value of a word is always conditioned by the word which expresses its opposite. For us, the opposite of play is *earnest*, also used in the more special sense of *work*; while the opposite of earnest can either be play or jesting, joking. However, the complementary pair of opposites *play-earnest* is the more important. Not every language expresses the contrast as simply or as completely as the Germanic group, where the equivalent of "earnest" is found in German and Dutch, while the Scandinavian languages use *alvara* in precisely the same way. Equally definite is the contrast in Greek between σπουδή and παιδιά. Other languages possess an adjective for the opposite of play, but no noun, as in Latin, for instance, where *serius* has no substantival equivalent. This would appear to indicate that the abstraction of an antonym for play is conceptually incomplete. *Gravitas*, *gravis* can sometimes mean earnest, but are not specific of it. The Romance languages also have to make do with a derivative of the adjective: *serietà* in Italian, *seriedad* in Spanish. French makes the concept substantival only with reluctance—*sériosité* is weak as a word, as also is "seriousness".

The semantic starting-point of the Greek σπουδή lies in "zeal" or "speed", that of *serius* in "heaviness", "weightiness". The Germanic word presents graver difficulties. The original meaning of *ernest*, *ernust*, *eornost* is generally given as "strife", "struggle". Actually it does mean "struggle" in many cases. The difficulty arises because in the English *earnest* two different forms appear to have coincided, one corresponding to the Old English *(e)ornest*, and the other to the Old Norse *orrusta*, meaning "battle, single combat, pledge or challenge". The etymological identity of these two words is a moot point, so we leave the issue undecided and pass to our general conclusion.

We can say, perhaps, that in language the play-concept seems to be much more fundamental than its opposite. The need for a comprehensive term expressing "not-play" must have been rather feeble, and the various expressions for "seriousness" are but a secondary attempt on the part of language to invent the conceptual opposite of "play". They are grouped round the ideas of "zeal", "exertion", "painstaking", despite the fact that in themselves all these qualities may be found associated with play as well.

The appearance of a term for "earnest" means that people have become conscious of the play-concept as an independent entity—a process which, as we remarked before, happens rather late. Small wonder, then, that the Germanic languages with their very pronounced and comprehensive play-concept, also stressed its opposite so forcefully.

Leaving aside the linguistic question and observing the play-earnest antithesis somewhat more closely, we find that the two terms are not of equal value: play is positive, earnest negative. The significance of "earnest" is defined by and exhausted in the negation of "play"—earnest is simply "not playing" and nothing more. The significance of "play", on the other hand, is by no means defined or exhausted by calling it "not-earnest", or "not serious". Play is a thing by itself. The play-concept as such is of a higher order than is seriousness. For seriousness seeks to exclude play, whereas play can very well include seriousness.

III

PLAY AND CONTEST AS CIVILIZING FUNCTIONS

WHEN speaking of the play-element in culture we do not mean that among the various activities of civilized life an important place is reserved for play, nor do we mean that civilization has arisen out of play by some evolutionary process, in the sense that something which was originally play passed into something which was no longer play and could henceforth be called culture. The view we take in the following pages is that culture arises in the form of play, that it is played from the very beginning. Even those activities which aim at the immediate satisfaction of vital needs—hunting, for instance—tend, in archaic society, to take on the play-form. Social life is endued with supra-biological forms, in the shape of play, which enhance its value. It is through this playing that society expresses its interpretation of life and the world. By this we do not mean that play turns into culture, rather that in its earliest phases culture has the play-character, that it proceeds in the shape and the mood of play. In the twin union of play and culture, play is primary. It is an objectively recognizable, a concretely definable thing, whereas culture is only the term which our historical judgement attaches to a particular instance. Such a conception approximates to that of Frobenius who, in his *Kulturgeschichte Afrikas*, speaks of the genesis of culture "als eines aus dem natürlichen 'Sein' aufgestiegenen 'Spieles' " (as a "play" emerging out of natural "being"). In my opinion, however, Frobenius conceives the relationship between play and culture too mystically and describes it altogether too vaguely. He fails to put his finger on the point where culture emerges from play.

As a culture proceeds, either progressing or regressing, the original relationship we have postulated between play and non-play does not remain static. As a rule the play-element gradually recedes into the background, being absorbed for the most part in the sacred sphere. The remainder crystallizes as knowledge: folklore, poetry, philosophy, or in the various forms of judicial and social life. The original play-element is then almost completely hidden behind cultural phenomena. But at any moment, even in a highly developed civilization, the play-"instinct" may reassert itself in full force, drowning the individual and the mass in the intoxication of an immense game.

Naturally enough, the connection between culture and play is particularly evident in the higher forms of social play where the latter consists in the orderly activity of a group or two opposed groups. Solitary play is productive of culture only in a limited degree. As we have indicated before, all the basic factors of play, both individual and communal, are already present in animal life—to wit, contests, performances, exhibitions, challenges, preenings, struttings and showings-off, pretences and binding rules. It is doubly remarkable that birds, phylogenetically so far removed from human beings, should have so much in common with them. Woodcocks perform dances, crows hold flying-matches, bower-birds and others decorate their nests, song-birds chant their melodies. Thus competitions and exhibitions as amusements do not proceed from culture, they rather precede it.

"Playing together" has an essentially antithetical character. As a rule it is played between two parties or teams. A dance, a pageant, a performance may, however, be altogether lacking in antithesis. Moreover "antithetical" does not necessarily mean "contending" or "agonistic". A part-song, a chorus, a minuet, the voices in a musical ensemble, the game of cat's cradle—so interesting to the anthropologist because developed into intricate systems of magic with some primitive peoples—are all examples of antithetical play which need not be agonistic although emulation may sometimes be operative in them. Not infrequently an activity which is self-contained—for instance the performance of a theatrical piece or a piece of music—may incidentally pass into the agonistic category by becoming the occasion of competition for prizes, either in respect of the arrangement or the execution of it, as was the case with Greek drama.

Among the general characteristics of play we reckoned tension and uncertainty. There is always the question: "will it come off?" This condition is fulfilled even when we are playing patience, doing jig-saw puzzles, acrostics, crosswords, diabolo, etc. Tension and uncertainty as to the outcome increase enormously when the antithetical element becomes really agonistic in the play of groups. The passion to win sometimes threatens to obliterate the levity proper to a game. An important distinction emerges here. In games of pure chance the tension felt by the player is only feebly communicated to the onlooker. In themselves, gambling games are very curious subjects for cultural research, but for the development of culture as such we must call them unproductive. They are sterile, adding nothing to life or the mind. The picture changes as soon as play demands application, knowledge, skill, courage and strength. The more "difficult" the game the greater the tension in the beholders. A game of chess may fascinate the onlookers although it still remains unfruitful for culture and devoid of visible charm. But once a game is beautiful to look at its cultural value is obvious; nevertheless its aesthetic value is not indispensable to culture. Physical, intellectual, moral or spiritual values can equally well raise play to the cultural level. The more apt it is to raise the tone, the intensity of life in the individual or the group the more readily it will become part of civilization itself. The two ever-recurrent forms in which civilization grows in and as play are the sacred performance and the festal contest.

Here the question broached in our first chapter arises once more: are we entitled to include all contests unreservedly in the play-concept? We saw how the Greeks distinguished ἀγών from παιδιά. This could be explained on etymological grounds, since in παιδιά the childish was evoked so vividly that it could hardly have been applied to the serious contests that formed the core of Hellenic social life. The word ἀγών, on the other hand, defined the contest from quite a different point of view. Its original meaning appears to have been a "gathering" (compare ἀγορά—"market-place"—to which ἀγών is related). Thus, as a term, it had nothing to do with play proper. The essential oneness of play and contest, however, still peeps through when, as we have seen, Plato uses παίγνιον for the armed ritual dances of the Kouretes (τά τῶν Κουρήτων ἐνόπλια παίγνια) and παιδιά for sacred performances in general. That the majority of Greek contests were fought out in deadly earnest is no reason for separating the agon from play, or for denying the play-character of the former. The contest has all the formal and most of the functional features of a game. Dutch and German both have a word which expresses this unity very clearly: *wedkamp* and *Wettkampf* respectively. It contains the idea of a play-ground (Latin *campus*) and that of a wager (*Wette*). It is, moreover, the normal word for "contest" in those languages. We would allude once more to the remarkable testimony from the Second Book of Samuel, where a fight to the death between two groups was still called "playing", the word used being taken from the sphere of laughter. On numerous Greek vases we can see that a contest of armed men is characterized as an agon by the presence of the flute-players who accompany it. At the Olympic games there were duels fought to the death.[1] The mighty *tours de force* accomplished by Thor and his companions in their contest with the Man of Utgardaloki are called *leika*, "play". For all these reasons it would not seem overbold to consider the terminological disparity between contest and play in Greek as the more or less accidental failure to abstract a general concept that would have embraced both. In short, the question as to whether we are entitled to include the contest in the play-category can be answered unhesitatingly in the affirmative.

Like all other forms of play, the contest is largely devoid of purpose. That is to say, the action begins and ends in itself, and the outcome does not contribute to the necessary life-processes of the group. The popular Dutch saying to the effect that "it is not the marbles that matter, but the game", expresses this clearly enough. Objectively speaking, the result of the game is unimportant and a matter of indifference. On a visit to England the Shah of Persia is supposed to have declined the pleasure of attending a race meeting, saying that he knew very well that one horse runs faster than another. From his point of view he was perfectly right: he refused to take part in a play-sphere that was alien to him, preferring to remain outside. The outcome of a game or a contest—except, of course, one played for pecuniary profit—is only interesting to those who enter into it as players or spectators, either personally and locally, or else as listeners by radio or viewers by television, etc., and accept its rules. They have become play-fellows and choose to be so. For them it is immaterial whether Oxford wins, or Cambridge.

"There is something at stake"—the essence of play is contained in that phrase. But this "something" is not the material result of the play, not the mere fact that the ball is in the hole, but the ideal fact that the game is a success or has been successfully concluded. Success gives the player a satisfaction that lasts a shorter or a longer while as the case may be. The pleasurable feeling of satisfaction mounts with the presence of spectators, though these are not essential to it. A person who gets a game of patience

[1]Plutarch deemed this form of contest contrary to the idea of the agon, in which Miss Harrison (*Themis*, pp. 221, 323) agrees with him, wrongly, as it seems to me.

"out" is doubly delighted when somebody is watching him. In all games it is very important that the player should be able to boast of his success to others. The angler is a familiar type in this respect. We shall have to return to this self-approbation later on.

Closely connected with play is the idea of winning. Winning, however, presupposes a partner or opponent; solitary play knows no winning, and the attainment of the desired objective here cannot be called by that name.

What is "winning", and what is "won"? Winning means showing oneself superior in the outcome of a game. Nevertheless, the evidence of this superiority tends to confer upon the winner a semblance of superiority in general. In this respect he wins something more than the game as such. He has won esteem, obtained honour; and this honour and esteem at once accrue to the benefit of the group to which the victor belongs. Here we have another very important characteristic of play: success won readily passes from the individual to the group. But the following feature is still more important: the competitive "instinct" is not in the first place a desire for power or a will to dominate. The primary thing is the desire to excel others, to be the first and to be honoured for that. The question whether, in the result, the power of the individual or the group will be increased, takes only a second place. The main thing is to have won. The purest example of a victory which has nothing visible or enjoyable about it save the mere fact of winning, is afforded by a game of chess.

We play or compete "for" something. The object for which we play and compete is first and foremost victory, but victory is associated with all the various ways in which it can be enjoyed—for instance, as a triumph celebrated by the group with massed pomps, applause and ovations. The fruits of victory may be honour, esteem, prestige. As a rule, however, something more than honour is associated with winning. We see this even in the "staking out" of a game: the marking of its limits. Every game has its stake. It can be of material or symbolical value, but also ideal. The stake can be a gold cup or a jewel or a king's daughter or a shilling; the life of the player or the welfare of the whole tribe. It can be a prize or a "gage". This is a most significant word. Etymologically and semantically it is related to the Latin *vadium* (German *Wette*), meaning a "pledge" in the sense of a purely symbolical object thrown down into the "ring" or play-ground as a token of challenge. It is not quite identical with "prize", which conveys the idea of something intrinsically valuable—for instance, a sum of money—though it may be simply a laurel-wreath. It is very curious how the words "prize", "price" and "praise" all derive more or less directly from the Latin *pretium* but develop in different directions. *Pretium* arose originally in the sphere of exchange and valuation, and presupposed a counter-value. The mediaeval *pretium justum* or "just price" corresponded approximately to the idea of the modern "market value". Now while *price* remains bound to the sphere of economics, *prize* moves into that of play and competition, and *praise* acquires the exclusive signification of the Latin *laus*. Semantically, it is next to impossible to delimit the field proper to each of the three words. What is equally curious is to see how the word *wage*, originally identical with *gage* in the sense of a symbol of challenge, moves in the reverse direction of *pretium*—i.e. from the play-sphere to the economic sphere and becomes a synonym for "salary" or "earnings". We do not *play* for wages, we *work* for them. Finally, "gains" or "winnings" has nothing to do with any of these words etymologically, though semantically it pertains to both play and economics: the player receives his winnings, the merchant makes them.

We might say that proper to all the derivations of the Latin root *vad* is a sense of passion, of chance, of daring, as regards both economic activity and play activity. Pure avarice neither trades nor plays; it does not gamble. To dare, to take risks, to bear uncertainty, to endure tension—these are the essence of the play spirit. Tension adds to the importance of the game and, as it increases, enables the player to forget that he is only playing.

The Greek word for "prize"—ἄθλον—is derived by some from the same fruitful root *vad* just discussed. ἄθλον yields ἀθλητής, the athlete. Here the ideas of contest, struggle, exercise, exertion, endurance and suffering are united. If we bear in mind that in savage society the majority of agonistic activities really are "agonizing", involving as they do mental and physical hardship; and if we remember also the intimate connection between ἀγών and ἀγωνία (which latter word originally meant simply "contest", but later "death-struggle" and "fear"), we shall see that in *athletics* we are still moving in that sphere of serious competition which forms our theme.

Competition is not only "for" something but also "in" and

"with" something. People compete to be the first "in" strength or dexterity, in knowledge or riches, in splendour, liberality, noble descent, or in the number of their progeny. They compete "with" bodily strength or force of arms, with their reason or their fists, contending against one another with extravagant displays, big words, boasting, vituperation and finally with cunning and deceit. To our way of thinking, cheating as a means of winning a game robs the action of its play-character and spoils it altogether, because for us the essence of play is that the rules be kept—that it be fair play. Archaic culture, however, gives the lie to our moral judgement in this respect, as also does the spirit of popular lore. In the fable of the hare and the hedgehog the beau role is reserved for the false player, who wins by fraud. Many of the heroes of mythology win by trickery or by help from without. Pelops bribes the charioteer of Oenomaus to put wax pins into the axles. Jason and Theseus come through their tests successfully, thanks to Medea and Ariadne. Gunther owes his victory to Siegfried. The Kauravas in the *Mahābhārata* win by cheating at dice. Freya double-crosses Wotan into granting the victory to the Langobards. The Ases of Eddic mythology break the oath they have sworn to the Giants. In all these instances the act of fraudulently outwitting somebody else has itself become a subject for competition, a new play-theme, as it were.[1]

The hazy border-line between play and seriousness is illustrated very tellingly by the use of the words "playing" or "gambling" for the machinations on the Stock Exchange. The gambler at the roulette table will readily concede that he is playing; the stock-jobber will not. He will maintain that buying and selling on the off-chance of prices rising or falling is part of the serious business of life, at least of business life, and that it is an economic function of society. In both cases the operative factor is the hope of gain; but whereas in the former the pure fortuitousness of the thing is generally admitted (all "systems" notwithstanding), in the latter the player deludes himself with the fancy that he can calculate the future trends of the market. At any rate the difference of mentality is exceedingly small.

In this connection it is worth noting that two forms of business

[1] I have failed to discover a direct connection between the hero of the legends who attains his objective by fraud and cunning, and the divine figure who is at once the benefactor and deceiver of man. Cf. W. B. Kristensen, *De goddelijke bedrieger*, Mededeelingen der K. Akad. van Wetenschappen, afd. Lett. No. 3; and J. P. B. Josselin de Jong, *De oorsprong van den goddelijken bedrieger*, *ibid.* Lett. No. 1.

agreement in the hope of future fulfilment have sprung directly from the wager, so that it is a moot point whether play or serious interest came first. Towards the close of the Middle Ages we see, in Genoa and Antwerp, the emergence of life-insurance in the form of betting on future eventualities of a non-economic nature. Bets were made, for instance, "on the life and death of persons, on the birth of boys or of girls, on the outcome of voyages and pilgrimages, on the capture of sundry lands, places or cities".[1] Such contracts as these, even though they had already taken on a purely commercial character, were repeatedly proscribed as illegal games of chance, amongst others by Charles V.[2] At the election of a new Pope there was betting as at a horse-race to-day.[3] Even in the 17th century dealings in life-insurances were still called "betting".

Anthropology has shown with increasing clarity how social life in the archaic period normally rests on the antagonistic and antithetical structure of the community itself, and how the whole mental world of such a community corresponds to this profound dualism. We find traces of it everywhere. The tribe is divided into two opposing halves, called "phratriai" by the anthropologist, which are separated by the strictest exogamy. The two groups are further distinguished by their totem—a term somewhat recklessly jargonized out of the special field to which it belongs, but very convenient for scientific use. A man may be a raven-man or a tortoise-man, thereby acquiring a whole system of obligations, taboos, customs, objects of veneration peculiar to raven or tortoise as the case may be. The mutual relationship of the two tribal halves is one of contest and rivalry, but at the same time of reciprocal help and the rendering of friendly service. Together they enact, as it were, the public life of the tribe in a never-ending series of ceremonies precisely formulated and punctiliously performed. The dualism that sunders the two halves extends over their whole conceptual and imaginative world. Every creature, every thing has its place on one side or the other, so that the entire cosmos is framed in this classification.

[1]Anthonio van Neulighem, *Openbaringe van 't Italiaens boeckhouden*, 1631, pp. 25, 26, 77, 86 f., 91 f.

[2]Verachter, *Inventaire des Chartes d'Anvers*, No. 742, p. 215; *Coutumes de la ville d'Anvers* ii, p. 400, iv, p. 8; cf. E. Bensa, *Histoire du contrat d'assurance au moyen âge*, 1897, p. 84 f.: in Barcelona 1435, in Genoa, 1467: decretum ne asseveratio fieri possit super vita principum et locorum mutationes.

[3]R. Ehrenberg, *Das Zeitalter der Fugger*, Jena 1896, II, p.19.

Along with the tribal division goes the sexual division, which is likewise the expression of a cosmic duality as in the Chinese *yin* and *yang*, the female and male principle respectively. These, alternating and collaborating with one another, maintain the rhythm of life. According to some, the origin of this sexual dualism as a philosophical system is supposed to have lain in the actual division of the tribe into groups of youths and maidens, who met at the great seasonal festivities to court one another in ritual form with alternate song and dance.

At these festivals the spirit of competition between the two opposing halves of the tribe or between the sexes comes fully into play. For no other great culture has the immensely civilizing influence of these multifarious festal competitions been more clearly elucidated than for ancient China, by Marcel Granet. Basing his reconstruction on an anthropological interpretation of ancient Chinese ritual songs, Granet was able to give an account of the early phases of Chinese culture as simple as it is convincing and scientifically accurate.

He describes the earliest phase of all as one in which rural clans celebrate the seasonal feasts by contests devised to promote fertility and the ripening of crops. It is a well-known fact that such an idea underlies most primitive ritual. Every ceremony well performed, every game or contest duly won, every act of sacrifice auspiciously concluded, fervently convinces archaic man that a boon and a blessing have thereby been procured for the community. The sacrifices or sacred dances have been successfully executed; now all is well, the higher powers are on our side, the cosmic order is safeguarded, social well-being is assured for us and ours. Of course this feeling is not to be imagined as the end-result of a series of reasonable deductions. It is rather a life-feeling, a feeling of satisfaction crystallized into faith more or less formulated in the mind.

According to Granet the winter festival, celebrated by the men in the men's house, bore a markedly dramatic character. In a state of ecstatic excitement and intoxication animal-dances were performed with masks, there were carousings and feastings, bets, tricks and *tours de force* of all kinds. Women were excluded, but the antithetical nature of the festival was still preserved. The effectiveness of the ceremonial depended on competition and regular alternation. There was a group of hosts and a group of guests. If one of them represented the *yang* principle, standing for sun, warmth and summer, the other embodied *yin*, comprising moon, coldness, winter.

Granet's conclusions, however, go far beyond this picture of a pastoral, almost idyllic existence lived by scattered tribes against a background of pure nature. With the rise of chieftains and regional kingdoms within the immense spaces of China there developed, over and above the original, simple dualisms each comprising a single clan or tribe, a system of many competing groups covering an area of several clans or tribes put together, but still expressing their cultural life mainly in the festal and ritual contests. From these age-old seasonal contests between the parts of a tribe and then between whole tribes, a social hierarchy was born. The prestige won by the warriors in these sacred contests was the beginning of the feudalizing process so long dominant in China. "The spirit of competition," says Granet, "which animated the men's societies or brotherhoods and set them against one another during the winter festivities in tournaments of dance and song, comes at the beginning of the line of development that led to State forms and institutions."[1]

Even if we hesitate to go all the way with Granet, who derives the whole hierarchy of the later Chinese state from these primitive customs, we must admit that he has demonstrated in an altogether masterly fashion how the agonistic principle plays a part in the development of Chinese civilization far more significant even than the agon in the Hellenic world, and in which the essentially *ludic* character shows up much more clearly there than in Greece. For in ancient China almost every activity took the form of a ceremonial contest; the crossing of a river, the climbing of a mountain, cutting wood or picking flowers. A typical Chinese legend about the founding of a kingdom shows the hero-prince vanquishing his opponents by miraculous proofs of strength or amazing feats, thus demonstrating his superiority. As a rule the tourney ends in the death of the vanquished party.

The point for us is that all these contests, even where fantastically depicted as mortal and titanic combats, with all their peculiarities still belong to the domain of play. This becomes particularly evident as soon as we compare the contests which Chinese tradition has in mythical or heroic form, with those seasonal contests still in living use to-day in various parts of the world, namely

[1]*Civilization*, p. 204. José Ortega y Gasset has also outlined the same theme in his essay on *El origen deportivo del estado, El Espictador vii*, pp. 103-143, Madrid, 1930.

the tournaments of songs and games between the young men and girls of a group at the spring or autumn festivals. Granet, when dealing with this theme for ancient China in the light of the love-songs in the *Shih Ching*, mentioned similar festivals in Tonking, Tibet and Japan. An Annamite scholar, Nguyen van Huyen, has taken up the theme for Annam, where these customs were in full flower until quite recently, and given an excellent description of them in a thesis written in French.[1] Here we find ourselves in the midst of the play-sphere: antiphonal songs, ball-games, courtship, question games, riddle-solving, *jeux d'esprit*, all in the form of a lively contest between the sexes. The songs themselves are typical play-products with fixed rules, varied repetition of words or phrases, questions and answers. Anyone who wishes to have a striking illustration of the connection between play and culture could not do better than read Nguyen's book with its wealth of examples.

All these forms of contest betray their connection with ritual over and over again by the constant belief that they are indispensable for the smooth running of the seasons, the ripening of crops, the prosperity of the whole year.

If the outcome of a contest as such, as a performance, is deemed to influence the course of nature, it follows that the particular kind of contest through which this result is obtained is a matter of small moment. It is the winning itself that counts. Every victory *represents*, that is, realizes for the victor the triumph of the good powers over the bad, and at the same time the salvation of the group that effects it. The victory not only represents that salvation but, by so doing, makes it effective. Hence it comes about that the beneficent result may equally well flow from games of pure chance as from games in which strength, skill or wit decide the issue. Luck may have a sacred significance; the fall of the dice may signify and determine the divine workings; by it we may move the gods as efficiently as by any other form of contest. Indeed, we may go one further and say that for the human mind the ideas of happiness, luck and fate seem to lie very close to the realm of the sacred. In order to realize these mental associations we moderns have only to think of the sort of futile auguries we all used to practise in childhood without really believing in them, and which a perfectly balanced adult not in the least given to superstition may sometimes catch himself doing. As a rule we do not

[1] *Les chants alternés des garçons et des filles en Annam*, Paris, 1933.

attribute much importance to them. It is rather rare to find such futilities actually recorded in literature, but as an example I would refer you to the passage in Tolstoy's *Resurrection*, where one of the judges on entering the court says silently to himself: "If I reach my seat with an even number of steps I shall have no stomach pains to-day".

With many peoples dice-playing forms part of their religious practices.[1] The dualistic structure of a society in phratria is sometimes reflected in the two colours of their playing-boards or their dice. In the Sanskrit word *dyūtam* the significations of fighting and dicing merge. Very remarkable affinities exist between dice and arrows.[2] In the *Mahābhārata* the world itself is conceived as a game of dice which Siva plays with his queen.[3] The seasons, *ṛtu*, are represented as six men playing with gold and silver dice. Germanic mythology also tells of a game played by the gods on a playing-board: when the world was ordained the gods assembled for dicing together, and when it is to be born again after its destruction the rejuvenated Ases will find the golden playing-boards they originally had.[4]

The main action of the *Mahābhārata* hinges on the game of dice which King Yudhiṣṭira plays with the Kauravas. G. J. Held draws ethnological inferences from this in the study noted below. For us the chief point of interest is the place where the game is played. Generally it is a simple circle, *dyūtamaṇḍalam*, drawn on the ground. The circle as such, however, has a magic significance. It is drawn with great care, all sorts of precautions being taken against cheating. The players are not allowed to leave the ring until they have discharged all their obligations.[5] But sometimes a special hall is provisionally erected for the game, and this hall is holy ground. The *Mahābhārata* devotes a whole chapter to the erection of the dicing-hall—*sabhā*—where the Pāndavas are to meet their partners.

Games of chance, therefore, have their serious side. They are included in ritual, and Tacitus was at fault in being astonished at the Germans casting dice in sober earnest as a serious occupation.

[1]Stewart Culin, *Chess and Playing Cards*, Annual Report of the Smithsonian Institute, 1896; G. J. Held, *The Mahābhārata: an Ethnological Study*, Leyden thesis, 1935—a work of interest for the understanding of the connection between culture and play.

[2]Held, *op. cit.*, p. 273.

[3]Book xiii, 2368, 2381.

[4]J. de Vries, *Altgermanische Religionsgeschichte*, ii, p. 154. Berlin, 1937.

[5]H. Lüders, *Das Würferspiel im alten Indien*, Abh. K. Gesellsch. d. Wissensch. Göttingen, 1907. Ph. H. Kl. ix, 2, p. 9.

But when Held concludes from the sacred significance of dicing that games in archaic culture are not entitled to be called "play",[1] I am inclined to deny this most strenuously. On the contrary, it is precisely the play-character of dicing that gives it so important a place in ritual.

The agonistic basis of cultural life in archaic society has only been brought to light since ethnology was enriched by an accurate description of the curious custom practised by certain Indian tribes in British Columbia, now generally known as the *potlatch.*[2] In its most typical form as found among the Kwakiutl tribe the potlatch is a great solemn feast, during which one of two groups, with much pomp and ceremony, makes gifts on a large scale to the other group for the express purpose of showing its superiority. The only return expected by the donors but incumbent on the recipients lies in the obligation of the latter to reciprocate the feast within a certain period and if possible to surpass it. This curious donative festival dominates the entire communal life of the tribes that know it: their ritual, their law, their art. Any important event will be the occasion for a potlatch—a birth, a death, a marriage, an initiation ceremony, a tattooing, the erection of a tomb, etc. A chieftain will give a potlatch when he builds a house or sets up a totem-pole. At the potlatch the families or clans are at their best, singing their sacred songs and exhibiting their masks, while the medicine-men demonstrate their possession by the clan-spirits. But the main thing is the distribution of goods. The feast-giver squanders the possessions of the whole clan. However, by taking part in the feast the other clan incurs the obligation to give a potlatch on a still grander scale. Should it fail to do so it forfeits its name, its honour, its badge and totems, even its civil and religious rights. The upshot of all this is that the possessions of the tribe circulate among the houses of the "quality" in an adventurous way. It is to be assumed that originally the potlatch was always held between two phratriai.

In the potlatch one proves one's superiority not merely by the lavish prodigality of one's gifts but, what is even more striking, by the wholesale destruction of one's possessions just to show that one can do without them. These destructions, too, are executed

[1] *Op. cit.* p. 255.

[2] The name was chosen more or less arbitrarily from a number of terms in different Indian dialects. Cf. G. Davy, *La Foi jurée*, Thèse, Paris, 1923; *Des Clans aux Empire* (*L'Evolution de l'Humanité*, No. 6), 1923; M. Mauss, *Essai sur le Don, Forme archaique de l'échange* (*L'Année Sociologique*, N.S. i), 1923–4.

with dramatic ritual and are accompanied by haughty challenges. The action always takes the form of a contest: if one chieftain breaks a copper pot, or burns a pile of blankets, or smashes a canoe, his opponent is under an obligation to destroy at least as much or more if possible. A man will defiantly send the potsherds to his rival or display them as a mark of honour. It is related of the Tlinkit, a tribe akin to the Kwakiutl, that if a chieftain wanted to affront a rival he would kill a number of his own slaves, whereupon the other, to avenge himself, had to kill an even greater number of his.[1]

Such competitions in unbridled liberality, with the frivolous destruction of one's own goods as the climax, are to be found all over the world in more or less obvious traces. Marcel Mauss was able to point to customs exactly like the potlatch, in Melanesia. In his *Essai sur le don* he found traces of similar customs in Greek, Roman and Old Germanic culture. Granet has evidence of both giving and destroying matches in Ancient Chinese tradition.[2] In the pagan Arabia of pre-Islamic times they are to be met with under a special name, which proves their existence as a formal institution. They are called *mu'āqara*, a *nomen actionis* of the verb *'aqara* in the third form, rendered in the old lexicons, which knew nothing of the ethnological background, by the phrase "to rival in glory by cutting the feet of camels".[3] Mauss neatly sums up Held's theme by saying: "The *Mahābhārata* is the story of a gigantic potlatch".

The potlatch and everything connected with it hinges on winning, on being superior, on glory, prestige and, last but not least, revenge. Always, even when only one person is the feast-giver, there are two groups standing in opposition but bound by a spirit of hostility and friendship combined. In order to understand this ambivalent attitude we must recognize that the essential feature of the potlatch is the winning of it. The opposed groups do not contend for wealth or power but simply for the pleasure of parading their superiority—in a word, for glory. At the wedding of a Mamalekala chieftain described by Boas,[4] the guest-group declares itself "ready to begin the fray", meaning the ceremony at the end of which the prospective father-in-law gives away the

[1]Davy, *La Foi jurée*, p. 177.
[2]*Chinese Civilization*, p. 156.
[3]G. W. Freytag, *Lexicon Arabico-latinum*, Halle, 1830, i.v. *aqara:* de gloria certavit in incidendis camelorum pedibus.
[4]Quoted by Davy, *op. cit.*, p. 119 f.

bride. The proceedings at a potlatch also have something of a "fray" about them, an element of trial and sacrifice. The solemnity runs its course in the form of a ritual act accompanied by antiphonal songs and masked dances. The ritual is very strict: the slightest blunder invalidates the whole action. Coughing and laughing are threatened with severe penalties.

The mental world in which the ceremony takes place is the world of honour, pomp, braggadocio and challenge. The performers dwell in the realms of chivalry and heroism, where illustrious names and coats of arms and splendid lineages bulk large. This is not the ordinary world of toil and care, the calculation of advantage or the acquisition of useful goods. Aspiration here turns to the esteem of the group, a higher rank, marks of superiority. The mutual relations and obligations of the two phratriai of the Tlinkit are expressed by a word which means "showing respect". These relations are continually turned into actual deeds by an exchange of services and presents.

To the best of my knowledge, anthropology seeks the explanation of the potlatch mainly in magical and mythical ideas. G. W. Locker provides an excellent example of this in his book *The Serpent in Kwakiutl Religion* (Leyden, 1932).

No doubt there is an intimate connection between the potlatch and the religious preconceptions of the tribes observing it. All the characteristic notions about intercourse with ghosts, initiation, identification of men and animals, etc., are constantly displayed in the potlatch. But that does not prevent us from understanding it as a sociological phenomenon having no ties whatever with any definite system of religion. We have only to think ourselves into a society wholly dominated by those primary impulses and incentives which, in a more cultivated phase, are peculiar to boyhood. Such a society will be animated in the highest degree by things like group-honour, admiration for wealth and liberality, trust and friendship; it will lay great stress on challenges, bettings and "darings" of all kinds, competitions, adventures and the everlasting glorification of the self by displays of studied indifference to material values. In brief, the potlatch spirit is akin to the thoughts and feelings of the adolescent. Quite apart from any connections it may have with the genuine, technically organized potlatch as a ritual performance, a contest in the giving away or destruction of one's own property is psychologically quite understandable. That is why instances of this kind which are not based on a definite system of religion are of particular importance, as, for example, the one described by R. Maunier from a report appearing some years ago in an Egyptian newspaper. Two gypsies had a quarrel. In order to settle it they solemnly called the whole tribe together and then proceeded each one to kill his own sheep, after which they burned all the bank-notes they possessed. Finally the man who saw that he was going to lose, immediately sold his six asses, so as to become victor after all by the proceeds. When he came home to fetch the asses his wife opposed the sale, whereupon he stabbed her.[1] It is obvious that in this whole sad affair we are dealing with something quite different from a spontaneous outburst of passion. It is manifestly a formalized custom with a special name of its own, which Maunier renders by the word *vantardise*; and it seems to me to have the closest affinities with the pre-Islamic *mu'aqara* mentioned above. There is no reason to look for a specifically religious foundation.

The underlying principle in all the strange usages associated with the potlatch is, in my view, the agonistic "instinct" pure and simple. They must all be regarded first and foremost as a violent expression of the human need to fight. Once this is admitted we may call them, strictly speaking, "play"—serious play, fateful and fatal play, bloody play, sacred play, but nonetheless that playing which, in archaic society, raises the individual or the collective personality to a higher power. Mauss and Davy pointed to the play-character of the potlatch long ago, though considering it from quite a different angle. "Le potlatch," says Mauss, "est en effet un jeu et une preuve." Davy, who approaches it from the juristic side and is only concerned to demonstrate the potlatch as a law-creating custom, likens the communities that practise it to big gambling dens where, as a result of bets and challenges, reputations are made and whole fortunes exchange hands. Consequently, when Held comes to the conclusion that dicing and primitive games of chess are not genuine games of chance because they pertain to the realm of the sacred and are an expression of the potlatch principle, I am inclined to put his argument the other way about and say that they pertain to the realm of the sacred precisely because they are genuine games.

[1]R. Maunier, *Les echaufes rituels en Afrique du Nord* (*L'Année Sociologique*, N.S. ii), 1924–5, p. 81, n. i.

Livy complaining of the prodigal luxury of the *ludi publici* as degenerating into crazy rivalry;[1] Cleopatra going one better than Mark Anthony by dissolving her pearl in vinegar; Philip of Burgundy crowning a series of banquets given by his nobles with his own Gargantuan feast at Lille, when the *voeux du faisan*, or "students" as we would call them, indulged in a ceremonial smashing of glassware—all these instances display, in the forms appropriate to their respective times and civilizations, the real *potlatch* spirit, if you like. Or would it not be truer and simpler to refrain from making a cant-word of this term and to regard the potlatch proper as the most highly developed and explicit form of a fundamental human need, which I would call playing for honour and glory? A technical term like potlatch, once accepted in scientific parlance, all too readily becomes a label for shelving an article as filed and finally accounted for.

The play quality of the "gift ritual" found all over the earth has emerged with singular clarity since Malinowski gave a vivacious and extremely circumstantial account in his masterly *Argonauts of the Western Pacific*, of the so-called *kula* system which he observed among the Trobriand Islanders and their neighbours in Melanesia. The *kula* is a ceremonial voyage starting at fixed times from one of the island groups east of New Guinea and going in two opposite directions. Its purpose is the mutual exchange, by the various tribes concerned, of certain articles having no economic value either as necessities or useful implements, but highly prized as precious and notorious ornaments. These ornaments are necklaces of red, and bracelets of white, shells. Many of them bear names, like the famous gems of Western history. In the *kula* they pass temporarily from the possession of one group into that of the other, which thereby takes upon itself the obligation to pass them on within a certain space of time to the next link in the *kula* chain. The objects have a sacred value, are possessed of magic powers, and each has a history relating how it was first won, etc. Some of them are so precious that their entry into the gift-cycle causes a sensation.[2] The whole proceeding is accompanied by all kinds of formalities interspersed with feasting and magic, in an atmosphere of mutual obligation and trust. Hospitality abounds, and at the end of the ceremony everybody feels he has had his

[1]Book vii, 2, 13.

[2]The objects in the *kula* custom may perhaps be compared with what the ethnologists call *Renommiergeld*—bragging-money.

full share of honour and glory. The voyage itself is often adventurous and beset with perils. The entire cultural treasury of the tribes concerned is bound up with the *kula*, it comprises their ornamental carving of canoes, their poetry, their code of honour and manners. Some trading in useful articles attaches itself to the *kula* voyages, but only incidentally. Nowhere else, perhaps, does an archaic community take on the lineaments of a noble game more purely than with these Papuans of Melanesia. Competition expresses itself in a form so pure and unalloyed that it seems to excel all similar customs practised by peoples much more advanced in civilization. At the root of this sacred rite we recognize unmistakably the imperishable need of man to live in beauty. There is no satisfying this need save in play.

From the life of childhood right up to the highest achievements of civilization one of the strongest incentives to perfection, both individual and social, is the desire to be praised and honoured for one's excellence. In praising another each praises himself. We want to be honoured for our virtues. We want the satisfaction of having done something well. Doing something well means doing it better than others. In order to excel one must prove one's excellence; in order to merit recognition, merit must be made manifest. Competition serves to give proof of superiority. This is particularly true of archaic society.

In archaic periods, of course, the virtue that renders one worthy of honour is not the abstract idea of moral perfection as measured by the commandments of a supreme heavenly power. The idea of virtue, as the word for it in the Germanic languages shows, is still, in its current connotation, inextricably bound up with the *idiosyncrasy* of a thing. *Tugend* in German (*deugd* in Dutch) corresponds directly to the verb *taugen* (*deugen*), meaning to be fit or apt for something, to be the true and genuine thing in one's kind. Such is the sense of the Greek ἀρετή and the Middle High German *tugende*. Every thing has its ἀρετή that is specific of it, proper to its kind.[1] A horse, a dog, the eye, the axe, the bow—each has its proper virtue. Strength and health are the virtues of the body; wit and sagacity those of the mind. Etymologically, ἀρετή is connected with ἄριστος: the best, the most excellent.[2]

[1]One might suggest that the closest English equivalent of the German *Tugend*, apart from the word "virtue" itself, is "property". Trans.

[2]Cf. Werner Jaeger, *Paideia* i, Oxford, 1939, p. 3 ff.; R. W. Livingstone, *Greek Ideals and Modern Life*, Oxford, 1935, p. 102 f.

The virtue of a man of quality consists in the set of properties which make him fit to fight and command. Among these liberality, wisdom and justice occupy a high place. It is perfectly natural that with many peoples the word for virtue derives from the idea of manliness or "virility", as for instance the Latin *virtus*, which retained its meaning of "courage" for a very long time—until, in fact, Christian thought became dominant. The same is true of the Arabic *muru'a*, comprising, like the Greek ἀρετή, the whole semantic complex of strength, valour, wealth, right, good management, morality, urbanity, fine manners, magnanimity, liberality and moral perfection. In every archaic community that is healthy, being based on the tribal life of warriors and nobles, there will blossom an ideal of chivalry and chivalrous conduct, whether it be in Greece, Arabia, Japan or mediaeval Christendom. And this virile ideal of virtue will always be bound up with the conviction that honour, to be valid, must be publicly acknowledged and forcibly maintained if need be. Even in Aristotle honour is called the "prize of virtue".[1] His thought is, of course, far above the level of archaic culture. He does not call honour the aim or basis of virtue, but the natural measure of it. "Men crave honour," he says, "in order to persuade themselves of their own worth, their virtue. They aspire to be honoured by persons of judgement and in virtue of their real value."[2]

Consequently virtue, honour, nobility and glory fall at the outset within the field of competition, which is that of play. The life of the young warrior of noble birth is a continual exercise in virtue and a continual struggle for the sake of the honour of his rank. The ideal is perfectly expressed in the well-known line of Homer: αἰὲν ἀριστεύειν καὶ ὑπείροχον ἔμμεναι ἄλλων ("always to be the best and to excel others"). Hence the interest of the epic depends not on the war exploits as such but on the ἀριστεία of the individual heroes.

Training for aristocratic living leads to training for life in the State and for the State. Here too ἀρετή is not as yet entirely ethical. It still means above all the *fitness* of the citizen for his tasks in the *polis*, and the idea it originally contained of exercise by means of contests still retains much of its old weight.

That nobility is based on virtue is implicit from the very beginning of both concepts and right through their evolution, only the meaning of virtue changes as civilization unfolds. Gradually the

[1] *Eth. Nic.* iv, 1123 D 35. [2] *Ibid.* i, 1095 D 26.

idea of virtue acquires another content: it rises to the ethical and religious plane. The nobility, who once lived up to their ideal of virtue merely by being brave and vindicating their honour, must now, if they are to remain true to their tasks and to themselves, either enrich the ideal of chivalry by assimilating into it those higher standards of ethics and religion (an attempt which usually turned out lamentably enough in practice!) or else content themselves with cultivating an outward semblance of high living and spotless honour by means of pomp, magnificence and courtly manners. The ever-present play-element, originally a real factor in the shaping of their culture, has now become mere show and parade.

The nobleman demonstrates his "virtue" by feats of strength, skill, courage, wit, wisdom, wealth or liberality. For want of these he may yet excel in a contest of words, that is to say, he may either himself praise the virtues in which he wishes to excel his rivals, or have them praised for him by a poet or a herald. This boosting of one's own virtue as a form of contest slips over quite naturally into contumely of one's adversary, and this in its turn becomes a contest in its own right. It is remarkable how large a place these bragging and scoffing matches occupy in the most diverse civilizations. Their play-character is beyond dispute: we have only to think of the doings of little boys to qualify such slanging-matches as a form of play. All the same, we must distinguish carefully between the formal boasting or scoffing tournament and the more spontaneous bravado which used to inaugurate or accompany a fight with weapons, though it is not at all easy to draw the line. According to ancient Chinese texts, the pitched battle is a confused mêlée of boasts, insults, altruism and compliments. It is rather a contest with moral weapons, a collision of offended honours, than an armed combat.[1] All sorts of actions, some of the most singular nature, have a technical significance as marks of shame or honour for him who perpetrates or suffers them. Thus, the contemptuous gesture of Remus in jumping over Romulus' wall at the dawn of Roman history constitutes, in Chinese military tradition, an obligatory challenge. A variant of it shows the warrior riding up to his enemy's gate and calmly counting the planks with his whip.[2] In the same tradition are the citizens of Meaux, standing on the wall and shaking the

[1] Granet, *Chinese Civilization*, p. 270. [2] *Ibid.* p. 267.

dust off their caps after the besiegers have fired their cannons. We shall have to revert to this kind of thing when treating of the agonistic, or even the play, element in war. What interests us at this juncture is the regular "joute de jactance".

It need hardly be said that these practices are closely related to the potlatch. Forms mid-way between boasting-matches and competitions in wealth (or what we might call "squandering-matches"), are to be found in the following, as reported by Malinowski. Foodstuffs, he says, are not valued among the Trobriand Islanders solely on account of their usefulness, but also as a means for parading wealth. Yam-houses are so constructed that one can compute from outside how much they contain, and make a shrewd guess as to the quality of the fruit by looking through the wide interstices between the beams. The best fruits are the most conspicuous, and particularly fine specimens are framed, decorated with paint, and hung up outside the yam-stores. In villages where a high-ranking chieftain resides, the commoners have to cover their store-houses with coconut leaves, so as not to compete with his.[1] In Chinese lore we find an echo of such customs in the tale of the bad King Shou-sin, who caused a mountain of foodstuffs to be piled up on which chariots could be driven, and a pond to be dug full of wine for sailing boats on.[2]

Competition for honour may also take, as in China, an inverted form by turning into a contest in politeness. The special word for this—*iang*—means literally "to yield to another"; hence one demolishes one's adversary by superior manners, making way for him or giving him precedence. The courtesy-match is nowhere as formalized, perhaps, as in China, but it is to be met with all over the world.[3] We might call it an inverted boasting-match, since the reason for this display of civility to others lies in an intense regard for one's own honour.

Formal contests in invective and vituperation were widespread in pre-Islamic Arabia, and their connection with the contests in destruction of property, so prominent a feature of the potlatch, is particularly striking. We have already mentioned the custom called *mu'āqara*, where the competing parties cut the tendons of their camels. The basic form of the verb to which *mu'āqara* belongs

[1]Malinowski, *Argonauts of the Western Pacific*, p. 168.
[2]Granet, *Chinese Civilization*, p. 202.
[3]Cf. my *Waning of the Middle Ages*, ch. 2.

in the third degree, means to wound or to mutilate. Now among the significations of *mu'āqara* we also find: "conviciis et dictis satyricis certavit cum aliquo"—to fight with invective and opprobious language; which reminds us of the Egyptian gypsies whose destroying-match bore the name of *vantardise*. But besides the term *mu'āqara* the pre-Islamic Arabs had two other technical terms for the slanging-match and its allied forms, namely, *munāfara* and *mufākhara*. It will be noted that all three words are formed in the same way. They are verbal substantives derived from the so-called third form of the verb, and this is perhaps the most interesting feature of the whole business. For Arabic possesses a special verbal form which can give to any root the sense of *competing in something* or excelling somebody in something. I am almost tempted to call it a kind of *verbal superlative* of the root itself. In addition, the so-called "sixth form", derived from the third, expresses the idea of reciprocal action. Thus the root *hasaba*—to count, to enumerate—becomes *muhāsaba*, a competition in good repute; *kathara*—to excel in numbers, to outnumber—becomes *mukāthara*, a competition in numbers. But to return to our point: *mufākhara* comes from a root meaning "to boast", while *munāfara* comes from the semantic field of "defeat" and "rout".

Honour, virtue, praise and glory are, in Arabic, semantically akin, just as the equivalent ideas in Greek gravitate round ἀρετή.[1] With the Arabs the central idea is *'irḍ*, which can best be translated by "honour", provided that we take it in an extremely concrete sense. The highest demand of a noble life is the obligation to preserve your honour safe and unsullied. Your adversary, on the other hand, is supposed to be animated by a consuming desire to damage and demolish your *'irḍ* with an insult. Here too, as in Greece, any physical, social, or moral excellence constitutes a basis for honour and glory, hence is an element of virtue. The Arab glories in his victories and his courage, he takes an inordinate pride in the numerousness of his clan or his children, in his liberality, his authority, his strength, his eyesight, or the beauty of his hair. All this makes up his *'izz*, *'izza*, i.e. his excellence, superiority over others, hence his authority and prestige.

The abuse and derision of your adversary, which is carried on with particular zeal when you are extolling your own *'izz*, is

[1]Cf. Bichr Farès, *L'Honneur chez les Arabes avant l'Islam, Etude de Sociologie*, Paris, 1933; ed. Encyclopédie de l'Islam, s.v. *mufākhara*.

properly called *hidja'*. Contests for honour, the *mufākhara*, used to be held at fixed times, simultaneously with the yearly fairs and after the pilgrimages. Whole tribes or clans might compete, or simply individuals. Whenever two groups happened to meet they opened the proceedings with a match of honour. There was an official spokesman for each group, the *sha'ir*—poet or orator—who played an important part. The custom clearly had a ritual character. It served to keep alive the powerful social tensions that held the pre-Islamic culture of Arabia together. But the onset of Islam opposed this ancient practice by giving it a new religious trend or reducing it to a courtly game. In pagan times the *mufākhara* frequently ended in murder and tribal war.

The *munāfara* is primarily a form of contest in which the two parties dispute their claims to honour before a judge or arbitrator: the verb from which the word is derived has the connotations of decision and judgement. A stake is set, or a theme for discussion fixed; for instance, who is of the noblest descent?—the prize being a hundred camels.[1] As in a lawsuit the parties stand up and sit down in turns while, to make the proceedings more impressive, each is supported by witnesses acting under oath. Later, in Islamic times, the judges frequently refused to act: the litigious pair were derided as being "two fools desiring evil". Sometimes the *munāfara* were held in rhyme. Clubs were formed for the express purpose first of staging a *mufākhara* (match of honour), then a *munāfara* (mutual vilification) which often ended in the sword.[2]

Greek tradition has numerous traces of ceremonial and festal slanging-matches. The word *iambos* is held by some to have meant originally "derision", with particular reference to the public skits and scurrilous songs which formed part of the feasts of Demeter and Dionysus. The biting satire of Archilochus is supposed to have developed out of this slating in public. Thus, from an immemorial custom of ritual nature, iambic poetry became an instrument of public criticism. Further, at the feasts of Demeter and Apollo, men and women chanted songs of mutual derision, which may have given rise to the literary theme of the diatribe against womankind.

Old Germanic tradition, too, affords a very ancient vestige of

[1]G. W. Freytag, *Einleitung in das Studium der arabischen Sprache bis Mohammed*, p. 184, Bonn, 1861.

[2]*Kitāb al Aghānī*, Cairo, 1905–6, iv, 8; viii, 109 *sq.*; xv, 52, 57.

the slanging-match in the story of Alboin at the Court of the Gepidæ, evidently rescued by Paulus Diaconus from the old epics.[1] The Langobard chieftains have been invited to a royal banquet by Turisind, King of the Gepidæ. When the king falls to lamenting his son Turismond, slain in battle against the Langobards, another of his sons stands up and begins to bait the Langobards with taunts (*iniuriis lacessere coepit*). He calls them white-footed mares, adding that they stink. Whereupon one of the Langobards answers: "Go to the field of Asfeld, there you will surely learn how valiantly those 'mares' of yours can put about them, where your brother's bones lie scattered like an old nag's in the meadow". The king restrains the two from coming to blows, and "then they bring the banquet to a merry end" (*laetis animis convivium peragunt*). These last words clearly reveal the playful character of the altercation. It is undoubtedly a specimen of the slanging-match. Old Norse literature has it in a special form called *mannjafnadr*—the comparing of men. It is part of the Jul-feast, as is also the competition in swearing vows. The Saga of Orvar Odd gives a detailed example. Orvar Odd is staying incognito at the court of a foreign king and takes on a wager, with his head at stake, to beat two of the king's men at drinking. As each proffers the drinking-horn to his rival, he boasts of some doughty exploit of war at which he, but not the other, was present, because the latter was sitting in shameful peace with the women at the hearth.[2] Sometimes two kings try to outdo one another in boastful language. One of the Edda songs, the *Harbardslojod*, deals with a contest of this kind between Thor and Odin.[3] To the same genre we must also add Loki's disputations with the Ases at a drinking-bout.[4] The ritual nature of all these contests is revealed by the express mention of the fact that the hall where the wassailing and disputing are held is a "great place of peace" (*griáastadr mikill*), and that in it nobody is allowed to do any violence to another whatever he says. Even if these instances are literary redactions of a theme harking back to a remote past, the ritualistic background is too obvious for them to be passed off as specimens of a later poetic fiction. The Old Erse legends of MacDatho's swine and the Feast of Bricreud have a similar "comparing of men". De Vries has no doubt of the religious origin of the

[1] *Historia Langobardorum* (Mon. Germ. Hist. SS. Langobard.), i, 24.
[2] *Edda* i, Thule i, 1928, No. 29, cf. x, pp. 298, 313.
[3] *Edda* i, Thule ii, No. 9.
[4] No. 8.

Mannjafnadr.[1] How much weight was attached to obloquy of this kind is clearly illustrated in the case of Harald Gormsson, who wanted to undertake a punitive expedition against Iceland on account of a single lampoon.

Beowulf, in the saga of that name, while staying at the court of the Danish king, is challenged by Unferd with taunts to recount his former exploits. The Old Germanic languages have a special word for this ceremony of mutual bragging and execration, be it the prelude to armed combat in connection with a tournament, or only part of the entertainment at a feast. They call it *gelp*, *gelpan*. The substantive, in Old English, means glory, pomp, arrogance, etc., and in Middle High German, clamour, mockery, scorn. The English dictionary still gives "to applaud, to praise" as obsolete meanings of "yelp", now reduced to the yapping of dogs; and "vainglory" for the substantive.[2]

Old French has the approximate equivalent of *gelp*, *gelpan* in *gab*, *gaber*, of uncertain origin. *Gab* means mockery and derision, particularly as a prelude to combat or as part of a banquet. *Gaber* is considered an art. On their visit to the Emperor at Constantinople, Charlemagne and his twelve paladins find twelve couches made ready after the meal, upon which, at Charlemagne's suggestion, they hold a *gaber* before going to sleep. He himself gives the lead. Next comes Roland, who accepts willingly, saying: "Let king Hugo lend me his horn and I will stand outside the town and blow so hard that the gates will fly off their hinges. And if the king attacks me I will spin him round so fast that his ermine cloak will vanish and his moustache catch fire".[3]

Geoffroi Gaimar's rhymed chronicle of King William Rufus of England shows him indulging in similar braggadocio with Walter Tyrel, shortly before the latter's fatal bow-shot in the New Forest that cost the king his life.[4] Later, in the Middle Ages, this convention of boasting and scoffing seems to have dwindled to an affair between heralds at tournaments. They glorify the feats of arms performed by their masters, praise their ancestry and some-

[1] *Altgermanische Religionsgeschichte*, ii, p. 153.

[2] An instance of *gilp-cwida* from the 11th century is given in the *Gesta Herwardi*, edited Duffus Hardy and C. T. Martin (in an appendix to Geffrei Gaimar, *Lestoire des Engles*), Rolls Series 1, 1888, p. 345.

[3] *Le Pèlerinage de Charlemagne* (11th century), ed. E. Koschwitz, Paris, 1925, pp. 471–81.

[4] F. Michel, *Chroniques anglo-normandes*, i, Rouen, 1836, p. 52; cf. Wace, *Le Roman de Rou*, ed. H. Andresen, Heilbronn, 1877, vv. 15038 *sq.* and William of Malmesbury, *De Gestis Regum Anglorum*, ed. Stubbs, London, 1888, iv, p. 320.

times mock the ladies. On the whole heralds are a despised tribe, a rabble of braggers and vagabonds.[1] The 16th century still knew the *gaber* as a social diversion, which at bottom it had always been despite its origins in ritual. The Duke of Anjou, it is said, found this game mentioned in *Amadis de Gaule* and decided to play it with his courtiers. But Bussy d'Amboise was loth to answer the Duke back. So a rule was made that all parties should be equal and no word be taken ill (just as in Aegir's hall where Loki starts a slanging-match). Nevertheless the Duke's *gab*-party becomes the occasion of a despicable intrigue through which the perfidious Anjou brings about Bussy's downfall.[2]

The contest as one of the chief elements of social life has always been associated in our minds with the idea of Greek civilization. Long before sociology and anthropology became aware of the extraordinary importance of the agonistic factor in general, Jacob Burckhardt coined the word "agonal" and described the purport of it as one of the main characteristics of Hellenic culture. Burckhardt, however, was not equipped to perceive the widespread sociological background of the phenomenon. He thought that the agonistic habit was specifically Greek and that its range was limited to a definite period of Greek history. According to him, the earliest type known to Greek history is the "heroic" man, who is followed by the "colonial" or "agonal" man, to be superseded in his turn by, successively, the man of the 5th century, the 4th century (who have no specific names) and finally, after Alexander, by the "Hellenistic man.[3] The "colonial" or "agonal" period is thus the 6th century B.C.—the age of Hellenic expansion and the national games. What he calls "the agonal" is "an impulse such as no other people has ever known".[4]

It is only to be expected that Burckhardt's views were limited by classical philology. His great work, published after his death as *Griechische Kulturgeschichte*, had taken shape from a series of lectures delivered at Basel University during the eighties, before any general sociology existed to digest all the ethnological and anthropological data, most of which, indeed, were only coming to light

[1]Jaques Bretel, *Le Tournoi de Chauvency*, ed. M. Delbouille, vv. 540, 1093–1158, etc., Liège, 1932; *Le Dit des Lérants*, Romania xliii, 1914, p. 218 *sq*.

[2]A. de Varillas, *Histoire de Henry III*, i, p. 574, Paris, 1694, reproduced in part in Fr. Godefroy's *Dictionnaire de l'ancienne langue française*, Paris, 1885, see *gaber* (p. 197).

[3]*Griechische Kulturgeschichte*, p. 111.

[4]iii, p. 68.

then. It is, however, rather disconcerting to find that Burckhardt's views have gained adherence from more than one scholar even to-day.[1] Victor Ehrenberg still regards the agonistic principle as specifically Greek. "To the Orient," he says, "it remained alien and antipathetic"; "we search the Bible in vain for evidence of agonistic contests".[2] In the foregoing we had frequent occasion to refer to the Far East, to the India of the *Mahābhārata* and to the world of savage peoples, so that we need not waste time refuting such assertions here. And it is precisely the Old Testament that affords one of the most convincing examples of the connection between the agonistic factor and play. Burckhardt admitted that primitive and barbaric peoples practise contests, but he attached little importance to it.[3] Ehrenberg condescends to recognize the agonistic principle as universally human, but at the same time he calls it "historically uninteresting and without significance"! The contest for sacred or magical purposes he completely ignores, and attacks what he calls "the folkloristic approach to Greek material".[4] According to him, the competitive impulse "hardly ever became a social and supra-personal force outside Greece".[5] It is true that after having written his book he grew aware at least of the Icelandic parallels to Greek tradition, and declared himself ready to attribute a certain significance to them.[6]

Ehrenberg also follows Burckhardt in focussing "the agonal" on the period that succeeded the "heroic" one, conceding at the same time that the latter already had a certain agonistic complexion. He says that on the whole the Trojan War was devoid of agonistic features; only after the "de-heroizing of the warrior-class" ("Entheroisierung des Kriegertums") did the need arise to create a substitute for heroism in "the agonal", which was therefore a "product" of a younger phase of culture.[7] All this is based more or less on Burckhardt's striking aphorism: "A people knowing war has no need of tournaments".[8] Such an assumption may sound plausible enough to our thinking but, as regards all archaic periods of culture, it has been proved absolutely wrong by

[1] H. Schäfer, *Staatsform und Politik*, Leipzig, 1932; V. Ehrenberg, *Ost und West: Studien zur geschichtlichen Problematik der Antike*, Schriften der Philos. Fak. der deutschen Univ. Prag, xv, 1935.

[2] *Ost und West*, pp. 93, 94, 90.

[3] *Gr. Kulturg.* iii, p. 68.

[4] *Ost und West*, pp. 65, 219.

[5] *Ibid.* p. 217.

[6] *Ibid.* pp. 69, 218.

[7] *Ibid.* pp. 71, 67, 70, 66, 72; cf. Burckhardt, *op. cit.* pp. 26, 43.

[8] *Gr. Kulturg.* iii, p. 69; cf. Ehrenberg, *op. cit.* p. 88.

sociology and ethnology alike. No doubt the few centuries of Greek history when the contest reigned supreme as the life-principle of society also saw the rise of the great sacred games which united all Hellas at Olympia, on the Isthmus, at Delphi and Nemea; but the fact remains that the spirit of contest dominated Hellenic culture both before those centuries, and after.

During the whole span of their existence the Hellenic games remained closely allied with religion, even in later times when, on a superficial view, they might have the appearance of national sports pure and simple. Pindar's triumphal songs celebrating the great contests belong wholly to the rich harvest of religious poetry he produced, of which, indeed, they are the sole survivors.[1] The sacred character of the agon was everywhere apparent. The competitive zeal of the Spartan boys in enduring pain before the altar is only one example of the cruel trials connected with initiation to manhood, such as can be found all over the earth among primitive peoples. Pindar shows a victor in the Olympic games breathing new life into the nostrils of his aged grandfather.[2]

Greek tradition divides contests in general into such as are public or national, military and juridical, and such as are concerned with strength, wisdom and wealth. The classification would seem to reflect an earlier, agonistic phase of culture. The fact that litigation before a judge is called an "agon" should not be taken, with Burckhardt,[3] as a mere metaphorical expression of later times but, on the contrary, as evidence of an immemorial association of ideas, about which we shall have more to say. The lawsuit had in fact once been an agon in the strict sense of the word.

The Greeks used to stage contests in anything that offered the bare possibility of a fight. Beauty contests for men were part of the Panathenaean and Thesean festivals. At symposia contests were held in singing, riddle-solving, keeping awake and drinking. Even in the last-named the sacred element is not lacking: πολυποσία and ἀκρατοποσία (bulk-drinking and drinking neat) formed part of the Choen festival—or feast of pitchers. Alexander celebrated the death of Kalanos by a gymnastic and musical agon with prizes for the doughtiest drinkers, with the result that thirty-five of the competitors died on the spot, six afterwards, among them the prize-winner.[4] We may note in passing that contests

[1] Jaeger, *Paideia*, i, p. 208. [2] *Olympica*, viii, 92 (70). [3] *Op. cit.* iii, p. 85.
[4] After Chares, cf. Pauly Wissowa, s.v. Kalanos, c. 1545.

in swallowing large quantities of food and drink, or guzzling-matches, also occur in connection with the potlatch.

A too narrow conception of the agonistic principle has induced Ehrenberg to deny it to Roman civilization, or actually to attribute to it an anti-agonistic character.[1] It is true that contests between free men played a comparatively small part here, but this is not to say that the agonistic element was altogether lacking in the structure of Roman civilization. Rather we are dealing with the singular phenomenon showing how the competitive impulse shifted, at an early period, from the protagonist to the spectator, who merely watches the struggles of others appointed for that purpose. Without a doubt this shift is closely connected with the profoundly ritualistic character of the Roman games themselves, for this vicarious attitude is quite in place in ritual, where the contestants are regarded as representing—i.e. fighting on behalf of—the spectators. Gladiatorial games, contests between wild beasts, chariot-races, etc., lose nothing of their agonistic nature even when carried out by slaves. The *ludi* were either associated with the regular yearly festivals or were *ludi votivi*, held in honour of some vow, usually to pay homage to the deceased or, more particularly, to avert the wrath of the gods. The slightest offence against the ritual or the most accidental disturbance invalidated the whole performance. This points to the sacred character of the action.

It is of the utmost significance that these Roman gladiatorial combats, bloody, superstitious and illiberal as they were, nevertheless kept to the last the simple word "ludus" with all its associations of freedom and joyousness. How are we to understand this?

We shall have to revert once more to the place occupied by the agon in Greek civilization. According to the view expressed by Burckhardt and taken up again by Ehrenberg, there is a sequence of stages as follows: first an archaic period, also called the "heroic", which saw the rise of Hellas by serious combat and war, but lacking the agonistic principle as a social factor. Then, as the nation had consumed its best forces in these heroic struggles and was gradually losing its heroic temper, Greek society began to move in the direction of "the agonal", which thereupon became dominant in social life for some centuries. It is a transition from "battle to play", as Ehrenberg puts it, hence a sign of decadence. And undoubtedly the predominance of the agonistic principle

[1] *Op. cit.* p. 91.

does lead to decadence in the long run. Ehrenberg goes on to say that the very pointlessness and meaninglessness of the agon finally led to the "loss of all the serious qualities in life, in thought, and in action; indifference to all impulses from without, and the squandering of national forces merely for the sake of winning a game".[1] In the last words of this sentence there is much truth; but even admitting that Greek social life did at times degenerate into mere passion for emulation, Greek history as a whole follows a very different course from that supposed by Ehrenberg. We have to put the significance of the agonistic principle for culture in quite another way. There was no transition from "battle to play" in Greece, nor from play to battle, but a development *of* culture *in* play-like contest. In Greece as elsewhere the play-element was present and significant from the beginning. Our point of departure must be the conception of an almost childlike play-sense expressing itself in various play-forms, some serious, some playful, but all rooted in ritual and productive of culture by allowing the innate human need of rhythm, harmony, change, alternation, contrast and climax, etc., to unfold in full richness. Coupled with this play-sense is a spirit that strives for honour, dignity, superiority and beauty. Magic and mystery, heroic longings, the foreshadowings of music, sculpture and logic all seek form and expression in noble play. A later generation will call the age that knew such aspirations "heroic".

In play, therefore, the antithetical and agonistic basis of civilization is given from the start, for play is older and more original than civilization. So to return to our starting-point, the Roman *ludi*, we can affirm that Latin was right in calling the sacred contests by the simple word "play", because it expresses as purely as possible the unique nature of this civilizing force.

During the growth of a civilization the agonistic function attains its most beautiful form, as well as its most conspicuous, in the archaic phase. As a civilization becomes more complex, more variegated and more overladen, and as the technique of production and social life itself become more finely organized, the old cultural soil is gradually smothered under a rank layer of ideas, systems of thought and knowledge, doctrines, rules and regulations, moralities and conventions which have all lost touch with play. Civilization, we then say, has grown more serious; it assigns only a secondary place to playing. The heroic period is over, and the agonistic phase, too, seems a thing of the past.

[1] *Op. cit.* p. 96.

IV

PLAY AND LAW

AT FIRST sight few things would seem to be further apart than the domain of law, justice and jurisprudence, and play. High seriousness, deadly earnest and the vital interests of the individual and society reign supreme in everything that pertains to the law. The etymological foundation of most of the words which express the ideas of law and justice lies in the sphere of setting, fixing, establishing, stating, appointing, holding, ordering, choosing, dividing, binding, etc. All these ideas would seem to have little or no connection with, indeed to be opposed to, the semantic sphere which gives rise to the words for play. However, as we have observed all along, the sacredness and seriousness of an action by no means preclude its play-quality.

That an affinity may exist between law and play becomes obvious to us as soon as we realize how much the actual practice of the law, in other words a lawsuit, properly resembles a contest whatever the ideal foundations of the law may be. We have already touched on the possible relationship of the contest to the rise of a law-system in our description of the potlatch, which Davy approaches exclusively from the juristic point of view as a primitive system of contract and obligation.[1] In Greece, litigation was considered as an agon, a contest bound by fixed rules and sacred in form, where the two contending parties invoked the decision of an arbiter. Such a conception of the lawsuit must not be regarded as a later development, a mere transfer of ideas, let alone the degeneration that Ehrenberg seems to think it is.[2] On the contrary, the whole development goes in the opposite direction, for the juridical process started by being a contest and the agonistic nature of it is alive even to-day.

Contest means play. As we have seen, there is no sufficient reason to deny any contest whatsoever the character of play. The playful and the contending, lifted on to the plane of that sacred seriousness which every society demands for its justice, are still discernible to-day in all forms of judicial life. The pronouncement

[1]Davy, *La Foi jurée*.

[2]*Ost und West*, p. 76; cf. p. 71.

of justice takes place in a "court", for a start. This court is still, in the full sense of the word, the ἱερὸς κύκλος, the sacred circle within which the judges are shown sitting, in the shield of Achilles.[1] Every place from which justice is pronounced is a veritable *temenos*, a sacred spot cut off and hedged in from the "ordinary" world. The old Flemish and Dutch word for it is *vierschaar*, literally a space divided off by four ropes or, according to another view, by four benches. But whether square or round it is still a magic circle, a play-ground where the customary differences of rank are temporarily abolished. Whoever steps inside it is sacrosanct for the time being. Before Loki launched forth on his slanging-match he made sure that the spot on which he did so was a "great place of peace".[2] The English House of Lords is virtually still a court of justice; hence the Woolsack, the seat of the Lord Chancellor who really has no business there, is reckoned as "technically outside the precincts of the House".

Judges about to administer justice step outside "ordinary" life as soon as they don wig and gown. I do not know whether the costume of the English judge and barrister has been the subject of ethnological investigation. It seems to me that it has little to do with the vogue for wigs in the 17th and 18th centuries. The judge's wig is rather a survival of the mediaeval head-dress worn by lawyers in England, called the coif, which was originally a close-fitting white cap. A vestige of this is still present in the little white edging at the rim of the wig. The judge's wig, however, is more than a mere relic of antiquated professional dress. Functionally it has close connections with the dancing masks of savages. It transforms the wearer into another "being". And it is by no means the only very ancient feature which the strong sense of tradition so peculiar to the British has preserved in law. The sporting element and the humour so much in evidence in British legal practice is one of the basic features of law in archaic society. Of course this element is not wholly lacking in the popular tradition of other countries as well. Even law proceedings on the Continent, though much more persistently serious than in England, bear traces of it. The style and language in which the juristic wranglings of a modern lawsuit are couched often betray a sportsmanlike passion for indulging in argument and counter-

[1] *Iliad*, xviii, 504.

[2] Cf. Jaeger, *Paideia*, i, p. 104: ". . . the ideal of *dike* is used as a standard in public life by which both high-born and low-born men are measured as 'equals'."

argument, some of them highly sophistical, which has reminded a legal friend of mine, a judge, of the Javanese *adat*. Here, he says, the spokesmen poke little sticks into the ground at each well-aimed argument, so that he who has accumulated most sticks carries the day victoriously. The play-character of legal proceedings was faithfully observed by Goethe in his description of a sitting of a Venetian court in the Doge's Palace.[1]

These few random remarks may prepare us for the very real connection between jurisdiction and play. Let us turn back once more to the archaic forms of legal procedure. Any proceeding before a judge will always and in all circumstances be dominated by the intense desire of each party to gain his cause. The desire to win is so strong that the agonistic factor cannot be discounted for a single moment. If this does not of itself suffice to disclose the connection between legal justice and play, the formal characteristics of the law as practised lend added weight to our contention. The judicial contest is always subject to a system of restrictive rules which, quite apart from the limitations of time and place, set the lawsuit firmly and squarely in the domain of orderly, antithetical play. The active association of law and play, particularly in archaic culture, can be seen from three points of view. The lawsuit can be regarded as a game of chance, a contest, or a verbal battle.

We moderns cannot conceive justice apart from abstract righteousness, however feeble our conception of it may be. For us, the lawsuit is primarily a dispute about right and wrong; winning and losing take only a second place. Now it is precisely this preoccupation with ethical values that we must abandon if we are to understand archaic justice. Turning our eyes from the administration of justice in highly developed civilizations to that which obtains in less advanced phases of culture, we see that the idea of right and wrong, the ethical-juridical conception, comes to be overshadowed by the idea of winning and losing, that is, the purely agonistic conception. It is not so much the abstract question of right and wrong that occupies the archaic mind as the very concrete question of winning or losing. Once given this feeble ethical standard the agonistic factor will gain enormously in legal practice the further back we go; and as the agonistic element increases so does the element of chance, with the result that we soon find ourselves in the play-sphere. We are confronted by a

[1] *Italienische Reise*, Oct. 3rd.

mental world in which the notion of decision by oracles, by the judgement of God, by ordeal, by sortilege—i.e. by *play*—and the notion of decision by judicial sentence, fuse in a single complex of thought. Justice is made subservient—and quite sincerely—to the rules of the game. We still acknowledge the incontrovertibility of such decisions when, failing to make up our minds, we resort to drawing lots or "tossing up".

Divine Will, destiny and chance seem more or less distinct to us, at least we try to distinguish between them as concepts. To the archaic mind, however, they are more or less equivalent. "Fate" may be known by eliciting some pronouncement from it. An oracular decision of this kind is arrived at by trying out the uncertain prospects of success. You draw sticks, or cast stones, or prick between the pages of the Holy Book, and the oracle will respond. In Exodus xxviii 30, Moses is bidden "to put in the breastplate of judgement the Urim and Thummim" (whatever they were), so that Aaron "shall bear the judgement of the children of Israel upon his heart before the Lord continually". The breastplate is worn by the High Priest, and it is with this that the priest Eleazer asks for advice, in Numbers xxvii 21, on behalf of Joshua, "after the judgement of Urim". Likewise in 1 Samuel xiv 42, Saul orders lots to be cast as between himself and his son Jonathan. The relations between oracle, chance and judgement are illustrated very clearly in these instances. Pre-Islamic Arabia also knew this kind of sortilege.[1] Finally, is not the sacred balance in which Zeus, in the Iliad, weighs men's chances of death before the battle begins, much the same? "Then the Father strung the two golden scales and put into them the two portions of bitter death, one for the stallion-subduing Trojans and one for the bronze-bearing Achaeans."[2]

This weighing or *pondering* of Zeus is at the same time his judging (δικάζειν). The ideas of Divine Will, fate and chance are perfectly fused here. The scales of justice—a metaphor born undoubtedly of this Homeric image—are the emblem of uncertain chance, which is "in the balance". There is no question at this stage of the triumph of moral truth, or any idea that right weighs more heavily than wrong—a notion that was to come much later.

One of the devices on the shield of Achilles as described in the eighteenth book of the Iliad, represents a legal proceeding with

[1] J. Wellhausen, *Reste arabischen Heidentums*, Berlin, 1927, p. 132.
[2] *Iliad*, viii, 69; cf. xx, 209; xvi, 658; xix, 223.

judges sitting within the sacred circle, and at the centre of this there are "two talents of gold" (δύο χρυσοῖο τάλαντα) for him who pronounces the most righteous judgement.[1] These are commonly interpreted as being the sum of money for which the parties concerned are pleading. But, all things considered, they would seem to be rather a stake or a prize than an object of litigation; hence they are better suited to a game of lots than to a judicial session. Further, it is worth noting that *talanta* originally meant "scales". I am inclined to think, therefore, that the poet had a vase-painting in mind which showed two litigants sitting on either side of an actual pair of scales, the veritable "scales of justice" where judgement was done by weighing according to the primitive custom—in other words by oracle of lot. This custom was no longer understood at the time of the making of those lines, with the result that *talanta* were conceived, by a transposition of meanings, as money.

The Greek δίκη (right, justice) has a scale of meanings which range from the purely abstract to something very concrete indeed. It may signify justice as an abstract concept, or an equitable share, or indemnification, or even more: the parties to a lawsuit give and take δίκη, the judge allots δίκη. It also means the legal process itself, the verdict and the punishment. Though we might suppose the more concrete significations of a word to be the more original, as regards *diké* Werner Jaeger takes the opposite view. According to him, the abstract meaning is the primary one, from which the concrete is derived.[2] This does not seem to me to be compatible with the fact that it is precisely the abstractions—δίκαιος, righteous, and δικαιοσύνη, righteousness—that were subsequently formed from *diké*. The relationship discussed above between the administration of justice and the casting of lots ought surely to dispose us, rather, in the direction of the etymology expressly rejected by Jaeger, which derives δίκη from δικεῖν, to cast or throw, although there is obviously an affinity between δίκη and δείκνυμι. Hebrew, too, has a similar association of "right" and "casting", for *thorah* (right, justice, law) has unmistakable affinities with a root that means casting lots, shooting, and the pronouncement of an oracle.[3]

It is also significant that, on coins, the figure of Diké sometimes turns into that of Tyche, the goddess of uncertain fate. She too

[1] xviii, 497–509. [2] *Paideia*, i, p. 103.
[3] The word *urim* may perhaps come from this root.

holds a balance. "It is not," says Miss Harrison in her *Themis*, "that there is a late 'syncretism' of these divine figures; they start from one and the same conception and then diverge."

The primitive association of justice, fate and chance can also be seen in Germanic lore. The word *lot* in Dutch retains to this day the sense of man's destiny—that which is "allotted" or "sent" to him ("Schicksal" in German)—and also means the visible token of his chances in a lottery, i.e. the longest or shortest match-stick, or a ticket. One can hardly say which of the two significations is the more original, because in archaic thought the two ideas merge in one. Zeus holds the divine decrees of fate and justice in one and the same balance. The Ases of Eddic mythology cast the world's fate by throwing dice. Whether the Divine Will manifests itself in the outcome of a trial of strength, or in the issue of armed combat, or in the fall of sticks and stones, it is all one to the archaic mind. The practice of telling fortunes by cards is rooted deep in our past, in a tradition far older than the cards themselves.

Sometimes an armed combat is accompanied by a game of dice. While the Heruli are fighting the Langobards their king sits at the playing-board, and dice was played in King Theoderich's tent at Quierzy.[1]

The concept of judgement ("Urteil" in German) naturally leads us to consider the *ordeal* ("Gottesurteil"—God's judgement). The etymological connection can be seen at a glance if we thus compare the words in both languages. The word "ordeal" means nothing more nor less than divine judgement. But it is not so easy to determine what exactly the ordeal meant for the archaic mind. At first sight it might appear as if primitive man believed that the gods showed by the outcome of a trial or casting, which of the parties is right or—what amounts to the same thing—in which direction they have disposed fate. Of course the idea of a *miracle* proving which side is right is only a secondary Christian interpretation. But the above view—of divine judgement—is itself probably an interpretation coming from a still earlier phase of culture. The original starting-point of the ordeal must have been the contest, the test as to who will win. The winning *as such* is, for the archaic mind, proof of truth and rightness. The outcome

[1]Paulus Diaconus, *Hist. Langob.* i, 20; Fredegarius, *Chronicarum liber* (Mon. Germ. Hist. SS. rer. Merov. ii, p. 131); cf. iv, 27. Cf. also H. Brunner, *Deutsche Rechtsgeschichte*, Leipzig, 1912, p. 75.

of every contest, be it a trial of strength or a game of chance, is a sacred decision vouchsafed by the gods. We still fall into this habit of thought when we accept a rule that runs: unanimity decides the issue, or when we accept a majority vote. Only in a more advanced phase of religious experience will the formula run: the contest (or ordeal) is a revelation of truth and justice because some deity is directing the fall of the dice or the outcome of the battle. So that when Ehrenberg says that "secular justice springs from the ordeal"[1] he would seem to be inverting, or at least straining, the historical sequence of ideas. Would it not be truer to say that the pronouncing of judgement (and hence legal justice itself) and trial by ordeal both have their roots in agonistic decision, where the outcome of the contest—whether by lots, chance, or a trial of some kind (strength, endurance, etc.)—speaks the final word? The struggle to win is itself holy. But once it is animated by clear conceptions of right and wrong the struggle rises into the sphere of law; and seen in the light of positive conceptions regarding Divine Power it rises into the sphere of faith. In all this, however, the primary thing is play, which is the seed of that ideal growth.

Sometimes the legal dispute in archaic society takes the form of a wager or even a race. The idea of a wager is always forcing itself upon us in this connection, as we saw when describing the potlatch, where the mutual challenges bring about a primitive system of contract and liability. But apart from the potlatch and the ordeal proper, over and over again in primitive legal customs we come across the contest for justice, that is to say, for a decision and the recognition of a stable relationship in a particular instance. Otto Gierke collected a great many strange examples of this blending of play and justice under the title of "Humour in Law". He considered them merely as illustrating the playfulness of the "popular spirit", but actually they only find their rightful explanation in the agonistic origin of the legal function. The popular spirit is certainly playful, though in a far deeper sense than Gierke supposed; and this playfulness is pregnant with meaning. Thus, for example, it was an old Germanic legal custom to establish the "marke" or boundary of a village or piece of land by running a race or throwing an axe. Or else the justice of a person's claim was tested by making him touch, blindfolded, a particular person or object, or roll an egg. In all these instances we are dealing with judgement by trial of strength or play of chance.

[1] *Die Reichtsidee im frühen Griechentum*, Leipzig, 1912, p. 75.

It is certainly no accident that contests play a particularly important part in the choosing of a bride or bridegroom. The English word "wedding", like the Dutch "bruiloft", harks back to the dawn of legal and social history. "Wedding," derived from the Anglo-Saxon *wed* and ultimately from the Latin *vadium*, speaks of the "pledge" or "gage" with which one bound oneself to keep an "engagement" already contracted. *Bruiloft*—wedding-party—is the exact equivalent of the Old English *brydhleap*, Old Norse *brudhlaup*, Old High German *brutlouft*, meaning the race run for the bride, this being one of the trials on which the contract depended. The Danaids were won by a race and so, according to tradition, was Penelope.[1] The point is not whether such actions are mythical or legendary merely, or can be proved to have been a living custom, but the fact that the idea of a race for the bride exists at all. To archaic man marriage is a "contrat à épreuves, a potlatch custom", as the ethnologists say. The *Mahābhārata* describes the trials of strength which the wooers of Draupadi have to undergo, the *Ramayana* likewise with regard to Sita, and the *Nibelungenlied* does the same for Brunhild.

But it is not necessarily in strength and courage alone that the wooer is tested in order to win the bride. Sometimes he is also tested in knowledge and ready wit by having to answer difficult questions. According to Nguyen van Huyen, such contests play a large part in the festivities of young men and girls in Annam. Very often the girl holds a regular examination of her swain. In Eddic lore, though of course in somewhat different form, there is an instance of a similar trial in knowledge for the sake of the bride. Alvis, the all-wise dwarf, is promised Thor's daughter if he can answer all the questions that Thor puts to him regarding the secret names of things. There is a further variation of the theme in the *Fjölsvinnsmal*, where the young man venturing forth on his perilous courtship puts questions to the giant who guards the virgin.

Let us now pass from the contest to the wager, which in its turn is closely connected with the vow. The wagering element in legal proceedings expresses itself in two ways. Firstly, the principal person in a lawsuit "wagers his right", i.e. he challenges the other party to dispute it, by laying a "gage"—*vadium*. Right up to the 19th century, English law knew two forms of action in civil suits

[1] J. E. Harrison, *Themis*, p. 232. Cf. Frobenius, *Kulturgeschichte Afrikas*, p. 429, for a Nubian tale to this effect.

which bore the name "wager": the "wager of battle", in which the party initiating the proceedings offered judicial combat; and the "wager of law", in which he bound himself to swear the "oath of purgation" on a certain day, that is, to attest his innocence. Though they had long been out of use, these forms were only officially abolished in 1819 and 1833.[1] Secondly, and apart from the wagering element in the lawsuit proper, we find that it used to be a common practice, particularly in England, for the public both in court and at large to lay regular bets on the issue of a suit. When Anne Boleyn and her fellow-accused were on trial, the odds in Tower Hall were ten to one on the acquittal of her brother Rochford because of his vigorous defence. In Abyssinia, betting on the sentence was a constant practice in the course of a legal session, and took place between the defence and the hearing of witnesses. Even under Italian rule, litigation still continued to be a passion and a sport that delighted the natives. According to an English newspaper, a judge received a visit from a man who had lost his case on the previous day, but now said contentedly: "I had a very bad lawyer, you know, all the same I'm glad to have had a good run for my money!"

We have tried to distinguish three play-forms in the lawsuit by comparing it as we know it to-day with the legal proceedings in archaic society: the game of chance, the contest, the verbal battle. The lawsuit remains, in the nature of things, a verbal battle even when it has lost its play-quality wholly or in part, actually or in appearance, with the progress of civilization. For the purposes of our theme, however, we are concerned only with the archaic phase of this verbal battle, where the agonistic factor is at its strongest and the ideal foundation of justice at its weakest. Here it is not the most meticulously deliberated juristic argument that tips the balance, but the most withering and excoriating invective. The agon in this case consists almost exclusively in the endeavour of each party to exceed the other in choice vituperation and so to keep the upper hand. We have discussed the slanging-match as a social phenomenon for the sake of honour and prestige, under the guise of the *iambos*, the *mufakhara*, the *mannjafnadr*, etc. The transition from the *joute de jactance* proper to the reviling-match as a legal proceeding is, however, not very clear. It may become clearer if we now turn our attention to one of the most cogent

[1] W. Blackstone, *Commentaries on the Laws of England*, ed. Kerr, iii, London, 1857, p. 337 *sq.*

arguments for the intimate connections between culture and play, namely the drumming-matches or singing-matches of the Greenland Eskimo. We shall deal rather more extensively with this because here we have a practice still in living use (at least it was until recently) in which the cultural function we know as jurisdiction has not yet separated from the sphere of play.[1]

When an Eskimo has a complaint to make against another he challenges him to a drumming-contest (Danish: *Trommesang*). The clan or tribe thereupon gathers at a festal meeting, all in their finest attire and in joyful mood. The two contestants then attack one another in turn with opprobious songs to the accompaniment of a drum, each reproaching the other with his misdemeanours. No distinction is made between well-founded accusations, satirical remarks calculated to tickle the audience, and pure slander. For instance one singer enumerated all the people who had been eaten by his opponent's wife and mother-in-law during a famine, which caused the assembled company to burst into tears. This offensive chanting is accompanied throughout by all kinds of physical indignities directed against your opponent, such as breathing and snorting into his face, bumping him with your forehead, prizing his jaws open, tying him to a tent-pole—all of which the "accused" has to bear with equanimity and a mocking laugh. Most of the spectators join in the refrains of the song, applauding and egging the parties on. Others just sit there and go to sleep. During the pauses the contestants converse in friendly terms. The sessions of such a contest may extend over a period of years, during which the parties think up new songs and new misdeeds to denounce. Finally the spectators decide who the winner is. In most cases friendship is immediately re-established, but it sometimes happens that a family emigrates from shame at having been defeated. A person may have several drumming-matches running at the same time. Women too can take part.

It is of first-rate importance here that among the tribes that practise them these contests take the place of judicial decisions. Apart from the drumming-matches there is no form of jurisdiction whatsoever. They are the sole means of settling a dispute, and

[1]Thalbitzer, *The Ammassalik Eskimo*, Meddelelser om Gronland xxxix, 1914; Birket Smith, *The Caribou Esquimaux*, Copenhagen, 1929; Knud Rasmussen, *Fra Gronland till Stille Havet*, i–ii, 1925–6; *The Netsilik Eskimo*, Report of the Fifth Thule Expedition 1921–4, viii, 1, 2; Herbert König, *Der Rechtsbruch und sein Ausgleich bei den Eskimos*, Anthropos xix–xx, 1924–5.

there is no other way of moulding public opinion.[1] Even murders are delated in this curious manner. No sentence of any kind follows the victory in a drumming-match. In the great majority of cases these contests are occasioned by women's gossip. There is some distinction to be made between tribes which know the custom as a means of justice and those which know it only as a festal entertainment. Another difference concerns the licit degrees of violence: with some tribes beating is permitted, with others the plaintiff may only bind his opponent, etc. Finally, besides the drumming-match, boxing or wrestling occasionally serve to compose a quarrel.

Here, therefore, we are dealing with a cultural practice which fulfils the judicial function perfectly in agonistic form and yet is play in the most proper sense. Everything passes off amid laughter and in the greatest jollity, for the whole point is to keep the audience amused. "Next time," says Igsiavik in Thalbitzer's book,[1] "I shall make a new song. It will be extremely funny, and I shall tie the other fellow to a tent-pole." Indeed, the drumming-matches are the chief source of amusement for the whole community. Failing a quarrel, they are started for the sheer fun of the thing. Sometimes, as a special show of ingenuity, they are sung in riddles.

Not so far removed from the Eskimo drumming-matches are those satirical and comic sessions that used to be held in peasant courts, particularly in Germanic countries, where all sorts of minor offences were judged and punished, mostly sexual ones. The best known of these is the "Haberfeldtreiben". That they are situated midway between play and seriousness is evidenced by the "Saugericht" of the young men of Rapperswil, from which appeal could be made to the Petty Sessions of the town.[2]

It is clear that the Eskimo drumming-match belongs to the same sphere as the potlatch, the pre-Islamic bragging and slanging matches, the Old Norse *mannjafnaðr* and the Icelandic *nidsang* (hymn of hate), as well as the ancient Chinese contests. It is equally clear that these customs had originally little in common with the ordeal, in the sense of a divine judgement brought about by a miracle. The idea of divine judgement in the matter of

[1]Birket Smith, *op. cit.* p. 264, seems to define "judicial proceedings" too sharply when he says that among the Caribou Eskimos the drumming-matches are lacking in this respect because they were only "a simple act of vengeance" or for the purpose of "securing quiet and order".

[2]Stumpfl, *op. cit.* p. 16.

abstract right and wrong may, of course, attach itself to them, but only subsequently and secondarily; the primary thing is decision by the contest as such, that is to say, in and by play. The nearest approach to the Eskimo custom is the Arabic *munāfāra* or *nifar*, the competition for fame and honour in the presence of an arbiter. The Latin word *iurgum* also shows the original connection between the lawsuit and invective. It is an elliptic form of *ius-igium* (*ius* + *agere*), quite literally "law proceeding"; the connection still echoes faintly in the English "objurgation". Compare also "litigation" (*litigium:* quarrel-proceeding). In the light of the drumming-matches purely literary productions like Archilochus' scurrilous songs aimed at Lycambes, now fall into perspective, and even Hesiod's admonitions to his brother Perses may be seen from this point of view. Werner Jaeger points out that political satire with the Greeks was not mere moralizing or the ventilation of personal grudges, but originally served a social purpose.[1] We can confidently add: not unlike that of the Eskimo drumming-match.

And it is quite true that the classical age of Greek and Roman civilization had not wholly outgrown the phase in which the legal oration is hardly distinguishable from the reviling-match. Juristic eloquence in the Athens of Pericles and Phidias was still mainly a contest in rhetorical dexterity, allowing for every conceivable artifice of persuasion. The court and the public rostrum were reckoned the two places where the art could be learned. This art, together with military violence, robbery and tyranny, constitutes that "man-hunting" defined in Plato's *Sophist.*[2] With the Sophists you could take lessons in turning a bad cause into a good one, or even in making it victorious. A young man going in for politics generally opened his career by prosecuting somebody in an action for scandal.

In Rome, too, any and every means of undoing the other party in a lawsuit was held as licit for a long time. The parties draped themselves in mourning, sighed, sobbed, loudly invoked the common weal, packed the court with witnesses and clients to make the proceedings more impressive.[3] In short, they did everything that we do to-day. One thinks of the lawyer who thumped the Bible in the Hauptmann trial and waved the American flag, or of his Dutch colleague who, in a sensational criminal case, tore up the report of the psychiatrist's findings. Littmann describes an

[1] *Paideia*, i. p. 119.
[2] 222 D.
[3] Cicero, *De oratione*, i, 229 *sq*.

Abyssinian court-sitting as follows: "With carefully studied and extremely able oratory the prosecutor develops his indictment. Humorous sallies, satire, apt allusions, proverbs, withering scorn and cold contempt are all enlisted, accompanied the while by the liveliest gesticulations and the most fearful bellowings calculated to strengthen the accusation and utterly confound the accused".

It was only when Stoicism became the fashion that efforts were made to free juristic eloquence of the play-character and purify it in accordance with the severe standards of truth and dignity professed by the Stoics. The first man who attempted to put this new approach into practice was a certain Rutilius Rufus. He lost his cause and had to retreat into exile.

V

PLAY AND WAR

EVER since words existed for fighting and playing, men have been wont to call war a game. We have already posed the question whether this is to be regarded only as a metaphor, and come to a negative conclusion. Language everywhere must have expressed matters in that way from the moment words for combat and play existed.

The two ideas often seem to blend absolutely in the archaic mind. Indeed, all fighting that is bound by rules bears the formal characteristics of play by that very limitation. We can call it the most intense, the most energetic form of play and at the same time the most palpable and primitive. Young dogs and small boys fight "for fun", with rules limiting the degree of violence; nevertheless the limits of licit violence do not necessarily stop at the spilling of blood or even at killing. The mediaeval tournament was always regarded as a sham-fight, hence as play, but in its earliest forms it is reasonably certain that the joustings were held in deadly earnest and fought out to the death, like the "playing" of the young men before Abner and Joab. As a striking instance of the play-element in fighting taken from a not too remote period of history, we would refer to the famous "Combat des Trente" fought in Brittany in 1351. I have not found it expressly styled as "play" in the sources, but the whole performance has the features of a game. So has the equally famous "Disfida di Barletta" of the year 1503, where thirteen Italian knights met thirteen French knights.[1] Fighting, as a cultural function, always presupposes limiting rules, and it requires, to a certain extent anyway, the recognition of its play-quality. We can only speak of war as a cultural function so long as it is waged within a sphere whose members regard each other as equals or antagonists with equal rights; in other words its cultural function depends on its play-quality. This condition changes as soon as war is waged outside the sphere of equals, against groups not recognized as human

[1]See my *Herbst des Mittelalters* (*The Waning of the Middle Ages*), 4th edition, Stuttgart, 1938, p. 141.

beings and thus deprived of human rights—barbarians, devils, heathens, heretics and "lesser breeds without the law". In such circumstances war loses its play-quality altogether and can only remain within the bounds of civilization in so far as the parties to it accept certain limitations for the sake of their own honour. Until recently the "law of nations" was generally held to constitute such a system of limitation, recognizing as it did the ideal of a community of mankind with rights and claims for all, and expressly separating the state of war—by declaring it—from peace on the one hand and criminal violence on the other. It remained for the theory of "total war" to banish war's cultural function and extinguish the last vestige of the play-element.

If we are right in considering the ludic function to be inherent in the agon, the question now arises how far war (in our view, a development of the agon) can be called an agonistic function of society? Several forms of combat at once suggest themselves as being non-agonistic: the surprise, the ambush, the raid, the punitive expedition and wholesale extermination cannot be described as agonistic forms of warfare, though they may be subservient to an agonistic war. Moreover the political objectives of war also lie outside the immediate sphere of contest: conquest, subjection or domination of another people. The agonistic element only becomes operative when the war-making parties regard themselves and each other as *antagonists* contending for something to which they feel they have a right. This feeling is almost always present, though it is often exploited only as a pretext. Even when sheer hunger moves to war—a comparatively rare phenomenon—the aggressors will interpret it, and perhaps sincerely feel it, as a holy war, a war of honour, divine retribution and what not. History and sociology tend to exaggerate the part played in the origin of wars, ancient or modern, by immediate material interests and the lust for power. Though the statesmen who plan the war may themselves regard it as a question of power-politics, in the great majority of cases the real motives are to be found less in the "necessities" of economic expansion, etc., than in pride and vainglory, the desire for prestige and all the pomps of superiority. The great wars of aggression from antiquity down to our own times all find a far more essential explanation in the idea of glory, which everybody understands, than in any rational and intellectualist theory of economic forces and political dynamisms. The modern outbursts of glorifying war, so lamentably familiar to us, carry us back to the Babylonian and Assyrian conception of war as a divine injunction to exterminate foreign peoples to the greater glory of God.

In certain archaic forms of warfare the play-element finds immediate and, comparatively speaking, more pleasant expression. We are once more dealing with that same sphere of archaic thought in which chance, fate, judgement, contest and play lie side by side as so many holy things. It is only natural that war too should fall under this head. One wages war in order to obtain a decision of holy validity. The test of the will of the gods is victory or defeat. So that instead of trying out your strength in a contest, or throwing dice, or consulting the oracle, or disputing by fierce words—all of which may equally well serve to elicit the divine decision—you can resort to war. As we have seen, the connection between decision and Deity is explicit in the German word for ordeal—"Gottesurteil", though fundamentally the ordeal is simply judgement, any judgement whatsoever. Every decision acquired by the ritually correct forms is a "judgement of God". It is only secondarily that the technical idea of the ordeal is associated with definite proofs of miraculous power. In order to understand these associations we have to look beyond our customary division between the juridical, the religious, and the political. What we call "right" can equally well, archaically speaking, be "might"—in the sense of "the will of the gods" or "manifest superiority". Hence an armed conflict is as much a mode of justice as divination or a legal proceeding. Finally, since a holy significance attaches to every decision, war itself might conceivably be regarded as a form of divination.[1]

The inextricable complex of ideas covering anything from the game of chance to the lawsuit can be seen most strikingly at work in the "single combat" in archaic culture. The single combat serves various purposes; it may be a demonstration of personal *aristeia*, or it may be the prelude to a general conflict, or it may go on during the battle as episodes of it. Poets and chroniclers glorify it in the history and literature of all ages, and it is known in all parts of the world. A very characteristic instance of this is

[1]The origin of the curious Dutch word for war, *oorlog*, is not altogether clear, but at any rate it belongs to the sacred or ritual sphere. The meaning of the Old Germanic words that correspond to it fluctuates between "conflict", "fate", and a condition of no longer being bound by an oath. But it is not certain that exactly the same word is being dealt with in all cases. Hnizinga's own English MS. replaces this third factor by "the cessation of normal social conditions". Trans.

Wakidi's description of the Battle of Badr, where Mohammed defeated the Koraishites. Three of Mohammed's warriors challenged a like number of heroes in the enemy ranks; they introduce themselves with due form and hail each other as worthy adversaries.[1] The First World War witnessed a revival of *aristeia* in the dropping of challenges by airmen. The single combat can also serve as an augury of battle, in which form it is known to both Chinese and Old Germanic literature. Before the battle begins the bravest men challenge their opposite numbers on each side. "Battle is a testing of fate. The first encounters are weighty presages."[2] The single combat, however, can also take the place of the battle itself. When the Vandals were at war with the Alemans in Spain the hostile parties decided to have their conflict settled by a single combat.[3] We must not regard this as having provided an omen or as being an humanitarian measure designed to avoid the spilling of blood, but simply as an appropriate substitute for war, a concise proof, in agonistic form, of the superiority of one of the parties: victory proves that the cause of the victors is favoured by the gods, is therefore a "just" cause. Needless to say, this archaic conception of war is soon vitiated by specifically Christian arguments advocating single combat as a means of avoiding unnecessary bloodshed. Even very early on, as in the case of the Merovingian king Theoderich at Quierzy on the Oise, the warriors say: "Better for one to fall than the whole army".[4] In the later Middle Ages it was quite customary for kings or princes at war to set about staging a single combat between themselves and so to end their "querelle". The preparations for it were made with great solemnity and in elaborate detail, the express motive always being "pour éviter effusion de sang chrestien et la destruction du peuple".[5] But, however pompously announced, the battle royal never came off. It had long been an international comedy, a piece of empty ceremonial between royal houses. Nevertheless the tenacity with which monarchs clung to this ancient custom and the mock-seriousness with which it was kept up betray its origin in the sphere of ritual. The archaic conception of a legal proceeding which gave a legitimate and even sacred

[1]Wakidi, ed. Wellhausen, p. 53.

[2]Granet, *Chinese Civilization*, p. 266; cf. J. de Vries, *Altgerman. Religionsg.* i, Berlin, 1934, p. 258.

[3]Gregory of Tours, ii, 2.

[4]Fredegar, *op. cit.* iv, 27.

[5]Cf. my *Herbst des Mittelalters*, p. 134 *sq.*

decision in this way, was still operative. The Emperor Charles V twice challenged François I to a single combat with due ceremony, and this case was by no means the last.[1]

Single combat as a substitute for battle is of course quite different from "trial by battle" in the strict sense of the words, as a legal means to the settlement of a dispute. The important place held by the "judicial duel" in Mediaeval law is well known. It is a moot point whether it is to be regarded as an "ordeal" or not. H. Brunner[2] and others consider it in this light, while R. Schröder[3] holds that it is simply a form of trial like any other. The fact that trial by battle is not to be found in the Anglo-Saxon laws and was only introduced by the Normans, points rather to the conclusion that it was not, subsequently, on the same footing as the ordeal, which was very common in England. The whole issue loses much of its importance if we view the judicial duel properly as a sacred agon, which of its own nature shows which side is right and where the favour of the gods lies. Hence a conscious appeal to heaven, as in the later forms of the ordeal, is not the primary meaning.

Though sometimes fought to the bitter end the judicial duel shows a tendency to assume the features of play. A certain formality is essential to it. The fact that it can be executed by hired fighters is itself an indication of its ritual character, for a ritual act will allow of performance by a substitute. Such professional fighters are, for instance, the *kempa* of the Old Frisian lawsuit. Also, the regulations concerning the choice of weapons and the peculiar handicaps designed to give equal chances to unequal antagonists—as when a man fighting a woman has to stand in a pit up to his waist—are the regulations and handicaps appropriate to armed play. In the later Middle Ages, it would seem, the judicial duel generally ended without much harm done. It remains an open question whether this play-quality is to be regarded as a sign of decadence or whether it is to be attributed to the nature of the custom itself, which did not, however, preclude deadly earnest.

The last "trial by battle" in a civil suit before the Court of Common Pleas was held in the year 1571 on Tothill Fields at Westminster, on a battle-ground sixty feet square specially marked off for the purpose. The combat was permitted to last from sunrise

[1] Erasmus, *Opus epistolarum* vii, No. 2024, 38 *sq.*, 2059, 9.
[2] *Op. cit.* p. 555.
[3] *Lehrbuch der deutschen Religionsg.* Leipzig, 1907, p. 89.

"until the stars grow visible", or until one of the combatants—each armed with buckler and staff as prescribed in the Carolingian capitulars—should utter "the dreadful word" *craven*, thereby avowing himself beaten. The whole "ceremony", as Blackstone calls it, [1] much resembled certain athletic entertainments at a village sports.

If a strong element of play is proper to both the judicial duel and the wholly fictitious royal duel, it is small wonder that the ordinary duel as found among many European peoples to this day should have the same ludic character. The private duel avenges outraged honour. Both ideas—honour that can be outraged and the need to avenge it—belong to the archaic sphere, notwithstanding their undiminished psychological and social significance in modern society. A person's honourable qualities must be manifest to all and, if their recognition is endangered, must be asserted and vindicated by agonistic action in public. Where recognition of personal honour is concerned the point is not whether honour is founded on righteousness, truthfulness or any other ethical principle. What is at stake is social appreciation as such. Nor is it of great importance to show that the private duel derives from the judicial duel. Essentially they are the same: the continual struggle for prestige, which is a fundamental value comprising both right and might. Vengeance is the satisfaction of the sense of honour, and honour will be satisfied no matter how perverse, criminal or morbid. In Greek iconography "Diké" (justice) frequently blends with the figure of Nemesis (vengeance) just as she does with "Tyché" (fortune). [2] The duel also reveals its deep-seated identity with the judicial decision in the fact that, like the judicial duel itself, it hands no blood-feud on to those who lose a kinsman by it—provided, of course, that the duel was fought in due form.

In periods that bear the stamp of a powerful military nobility the private duel may take on extremely sanguinary forms. The principals and their seconds may indulge in a group-fight on horseback with pistols—a regular cavalry engagement. Such were the proportions to which the duel had grown in France during the 16th century. A trifling difference of words between two noblemen might well involve six or even eight persons in a deadly encounter. Honour forbade refusal as a second. Montaigne speaks of such a duel between three of Henri's mignons and three noble-

[1] *Op. cit.* p. 337 *sq.*

[2] Harrison, *Themis*, p. 258.

men from the court of the Duc de Guise. Richelieu tried to abolish this fierce usage, but victims continued to fall to it right up to the time of Louis XIV.

On the other hand it is quite in accordance with the ritual character underlying the private duel that the fighting should not aim at killing but stop at the shedding of blood, when honour is satisfied. Hence the modern duel after the French fashion, which is not as a rule prosecuted beyond the wounding of one of the parties, should not be thought of as a rather ridiculous effeminization of a stern custom. Being essentially a play-form, the duel is symbolical; it is the shedding of blood and not the killing that matters. We can call it a late form of ritual blood-play, the orderly regulation of the death-blow struck unawares in anger. The spot where the duel is fought bears all the marks of a play-ground; the weapons have to be exactly alike as in certain games; there is a signal for the start and the finish, and the number of shots is prescribed. When blood flows, honour is vindicated and restored.

It is difficult to assess the agonistic element in warfare proper. In the very earliest phases of culture fighting lacked what we would call fair play—that is, it was largely non-agonistic. The violence of savage peoples expresses itself in predatory expeditions, assassinations, man-hunts, head-hunting, etc., whether it be from hunger, fear, religion or mere cruelty. Such killings can hardly be dignified by the name of warfare. The idea of warfare only enters when a special condition of general hostility solemnly proclaimed is recognized as distinct from individual quarrels and family feuds. This distinction places war at one stroke in the agonistic as well as the ritual sphere. It is elevated to the level of holy causes, becomes a general matching of forces and a revelation of destiny; in other words it now forms part of that complex of ideas comprising justice, fate, and honour. As a sacred institution it is henceforth invested with all the ideal and material imagery common to the tribe. This is not to say that war will now be waged strictly in accordance with a code of honour and in ritual form, for brutal violence will still assert itself; it only means that war will be seen as a sacred duty and in an honourable light, that it will be played out more or less in conformity with that ideal. It is always a difficult question to determine how far war has really been influenced by such conceptions. Most of the tales we hear of noble battles in beautiful style are based not so much on the sober relation of annalists and chroniclers as on literary vision, either of contemporaries or their successors, in epic and song. There is a good deal of heroic and romantic fiction about it. Nevertheless it would be wrong to conclude that this ennobling of war by viewing it in the light of ethics and aesthetics is but a "fair seeming", or cruelty in disguise. Even if it were no more than a fiction, these fancies of war as a noble game of honour and virtue have still played an important part in developing civilization, for it is from them that the idea of chivalry sprang and hence, ultimately, of international law. Of these two factors, chivalry was one of the great stimulants of mediaeval civilization, and however constantly the ideal was belied in reality it served as a basis for international law, which is one of the indispensable safeguards for the community of mankind.

The agonistic or ludic element in war may be illustrated by examples chosen at random from divers civilizations and periods. First of all, let us take two from Greek history. According to tradition, the war between the two Euboean cities, Chalcis and Eretria, in the 7th century B.C. was fought wholly in the form of a contest. A solemn compact in which the rules were laid down was deposited beforehand in the temple of Artemis. The time and place for the encounter were therein appointed. All missiles were forbidden: spears, arrows, slingstones; only the sword and the lance were allowed. The other example, though less naïve, is better known. After the battle of Salamis the victorious Greeks sailed to the Isthmus with a view to distributing the prizes, here called *aristeia*, to those who had conducted themselves most meritoriously during the battle. The naval commanders were to place their votes on the altar of Poseidon, one vote for the first victor, one for the second. Each commander voted himself first, though most of them voted for Themistocles as second, so that the latter had a majority. However, the jealousies which broke out among them frustrated a ratification of the verdict.

Speaking of the battle of Mycale Herodotus calls the Islands and the Hellespont the "prizes" (ἄεθλα) as between the Greeks and the Persians; but this may be no more than a popular metaphor. Herodotus himself evidently has some doubts about the value of the "match" point of view in war. Through the mouth of Mardonius, who takes part in the imaginary council of war at the court of Xerxes, he speaks disapprovingly of the unwisdom of the Greeks who solemnly announce their wars beforehand, then proceed to choose a fine level battlefield, finally repairing thither for mutual slaughter to the detriment of victors and vanquished alike. Far better, he says, to have their quarrels settled by envoys or heralds or, if this prove impossible and a battle be absolutely imperative, let them fight by all means, but each should then select the coign of vantage most difficult to attack.[1]

It would seem that wherever literature sings the praises of noble and chivalrous war, criticism raises its head, recommending tactical and strategical considerations above fine points of honour. But, as regards honour itself, it is astonishing to note how far Chinese military tradition resembles that of the West in mediaeval times. According to Granet's sketch of Chinese warfare in what he calls the feudal age, there can be no talk of victory unless the prince's honour emerges with enhanced splendour from the field of battle. This is not procured by gaining the advantage, still less by using it to the utmost, but by showing moderation. Moderation alone proves the victor's heroic virtue. Two noble lords, Chin and Ch'in, face one another encamped. The two armies are ranged and do not fight. At night a messenger from Ch'in comes to warn Chin to get ready: "There is no lack of warriors in the two armies! To-morrow I engage you to meet us!" But the people of Chin notice that the messenger has an unsteady gaze and that his voice has no assurance. Ch'in is beaten beforehand. "The Ch'in army is afraid of us! It will take to flight! Let us hem them in against the river! Certainly, we will beat them! Yet the Chin army does not move, and the enemy can decamp in peace. It has sufficed for someone to say: "It is inhuman not to gather up the dead and wounded! It is cowardly not to wait for the time arranged, or to press upon the enemy in a dangerous passage." So Chin's army keeps quiet and leaves the enemy to draw off in peace.[2]

A victorious captain also declines, with becoming modesty, to have a monument erected to him on the battlefield. "Such a thing was fitting in ancient times, when the famous kings resplendent in every virtue warred with the enemies of heaven and made an example of the wicked. But in our day there are no guilty, only vassals proving their fidelity to the death. Is that just cause for a monument?"

In making camp the lay-out is carefully orientated to the four

[1]Book viii, 123–125.
[2]*Chinese Civilization*, pp. 272–3.

zodiacal quarters. Everything pertaining to the arrangement of an army camp in cultural epochs as in ancient China was strictly prescribed and full of sacred significance, for the camp was modelled on the Imperial city and this was modelled on heaven. No doubt Roman camp-buildings too bore traces of their ritual origin; F. Muller and others seem to think so. Although these vestiges had completely disappeared in Mediaeval Christendom, the sumptuously built and gorgeously decorated camp of Charles the Bold at the siege of Neuss in 1475 betrays the close connection between warfare and the tournament, and hence play.

A custom that stems from the idea of war as a noble game of honour and still lingers even in the dehumanized wars of to-day, is the exchanging of civilities with the enemy. A certain element of satire is seldom lacking, and this makes the playful character of it still more evident. The Chinese war lords of ancient times used to exchange jugs of wine which were solemnly drunk amid reminiscences of a more peaceful past and protestations of mutual esteem.[1] They greeted one another with all manner of compliments and reverences, swapped weapons just like Glaucos and Diomedes. Even at the siege of Breda—not the famous one of 1625 immortalized by Velasquez' *Lances*, but that of 1637 when the town was recovered by the Dutch under Frederick Henry of Orange—the Spanish commandant caused a coach and four that had been captured by the beleaguered inhabitants to be civilly returned to its owner the Count of Nassau, with a present of 900 guilders for his soldiery. Sometimes the adversaries will give each other mocking advice. To quote another Chinese instance a warrior, on one of the innumerable campaigns of Chin against Ch'u, demonstrates with infuriating patience how a chariot should be extricated from the mud where it had stuck. All he gets by way of thanks from the enemy soldier is a venomous: "We are not so practised in the art of running away as the inhabitants of your great country!"[2]

In the year 1400 a certain Count of Virneburg offered battle to the town of Aachen on a fixed day and place, and counsels the people to bring the Bailiff of Jülich with them, the cause of the mischief.[3] Such appointments regarding the time and place of a battle are of the utmost importance in treating war as an honourable contest which is at the same time a judicial decision. The

[1] *Ibid.* p. 268. [2] *Ibid.* p. 269.
[3] W. Erben, *Kriegsgeschichte des Mittelalters*, Munich, 1929, p. 95.

"staking out" of a place for battle is identical with the "hedging in" (*hegen* in German) of a law court; it speaks quite literally and concretely of the proceeding as described in the Old Norse sources, where the battle-ground is marked out with wooden pegs or hazel-switches. The idea still lingers in the English expression "pitched battle", meaning one that is conducted according to military rules. It is difficult to say how far the demarcation of the ground actually went in serious warfare; being essentially ritualistic it might be fulfilled symbolically by putting up some token that represented a real fence or paling.[1] But as regards the ceremonial offer of time and place for a battle, mediaeval history abounds in examples. It is true that the rule was to decline or disregard the offer, which at once shows us the purely formal nature of the custom. Charles of Anjou sends word to Count William of Holland that "he and his army will wait on him for three days on the heath of Assche".[2] Similarly, in 1332 Duke John of Brabant dispatches a herald carrying a naked sword to King John of Bohemia with the offer of an appointed place for battle and withal on Wednesday, expressly requesting an answer and if need be a modified proposal. The King, though a paragon of chivalry, let the Duke hang about for three days in the rain. The battle of Crécy was preceded by an exchange of letters in which the King of France offered King Edward the choice of two places and four separate days for battle, or more if desired.[3] The English king sent answer that he was unable to cross the Seine and had been expecting the enemy for three days already. At Najera in Spain in 1367 Henry of Trastamara gave up his extremely favourable position in order to meet the enemy at any cost in open field, and was beaten. It was reported by the Domei agency that after the capture of Canton in December, 1938, the Japanese commander proposed to Chiang Kai-shek that the latter should fight an engagement, which would be decisive, in the plains of Southern China for the purpose of saving his military honour, and then acknowledge the decision as terminating the "incident".

There are other mediaeval military customs that are on the same level as the offer of a definite time and place, for instance the "place of honour" in the order of battle and the demand that the victor should remain on the battlefield for three days. The former

[1]Compare our expression "beyond the pale". Trans.
[2]Melis Stoke, *Rijmkroniek*, ed. W. V. Brill, iii, 1387.
[3]Cf. Erben, *op. cit.* p. 93; also my *Herbst des Mittelalters*, p. 142.

was eagerly contended for. Sometimes the right to vanguard action was fixed by charter or recognized as the hereditary privilege of certain families and counties. Disputes in this matter often had bloody consequences. When in 1396 a picked army of knights, whose lethal qualities had been proved by the recent wars in France, entered with uncommon pomp upon a crusade against the Turk, the chances of victory were thrown away in vain haggling for precedence at Nicopolis, with the result that the knightly host was annihilated. As to remaining in the field for three days, it is possible to trace in this constantly reiterated demand something of the juridical "sessio triduana". At any rate it is certain that in all these ceremonial and ritual usages as recorded by tradition from all parts of the world, we see war clearly originating in that primitive sphere of continuous and eager contest where play and combat, justice, fate, and chance are intimately commingled.[1]

The primitive ideal of honour and nobility—rooted in that first of sins, Superbia—is superseded in more advanced phases of civilization by the ideal of justice, or rather, this ideal attaches itself to it and, however miserably put into practice, henceforth becomes the recognized and desiderated norm of human society, which has now grown from a huddle of clans and tribes to an association of great nations and States. The "law of nations" derives from the agonistic sphere as the consciousness, or voice of conscience, which says: "This goes against honour, is against the rules". Once a thorough-going system of international obligations based on ethics has been developed, there is hardly any room for the agonistic element in the relations of States, for the system tries to sublimate the instinct of political struggle in a true sense of justice and equity. In a community of States bound by one international law universally recognized there is, in theory, no reason for agonistic warfare among its own members. Even so, such a community will not have lost all the features of a play-community. Its principle of reciprocal rights, its diplomatic forms, its mutual obligations in the matter of honouring treaties and, in the event of war, officially abrogating peace, all bear a formal resemblance to play-rules inasmuch as they are only binding while the game itself—i.e. the need for order in human affairs—is recognized. We might, in a purely formal sense, call all society a game, if we bear

[1] *Ibid.* p. 100; *ibid.* p. 140.

in mind that this game is the living principle of all civilization.

Things have now come to such a pass that the system of international law is no longer acknowledged, or observed, as the very basis of culture and civilized living. As soon as one member or more of a community of States virtually denies the binding character of international law and, either in practice or in theory, proclaims the interests and power of its own group—be it nation, party, class, church or whatsoever else—as the sole norm of its political behaviour, not only does the last vestige of the immemorial play-spirit vanish but with it any claim to civilization at all. Society then sinks down to the level of the barbaric, and original violence retakes its ancient rights.

The inference from all this is that in the absence of the play-spirit civilization is impossible. Yet, even in a society completely disintegrated by the collapse of all legal ties, the agonistic impulse is not lost, for it is innate. The innate desire to be first will still drive the power-groups into collision and may lead them to incredible extremes of infatuation and frenzied megalomania. It makes little difference whether one gives adherence to the doctrine of yesterday which interpreted history as the product of "inevitable and immutable" economic forces, or sets up brand-new "Weltanschauungen" which merely put a pseudo-scientific label on the eternal desire to succeed and excel. At bottom it is always a question of winning—though we know well enough that this form of "winning" can bring no gain.

In the beginnings of civilization rivalry for first rank was undoubtedly a formative and ennobling factor. Together with a genuine naiveté of mind and a lively sense of honour it produced that proud personal courage so essential to a young culture. And not only this: cultural forms will themselves develop in these ever-recurrent sacred contests, in them the structure of society will unfold. The noble life is seen as an exhilarating game of courage and honour. Unfortunately, even in archaic surroundings war with its grimness and bitterness offers but scant occasion for this noble game to become a reality. Bloody violence cannot be caught to any great extent in truly noble form; hence the game can only be fully experienced and enjoyed as a social and aesthetic fiction. That is why the spirit of society ever again seeks escape in fair imaginings of the life heroic, which is played out in the ideal sphere of honour, virtue, and beauty.

Such an ideal of noble strife, fulfilled in myth and legend, is one of the strongest incentives to civilization. It has more than once given rise to a system of martial athletics and ceremonial social play which together adorned real life with poetry, as in mediaeval chivalry and Japanese *bushido*. Here the power of imagination itself works on the personal bearing of the noble class, hardening their courage and heightening their sense of duty. The ideal of noble contest is particularly evident in a society where a military nobility with moderate landed property obeys a monarch regarded as divine or sacred, and where the central duty of life is loyalty to your lord. Only in such a feudally constructed society, in which no free man is required to work, can chivalry flourish and with it the tournament. Only under a feudal aristocracy are deadly serious vows made to accomplish unheard-of feats; only here do banners, crests and scutcheons become objects of veneration, chivalric orders bloom, and questions of rank and precedence become the most vital in life. Only a feudal aristocracy has time for such things. The fundamental character of this whole complex of ideals, manners and institutions is to be seen almost more clearly in the land of the Rising Sun than in Mediaeval Christendom or Islam. The Japanese samurai held the view that what was serious for the common man was but a game for the valiant. Noble self-restraint in face of danger and death is the supreme commandment for him. In this connection we may hazard the opinion that the competition in opprobrious language which we mentioned earlier may take the form of an endurance test, where controlled and chivalrous deportment is evidence of the heroic way of life. A mark of this heroism is the complete disdain felt by the noble-minded for all material things. A Japanese nobleman shows his education and superior culture by not knowing, or professing not to know, the value of coins. It is recorded that a Japanese Prince by name Kenshin, when warring with another Prince by name Shingen who dwelt in the mountains, was informed by a third party that he, though not in open feud with Prince Shingen, had cut the latter's supply of salt. Whereupon Prince Kenshin commanded his subjects to send salt to the enemy, expressing his contempt of such economic warfare by saying: "I fight not with salt but with the sword!"[1]

There can be no doubt that this ideal of chivalry, loyalty, courage and self-control has contributed much to the civilizations

[1] I. Nitobe, *The Soul of Japan*, Tokio, 1905, pp. 35, 98.

that upheld it. Even if the greater part of it was fiction and fantasy, in public life and in education it certainly raised the tone. But under the influence of epic and romantic fancy the historical image of such peoples as professed that ideal often underwent an enchanted transformation, which sometimes induced even the gentlest spirits to praise war, seen through this mirage of chivalrous tradition, more loudly than the reality of it has ever deserved. War as the fountain-head of human virtues and accomplishments—such was the theme that Ruskin rose to, doubtless with some effort, when he addressed the Woolwich cadets, holding it up as the absolute condition of all the pure and noble arts of peace. "No great art ever yet rose on earth, but among a nation of soldiers. . . . There is no great art possible to a nation but that which is based on battle," etc. "I found, in brief", he continues—not without a certain naive superficiality in his marshalling of the historical evidence—"that all the great nations learned their truth of word, and strength of thought, in war; that they were nourished in war, and wasted by peace; taught by war, and deceived by peace; trained by war, and betrayed by peace—in a word, that they were born in war, and expired in peace".

In all this there is a good deal of truth, and that truth is pungently stated. Only, Ruskin at once draws in the horns of his rhetoric by declaring that this is not true of *every* war. What he really has in mind, he says, is "the creative or foundational war in which the natural restlessness and love of contest among men are disciplined, by consent, into modes of beautiful—though it may be fatal—play". He sees mankind divided from the very beginning into "two races, one of workers, and the other of players: one tilling the ground, manufacturing, building, and otherwise providing for the necessities of life; the other part proudly idle, and continually therefore needing recreation, in which they use the productive and laborious orders partly as their cattle, and partly as their puppets or pieces in the game of death". There is a taint of the Superman in this declaration of Ruskin's, and a touch of cheap illusionism; but for our purposes the importance of the passage lies in the fact that Ruskin has correctly grasped the play-element in archaic warfare. In his opinion the ideal of the "creative or foundational" war was realized in Sparta and in mediaeval chivalry. Still, soon after the words we have just quoted his honesty, his seriousness and his gentleness get the better of him, and he arrests the flight of his thought so as to bring in a denunciation of "modern" war—war in 1865!—evidently thinking of the murderous civil war raging across the Atlantic.[1]

Among the human virtues—or had we better say "qualities"?—there is one that seems to have sprung direct from the aristocratic and agonistic warrior-life of archaic times: loyalty. Loyalty is the surrender of the self to a person, cause or idea without arguing the reasons for this surrender or doubting the lasting nature of it. Now this attitude has much in common with play. It would not be too far-fetched to derive this "virtue" —so beneficial in its pure form and so demoniacal a ferment when perverted—straight from the play-sphere. Be this as it may, it is certain that the soil in which chivalry flourished has yielded a rich harvest, the veritable first-fruits of civilization. Epic and lyrical expression of the noblest kind, brilliant decorative art, splendid ceremonial—all have sprung from this immemorial conception of war as a noble game. A direct line runs from the knight to the "honnête homme" of the 17th century and the modern gentleman. The Latin countries of the West added to this cult the ideal of the gallant, so that chivalry and courteous love are so interwoven that we can hardly tell which is warp and which woof.

One thing more remains to be said. In speaking of all this as "the first-fruits of civilization" we are in danger of forgetting their sacred origin. In history, art and literature everything that we perceive as beautiful and noble play was once sacred play. The tournaments and joustings, the orders, the vows, the dubbings are all vestiges of primaeval initiation-rites. The links in this long chain of development are lost to us. The chivalry of Mediaeval Christendom as we know it expends itself in artificially keeping up or even deliberately refurbishing certain cultural elements handed down from a long-forgotten past. But the sumptuous apparatus of codes of honour, courtly demeanour, heraldry, chivalric orders and tournaments had not lost all meaning even towards the close of the Middle Ages. It was in trying to describe the purpose of all this in my earlier book[2] that the intimate connection between culture and play first dawned on me.

[1] *The Crown of Wild Olive: Four Lectures on Industry and War*, iii: War.
[2] *The Waning of the Middle Ages*, chs. ii–x.

VI

PLAYING AND KNOWING

THE urge to be first has as many forms of expression as society offers opportunities for it. The ways in which men compete for superiority are as various as the prizes at stake. Decision may be left to chance, physical strength, dexterity, or bloody combat. Or there may be competitions in courage and endurance, skilfulness, knowledge, boasting and cunning. A trial of strength may be demanded or a specimen of art; a sword has to be forged or ingenious rhymes made. Questions may be put demanding an answer. The competition may take the form of an oracle, a wager, a lawsuit, a vow or a riddle. But in whatever shape it comes it is always play, and it is from this point of view that we have to interpret its cultural function.

The astonishing similarity that characterizes agonistic customs in all cultures is perhaps nowhere more striking than in the domain of the human mind itself, that is to say, in knowledge and wisdom. For archaic man, doing and daring are power, but knowing is magical power. For him all particular knowledge is sacred knowledge—esoteric and wonder-working wisdom, because any knowing is directly related to the cosmic order itself. The orderly procession of things, decreed by the gods and maintained in being by ritual for the preservation of life and the salvation of man—this universal order or *ṛtam* as it was called in Sanskrit, is safeguarded by nothing more potently than by the knowledge of holy things, their secret names, and the origin of the world.

For this reason there must be competitions in such knowledge at the sacred feasts, because the spoken word has a direct influence on the world order. Competitions in esoteric knowledge are deeply rooted in ritual and form an essential part of it. The questions which the hierophants put to one another in turn or by way of challenge are riddles in the fullest sense of the word, exactly resembling the riddles in a parlour-game but for their sacred import. The function of these ritual riddle-solving competitions is shown at its clearest in Vedic lore. At the great sacrificial festivals they were as essential a part of the ceremony as the sacrifice itself. The Brahmins competed in *jātavidyā*, knowledge of the origins, or in *brahmodya*, which might best be rendered by "utterance of holy things". From these appellations it is clear that the questions asked were primarily of a cosmogonic nature. Various hymns in the Rig-veda contain the direct poetical deposit of such competitions. For instance in the first hymn the questions relate partly to cosmic phenomena, partly to the details of sacrificial procedure:

"I ask you about the uttermost ends of the earth; I ask you, where is the navel of the earth? I ask you about the seed of the stallion; I ask you, where is the highest place of speech?"[1]

The eighth hymn describes the principal gods by their attributes in ten typical riddles, and the name of each has to follow as answer:

"One of them is ruddy-brown, many-formed, generous, a youth; he adorns himself with gold (Soma). Another descended refulgent into the womb, the wise among the gods (Agni), etc."

In these hymns the predominating element is their riddle-form, the solution of which depends on knowledge of ritual and its symbols. But in this riddle-form there lurks the profoundest wisdom concerning the origins of existence. Paul Deussen, not without justice, calls the tenth hymn "probably the most admirable piece of philosophy to have come down to us from ancient times".[2]

"Being then was not, nor not-being. The air was not, nor the sky above it. What kept closing in? Where? And whose the enclosure? And was the plunging abyss all water?

"Death then was not, nor not-death; and there was no distinction between day and night. Nothing breathed save That, windlessly of itself; there was nothing beyond That anywhere."[3]

The interrogative form of the riddle has here been partly superseded by the affirmative form, but the poetical structure of the hymn still reflects the original riddle-character. After verse 5 the interrogative form returns:

"Who knows it, and who shall declare where this Creation was born and whence it came?"

Once it is admitted that this hymn derives from the ritual

[1]Cf. *Hymns of the Rig-Veda*, Sacred Books of the East.
[2]*Allgemeine Geschichte der Philosophie*, i, Leipzig, 1894, p. 120.
[3]*Op. cit.* x, 129.

riddle-song which, in its turn, is the literary redaction of riddle-contests actually held, the genetic connection between the riddle-game and esoteric philosophy is established as convincingly as possible.

Some hymns of the *Atharvaveda*—for instance Nos. X, 7, and X, 8—appear to string together whole sequences of enigmatic questions under a common head, and either solved or left unanswered:

"Whither the moons and whither the half-moons, and the year to which they are joined? Whither the seasons—tell me the *skambha*[1] of them! Whither in their desire hasten the two maidens of divers form, day and night? Whither in their desire hasten the waters? Tell me the *skambha* of them!

"How does the wind not cease, nor the spirit rest? Why do the waters, desirous of truth, never at any time cease?"

Archaic thought, brooding in rapture on the mysteries of Being, is hovering here over the border-line between sacred poetry, profoundest wisdom, mysticism and sheer verbal mystification. It is not for us to account for each separate element in these outpourings. The poet-priest is continually knocking at the door of the Unknowable, closed to him as to us. All we can say of these venerable texts is that in them we are witnessing the birth of philosophy, not in vain play but in sacred play. Highest wisdom is practised as an esoteric *tour de force*. We may note in passing that the cosmogonic question as to how the world came about is one of the prime pre-occupations of the human mind. Experimental child-psychology has shown that a large part of the questions put by a six-year-old are actually of a cosmogonic nature, as for instance: What makes water run? Where does the wind come from? What is dead? etc.[2]

The enigmatic questions of the Vedic hymns lead up to the profound pronouncements of the Upanishads. Here, however, we are not concerned with the philosophic depth of the sacred riddle but rather with its play-character and its importance to civilization as such.

The riddle-contest is far from being a mere recreation; it is an integral part of the ceremonial of sacrifice. The solving of the

[1]Literally "pillar", but here used in the mystic sense as "ground of Being" or something of the sort. [For an arresting and unforgettable interpretation of this and similar cosmogonic myths see the works of H. S. Bellamy, *Moons, Myths and Man*, *Built Before the Flood*, etc. (Faber & Faber). Trans.]

[2]Piaget, *The Language and Thought of the Child*, ch. v, Routledge.

riddles is as indispensable as the sacrifice itself.[1] It forces the hand of the gods. An interesting parallel to the ancient Vedic custom is to be found among the Toradja of Central Celebes.[2] The posing of riddles at their feasts is strictly limited as to time, and begins the moment the rice becomes "pregnant", lasting until the harvest. The "coming out" of the riddles naturally promotes the coming out of the rice-ears. As often as a riddle is solved the chorus chimes in: "Come out, rice! come out, you fat ears high up in the mountains or low down in the valleys!" During the season immediately preceding the above period all literary activities are forbidden, as they might endanger the growth of the rice. The same word *wailo* means both riddle and millet (i.e. all fruit of the fields), which staple was supplanted by rice.[3] An exact parallel may be added from Grisons in Switzerland where, it is said,[4] "the inhabitants perform their foolish tricks that the corn may turn out better" ("thorechten abenteur treiben, dass ihnen das korn destobas geraten sölle").

It is well known to every student of Vedic literature, the *Brāhmanas* especially, that the explanations given there of the origin of things are as inconsistent as they are varied, and as subtle as they are often far-fetched. There is no general system, no discernible rhyme or reason. But, bearing in mind the fundamental play-character of these cosmogonic speculations and the fact that they all derive from the ritual riddle, it will then dawn upon us that their confusion need not rest so much on the hair-splitting habits of priests, each intent on exalting his particular sacrifice above others, or on capricious fancy,[5] as on the circumstance that the innumerable contradictory interpretations had once been so many different solutions to ritual riddles.

The riddle is a sacred thing full of secret power, hence a dangerous thing. In its mythological or ritual context it is nearly always what German philologists know as the *Halsrätsel* or "capital riddle", which you either solve or forfeit your head. The player's life is at stake. A corollary of this is that it is

[1]M. Winternitz, *Geschichte der indischen Literatur*, i, Leipzig, 1908, p. 160.

[2]N. Adriani en A. C. Kruyt, *De baree-sprekende Toradja's van Midden-Celebes*, iii. Batavia, 1914, p. 371.

[3]N. Adriani, *De naam der gierst in Midden-Celebes*, Tijdschrift van het Bataviaasch Genootschap xli, 1909, p. 370.

[4]Stumpfl, *Kultspide der Germanen*, p. 31.

[5]As H. Oldenburg, *Die Weltanschauung der Brahmantexte*, Göttingen, 1919, pp. 166, 182, is inclined to do.

accounted the highest wisdom to put a riddle nobody can answer. Both motifs are united in the Ancient Hindu tale of King Yanaka, who held a theological riddle-solving contest among the Brahmins attending his sacrificial feast, with a prize of a thousand cows.[1] The wise Yājñavalkya, anticipating certain victory, has the cows driven away for himself beforehand, and sure enough defeats all his opponents. One of these, Vidaghdha Sakalya, unable to answer, literally loses his head, which separates itself from his trunk and falls into his lap. The incident is doubtless a paedogogic version of the theme that the penalty for not being able to answer was a capital one. Finally, when nobody dares to put any more questions, Yājñavalkya cries out triumphantly: "Reverend brahmins, if any of you wishes to ask any questions let him do so, or all of you if you like; or let me ask a question of any of you, or all of you if you like!" The play-character of the whole proceeding is as clear as daylight. Sacred lore is having a game with itself. The degree of seriousness with which the story was accepted in the sacred canon is as indefinable and in the last resort as immaterial as the question whether anybody really lost his head for being unable to answer a riddle. That is not the most curious thing about it. The chief, the really remarkable thing is the play-motif as such.

Greek tradition, too, has the riddle-solving and death-penalty motif in the story of the seers Chalcas and Mopsos. It has been foretold of Chalcas that he will die if ever he meets a seer wiser than himself. He encounters Mopsos and they enter upon a riddle-contest, which Mopsos wins. Chalcas dies of grief or kills himself out of chagrin, and his followers attach themselves to Mopsos.[2] It is obvious in this case, I think, that the theme of the fatal riddle is there right enough, though in corrupt form.

The riddle-contest with life at stake is one of the main themes of Eddic mythology. In the *Vafthrúdnismal* Odin measures his wisdom against the all-wise giant, Vafthrúdnir, each asking questions in turn. The questions are of a mythological and cosmogonic nature, similar to those quoted from the Vedic texts: Where did Day and Night come from, Winter and Summer, and the Wind? In the *Alvissmál* Thor asks the dwarf Alvis how the various things are called among the Ases, the Vanes (the subsidiary Eddic pantheon), among men, giants, dwarfs and lastly

[1] *Satapatha-Brahmana*, xi, 6, 3, 3; *Bṛhadāranyaka-Upanishad*, iii, 1–9.
[2] Strabo, xiv, 642; Hesiod, *Fragm.*, 160.

in Hel; but before the end of the contest day breaks, and the dwarf is thrown into irons. The *Song of Fjölsvinn* has a similar form, also the *Riddles of King Heidrek*, who has vowed to reprieve from the death-sentence any who can propound a riddle that he cannot solve. Most of these songs are attributed to the later Edda, and the experts may be right in holding them to be no more than examples of deliberate poetic artifice. The fact remains, however, that their connection with the riddle-contests of a remote past is too obvious to be denied.

The answer to an enigmatic question is not found by reflection or logical reasoning. It comes quite literally as a sudden *solution*—a loosening of the tie by which the questioner holds you bound. The corollary of this is that by giving the correct answer you strike him powerless. In principle there is only one answer to every question. It can be found if you know the rules of the game. These are grammatical, poetical, or ritualistic as the case may be. You have to know the secret language of the adepts and be acquainted with the significance of each symbol—wheel, bird, cow, etc.—for the various categories of phenomena. Should it prove that a second answer is possible, in accord with the rules but not suspected by the questioner, then it will go badly with him: he is caught in his own trap. On the other hand, a thing may be figuratively represented in so many ways as to allow of concealment in the most diverse riddles. Often the solution depends wholly on the knowledge of the secret or sacred names of things, as in the *Alvissmál* cited above.

Here we are not concerned with the riddle as a literary form but only with its play-quality and its function in culture. Hence we need not go very deeply into the etymological and semantic connections between "riddle" (*Rätsel* in German) and *Rat* (advice) or *erraten* (to guess). In Dutch the verb *raden* comprises the meanings "to advise" and "to solve (a riddle)" even now. Similarly, αἶνος (a sentence or proverb) has affinities with αἴνιγμα (enigma). Culturally speaking, advice, riddle, myth, legend, proverb, etc., are closely connected. Let it suffice to recall these things to memory and then pass on to the various directions in which the riddle has developed.

The riddle, we may conclude, was originally a sacred game, and as such it cut clean across any possible distinction between play and seriousness. It was both at once: a ritual element of the highest importance and yet essentially a game. As civilization develops, the riddle branches out in two directions: mystic philosophy on the one hand and recreation on the other. But in this development we must not think of seriousness degenerating into play or of play rising to the level of seriousness. It is rather that civilization gradually brings about a certain division between two modes of mental life which we distinguish as play and seriousness respectively, but which originally formed a continuous mental medium wherein that civilization arose.

The riddle or, to put it less specifically, the set problem, is, apart from its magical effects, an important element in social intercourse. As a form of social recreation it adapts itself to all sorts of literary and rhythmical patterns, for instance the chain-question, where one question leads on to another, or the game of superlatives, each exceeding the other, of the well-known type: "What is sweeter than honey?" etc. The Greeks were very fond of the *aporia* as a parlour-game, i.e. the propounding of questions impossible to answer conclusively. It may be regarded as a weakened form of the fatal riddle. The "riddle of the Sphinx" still echoes faintly in the later forms of the riddle-game—the theme of the death-penalty is always in the background. A typical example of the way in which tradition modified it is afforded by the story of Alexander the Great's meeting with the Indian "gymnosophists". The conqueror has taken a town that dared to offer resistance, and accordingly sends for the ten wise men responsible for that advice. They are to answer a number of insoluble questions propounded by the conqueror himself. The penalty for a wrong answer will be death, and he who answers worst will die first. Of this one of the ten sages is to be the judge. If his judgement is deemed to be right he will save his life. Most of the questions are dilemmas of a cosmological nature, variants of the sacred Vedic riddles. For instance: Which is more—the living or the dead? Which is greater—the land or the sea? Which came first—day or night? The answers are tricks in logic rather than specimens of mystic wisdom. When, finally, the question is put: "Who has answered worst?" the wily judge replies: "Each worse than the other!" thus upsetting the whole plan, for now nobody can be killed.[1]

[1]U. Wilcken, *Alexander der Grosse und die indischen Gymnosophisten*, Sitzungsberichen der preuss. Akad. d. Wissensch. xxxiii, 1923, p. 164. The lacunae in the MS. which sometimes make the story difficult to follow have not, in my opinion, always been filled in very convincingly by the editor.

The question calculated to "catch" your opponent is properly called the dilemma, the answer to which, by forcing him to admit something else not covered by the original proposition, invariably falls out to his disadvantage.[1] The same is true of the riddle allowing of two solutions, of which the more obvious one is obscene. Such are to be found in the *Atharvaveda*.[2]

One of the literary derivatives of the riddle deserves particular attention because it shows the connection between the sacred and the ludic in a very striking manner. This is the philosophical or theological interrogative discourse. The theme is always the same: a sage is questioned by another sage or a number of sages. Thus Zarathustra has to answer the sixty sages of King Vistāspa, or Solomon replies to the questions of the Queen of Sheba. In the *Brāhmana* literature a favourite theme is the young disciple, the *brahmachārin*, who comes to the king's court and is there questioned by his elders until, by the wisdom of his answers, the roles are changed and he starts questioning them, thus showing himself master instead of pupil. It need hardly be said that this theme has the closest affinities with the ritual riddle-contest in archaic times. In this connection one story of the Mahābhārata is characteristic. The Pāndavas, in their wanderings, come to a beautiful pool in the forest. The indwelling water-spirit forbids them to drink until they have answered his questions. All those who ignore this injunction fall lifeless to the ground. Whereupon Yudhiṣṭhira declares himself ready to answer the spirit's questions, and there now ensues a game of question and answer in which nearly the whole system of Hindu ethics is expounded—a remarkable instance of the transition from the sacred cosmological riddle to the "jeu d'esprit". Properly viewed, the theological disputations of the Reformation, such as the one between Luther and Zwingli at Marburg in 1529 or between Theodore Beza with his Calvinist colleagues and a number of Catholic prelates at Poissy in 1561, are nothing less than a direct continuation of an age-old ritual custom.

The literary outcome of the interrogative discourse is particularly interesting in the case of the Pali treatise called *Milindapañha*—the Questions of King Menander, one of the Graeco-Indian princes who reigned in Bactria in the 2nd century B.C. The text,

[1] [E.g. from Aulus Gellius: Every woman is fair or ugly; it is not good to marry a fair wife, because she will flirt; it is not good to marry an ugly wife, because she will not be attractive; therefore, it is good not to marry at all. Trans.]

[2] xx, Nos. 133, 234.

though not officially incorporated in the *Tripiṭaka*, the canonical writings of the Southern Buddhists, was held in high esteem by them as well as by their Northern brethren, and must have been composed about the beginning of our era. It shows us Menander in disputation with the great Arhat, Nāgasena. The work is purely philosophical and theological in tenor, but in form and tone it is akin to the riddle-contest. The preamble is typical in this respect:

The King said: "Venerable Nāgasena, will you converse with me?"

Nāgasena: "If your Majesty will speak with me as wise men converse, I will; but if your Majesty speaks with me as kings converse, I will not".

"How then converse the wise, venerable Nāgasena?"

"The wise do not get angry when they are driven into a corner, kings do."

So the King consents to converse with him on an equal footing, just as in the *gaber* played by the Duke of Anjou. Sages from the king's court also take part; and five hundred Yonakas, i.e. Ionians and Greeks, not to speak of eighty thousand Buddhist monks, form the audience. Defiantly, Nāgasena proposes a problem "with two points to it, very profound, hard to unravel, tighter than a knot". The king's sages complain that Nāgasena is stumping them with catch-questions of an heretical tendency, and indeed many of them are typical dilemmas thrown out with a triumphant: "Find your way out of that one, your Majesty!" Thus the fundamental questions of Buddhist doctrine pass in review before us, expressed in simple Socratic form.

The opening tractate of the *Snorra Edda*, known as the *Gylfaginning*, also belongs to the genre of theological interrogative discourses. Gangleri enters upon his dispute with Har, which is in the form of a wager, after first having drawn King Gylf's attention to his abilities by juggling with seven swords.

Gradual transitions lead from the sacred riddle-contest concerning the origin of things to the catch-question contest, with honour, possessions, or dear life at stake, and finally to the philosophical and theological disputation. Closely related to the latter are other forms of dialogue, such as the litany and catechism of a religious doctrine. Nowhere are all these forms so inextricably mixed and jumbled together as in the canon of the *Zend-avesta* where doctrine is presented mainly in a series of questions and answers between Zarathustra and Ahura Mazda.[1] The *Yasnas* in particular—the liturgical texts for the rites of sacrifice—still bear many traces of the primitive play-form. Typically theological questions concerning doctrine, ethics and ritual rub shoulders with old cosmogonic enigmas of a remote, perhaps Indo-Iranian past, as in *Yasna* 44. Every verse begins by Zarathustra saying: "This I ask you, give me the right answer, O Ahura!", and the questions themselves lead off with: "Who is it that . . .?" For example: "Who is it that supported the earth below and the sky above that they did not fall?" "Who is it that joined speed with wind and welkin?" "Who is it that created blessed light and the darkness . . . sleeping and waking?" Towards the end there is a remarkable passage which clearly shows that we are dealing with the vestige of an ancient riddle-solving contest: "This I ask you, give me the right answer, O Ahura! Shall I obtain the prize of ten mares and a stallion and a camel, as was promised me?" Besides the cosmogonic questions there are others of a more catechetical nature concerning the origin and definition of piety, the distinction between good and evil, purity and impurity, and the best means of fighting the Evil One, etc.

Truly, the Swiss clergyman who, in the land and the century of Pestalozzi, wrote a catechism for children and named it "The Little Book of Riddles" (*Rätselbüchlein*), little knew how near this title led him to the actual fount of all catechisms and creeds!

The philosophical and theological disputation, like that of King Menander, was still alive in the courtly conversations of a scientific or scholastic character which the princes of a later age had with their courtiers or wise men from abroad. We know of two questionnaires from the hand of the Emperor Frederick II, the Hohenstaufen King of Sicily, the first addressed to his court-astrologer Michael Scotus,[2] the second to the Mohammedan scholar Ibn Sabin in Morocco. The former is of particular interest for our theme because it shows us the old cosmogonic conundrums mingling with theology and the new spirit of science so ardently fostered by Frederick. What does the earth rest on? How many heavens are there? How does God sit on His throne? What is the difference between the souls of the damned and fallen angels? Is the earth solid right through, or hollow in parts?

[1] C. Bartholomac, *Die Gatha's des Awesta*, Halle, 1879, ix, pp. 58–9.

[2] See *Isis*, iv, 2, 1921, No. 11; *Harvard Historical Studies*, xxvii, 1924, and K. Hampe, *Kaiser Friedrich II als Fragesteller*, Kultur—v. Universelfes, pp. 53–67, 1927.

What makes sea-water salt? Why does the wind blow from different directions? What are the causes of volcanic exhalations and eruptions? Why do the souls of the dead evidently not desire to return to earth? etc. The old voices are mingled with the new.

The second set of "Sicilian Questions" to Ibn Sabin is much more purely philosophical, and is sceptical and Aristotelian in tone. But it too shows traces of the old spirit. The young Mohammedan philosopher frankly lectures the Emperor: "Your questions are foolish and awkward and contradictory!" The Emperor takes this pertness in good part, and for this one of his German biographers, Hampe,[1] praises his "humanity". It is more likely that Frederick knew, as did Menander, that the game of question and answer must be played on an equal footing; hence the players conversed, in the words of old Nāgasena, "not as kings but as the wise".

The Greeks of the later period were perfectly well aware of the connection between riddle-solving and the origins of philosophy. Clearchus, a pupil of Aristotle, evolved a theory of the riddle in a treatise on proverbs, proving that the riddle had once been a subject of philosophy. "The ancients", he says, "used it as a proof of their education (παιδεία)",[2] a remark that clearly refers to the philosophical riddle-solving we dealt with above. Indeed, it would not be too strenuous or far-fetched to derive the earliest products of Greek philosophy from those immemorial riddle-questions.

Leaving aside the question of how far the word "problem" itself (πρόβλημα)—literally "what is thrown before you"—points to the *challenge* as the origin of philosophic judgement, we can say with certainty that the philosopher, from the earliest times to the late Sophists and Rhetors, always appeared as a typical champion. He challenged his rivals, he attacked them with vehement criticism and extolled his own opinions as the only true ones with all the boyish cocksureness of archaic man. In style and form the earliest samples of philosophy are polemical and agonistic. They invariably speak in the first person singular. When Zeno of Elea attacks his adversaries he does it with *aporias*—that is, he starts ostensibly from their premises only to arrive at two contradictory and mutually exclusive conclusions. The form points as clearly as anything can to the riddle. Zeno asks: "If

[1]See note *ante*.
[2]C. Prantl, *Geschichte der Logik im Abendlande*, i, Leipzig, 1855, p. 399.

space is something, what can it be in?"[1] For Heraclitus, the "dark philosopher", nature and life are a *griphos*, an enigma, and he himself is the riddle-solver.[2] The sayings of Empedocles often sound more like mystical solutions of conundrums than sober philosophy, and are still clothed in poetic form. His almost grotesque fancies concerning the origin of animal life would not seem out of place in the wild divagations of an Ancient Hindu *brāhmana* treatise. "From her (Nature) there proceeded many heads without necks, arms wandered about by themselves without shoulders, and eyes floated in mid-air without faces".[3]

The earliest philosophers speak in tones of prophecy and rapture. Their sublime self-assurance is that of the sacrificial priest or mystagogue. Their problems deal with the *fons et origo* of things, with ἀρχή—the Beginning, and φύσις—Nature; their solutions come not by reflection and argument but by flashes of insight. It is always the same old cosmogonic teasers, propounded since time immemorial in riddle-form and solved in myth. Before coming into its own as philosophy and science, speculation on the shape of the universe will have to break away from the wondrous imaginings of mythical cosmology, such as the Pythagorean conception of the 183 worlds lying side by side in the shape of an equilateral triangle.[4]

All these samples of early philosophizing are pervaded by a strong sense of the agonistic structure of the universe. The processes in life and the cosmos are seen as the eternal conflict of opposites which is the root-principle of existence, like the Chinese

[1]Aristotle, *Physics*, iv, 3, 210 b, 22 *sq.*, also W. Capelle, *Die Vorsokratiker: Die Fragmente und Quellenberichte*, Stuttgart, 1935, p. 172.

[2]Jaeger, *Paideia*, i, pp. 180–181.

[3]Capelle, *op. cit.* p. 216. Was Christian Morgenstern thinking of this when he wrote his fantastic poem: "Ein Knie geht einsam durch die Welt?" [For the benefit of readers not acquainted with this classic I am taking the liberty of giving a translation of it here:

A lone knee wanders through the world,
  A knee and nothing more;
It's not a tent, it's not a tree,
  A knee and nothing more.

In battle once there was a man
  Shot foully through and through;
The knee alone remained unhurt
  As saints are said to do.

Since then it's wandered through the world,
  A knee and nothing more.
It's not a tent, it's not a tree,
  A knee and nothing more.

Trans.]

[4]*Ibid.* p. 102.

yin and *yang*. For Heraclitus, strife was "the father of all things", and Empedocles postulated φιλία and νεῖκος—attraction and discord—as the two principles which rule the universal process from everlasting to everlasting. It was no accident that the antithetical trend of archaic philosophy was fully reflected in the antithetical and agonistic structure of archaic society. Man had long been accustomed to think of everything as cleft into opposites and dominated by conflict. Hesiod recognizes a *good* Eris—beneficial strife—as well as a destructive Eris.

It is consistent, therefore, with this outlook that the eternal strife of all things, the strife of *Physis*, should sometimes have been conceived as legal strife. Such a view shows up the play-character of archaic culture very clearly. According to Werner Jaeger, the ideas of *Kosmos, Diké* and *Tisis*—order, justice and punishment—were taken from the domain of law, where they belonged, and transferred to the universal process, so that this could be understood in terms of a lawsuit.[1] Similarly, he says, αἰτία originally meant guilt before the law, but only later became the generally accepted term for the idea of natural causality. Unfortunately the words in which Anaximander expresses this notion of the universal process as a legal process have been preserved only in very fragmentary form:[2]

"Things must necessarily perish in that same principle from which they arise (i.e. the Infinite). For they have to render expiation to one another and atone for the wrong they did according to the ordinance of time". This utterance can hardly be called exactly lucid. But at any rate it contains the idea of the cosmos having to seek expiation for some primordial wrong. However intended, it gives us a glimpse of a profound thought startlingly reminiscent of Christian doctrine. We have to ask ourselves, though, whether the dictum reflects the already mature stage of Greek thought about statecraft and justice as exemplified in the 5th century B.C. or rather a much older stratum of juridical thinking, the one discussed above, where the ideas of justice and punishment still mingled with those of sortilege and physical combat, where, in short, the legal process was still a sacred game? One of the Empedoclean fragments, referring to the mighty contest of the elements, speaks of the time being fulfilled which had been appointed for them "by a large oath".[3] It is impossible

[1] *Paideia*, i, p. 161. [2] Capelle, *op. cit.* p. 82.
[3] *Fragments*, No. 30; cf. Capelle, *op. cit.* p. 200.

to gauge the full significance of this mythico-mystical proposition. The only certain thing is that the thought of the philosopher-seer is still moving in that region of ritual combat which vouchsafes the divine decision and which, as we saw, was at the bottom of law and justice in archaic times.

VII

PLAY AND POETRY

In touching on the origins of Greek philosophy and its connection with the sacred contest in knowledge and wisdom, we inevitably touch the shadowy border-line between the religious or philosophical mode of expression and the poetic. It is therefore desirable to enquire into the nature of poetic creation. This question is, in a sense, at the heart of any discussion of the relations between play and culture, for while in the more highly organized forms of society religion, science, law, war and politics gradually lose touch with play, so prominent in the earlier phases, the function of the poet still remains fixed in the play-sphere where it was born. *Poiesis*, in fact, is a play-function. It proceeds within the play-ground of the mind, in a world of its own which the mind creates for it. There things have a very different physiognomy from the one they wear in "ordinary life", and are bound by ties other than those of logic and causality. If a serious statement be defined as one that may be made in terms of waking life, poetry will never rise to the level of seriousness. It lies beyond seriousness, on that more primitive and original level where the child, the animal, the savage and the seer belong, in the region of dream, enchantment, ecstasy, laughter. To understand poetry we must be capable of donning the child's soul like a magic cloak and of forsaking man's wisdom for the child's. Nobody has grasped, or expressed, the primordial nature of poetry and its relation to pure play more clearly than Vico, more than two hundred years ago.[1]

Poesis doctrinae tamquam somnium—poetry is like a dream of philosophic love,[2] says the deep-minded Francis Bacon. The mythical imaginings of savages, those children of nature, concerning the origins of existence often contain the seeds of a wisdom which will find expression in the logical forms of a later age. Philology and comparative religion are taking pains to penetrate

[1]Erich Auerbach, *Giambattista Vico und die Idee der Philologie*, Homenatge a Antoni Rubió i Lluch, Barcelona, 1936, i, p. 297 *sq*.
[2]Huizinga's English wording. Trans.

more and more deeply into the mythical origins of faith.[1] Ancient civilization is now being understood anew in the light of this fundamental unity of poetry, esoteric doctrine, wisdom and ritual.

The first thing we have to do to gain such an understanding is to discard the idea that poetry has only an aesthetic function or can only be explained in terms of aesthetics. In any flourishing, living civilization, above all in archaic cultures, poetry has a vital function that is both social and liturgical. All antique poetry is at one and the same time ritual, entertainment, artistry, riddle-making, doctrine, persuasion, sorcery, soothsaying, prophecy, and competition. Practically all the motifs proper to archaic ritual and poetry combined are to be found in the Third Canto of the Finnish epic, the *Kalevala*. The old and wise Väinämöinen *enchants* the young braggart who dares to challenge him to a sorcery-contest. First they contend in the knowledge of natural things, then in esoteric knowledge concerning the origins. At this point young Joukahainen pretends that part of the Creation was due to him; whereupon the old sorcerer *sings* him into the earth, into the bog, into the water, and the water rises to his waist, his armpits, then over his mouth until finally the young man promises him his sister Aino. Only then does Väinämöinen, sitting on the "stone of song", sing for another three hours to withdraw his strong magic and disenchant the reckless challenger. All the forms of contest we have mentioned earlier are united in this exploit: the bragging-match, the boasting-match, the "comparing of men", the competition in cosmogonic knowledge, the contest for the bride, the endurance-test, the ordeal—in one wild flight of poetic fancy.

The true appellation of the archaic poet is *vates*, the possessed, the God-smitten, the raving one. These qualifications imply at the same time his possession of extraordinary knowledge. He is the Knower, *sha'ir*, as the old Arabs called him. In Eddic mythology the mead that one has to drink to become a poet is prepared from the blood of Kvasir, the wisest of all creatures who was never yet questioned in vain. Gradually the poet-seer splits up into the figures of the prophet, the priest, the soothsayer, the mystagogue and the poet as we know him; even the philosopher, the legislator, the orator, the demagogue, the sophist and the rhetor spring from that primordial composite type, the *vates*. The

[1] E.g. the works of W. B. Kristensen or K. Kerényi.

early Greek poets all show traces of their common progenitor. Their function is eminently a social one; they speak as the educators and monitors of their people. They are the nation's leaders, whose place was later usurped by the sophists.[1]

The figure of the ancient *vates* is seen under many of its aspects in the *thulr* of Old Norse literature, *thyle* in Anglo-Saxon. Modern German philology renders the word by *Kultredner*, literally "cult orator".[2] The most typical example of the *thulr* is the *starkaðr*, which Saxo Grammaticus rightly translates as *vates*. The *thulr* sometimes appears as the speaker of liturgical formulae, sometimes as the performer in a sacred drama; sometimes as sacrificial priest, sometimes even as sorcerer. At other times he seems to be no more than a court-poet and orator, and his office no more than that of the *scurra*—buffoon or jester. The corresponding verb—*thylja*—means the reciting of religious texts, the practising of sorcery, or simply mumbling. The *thulr* is the repository of all mythological knowledge and poetic lore. He is the wise old man who knows the people's history and tradition, who acts as spokesman at the festivities and can recite the pedigrees of the heroes and other worthies by heart. His special office is the competitive peroration and the wisdom-match. In this capacity we meet him as Unferd in *Beowulf*. The *mannjafnaðr* which we discussed before and the wisdom-matches between Odin and the giants or dwarfs both properly belong to the *thulr*. The well-known Anglo-Saxon poems *Widsið* and *The Wanderer* seem to be typical products of the versatile court-poet. All the above-mentioned characteristics fit in quite naturally with our picture of the archaic poet, whose function at all times was both sacred and literary. But, sacred or profane, his function is always rooted in a form of play.

We can follow the primitive *vates* beyond the *thulr* of Germanic antiquity and find him, without straining our imaginations too much, in the "jongleur" of the feudal West (*joculator*) on the one hand and his companions of lower degree, the heralds, on the other. These latter, whom we mentioned in passing in connection with the reviling-match,[3] have many points in common with the ancient "cult orator". They too were the recorders of history, tradition and genealogies, the spokesmen and criers at public festivities and, above all, the official boasters and braggarts.

[1]Jaeger, *Paideia*, i, pp. 34–7, 72, 288–91.

[2]W. H. Vogt, *Stilgeschichte der eddischen Wissensdichtung*, i: Der Kultredner (Schriften der Baltischen Kommission zu Kiel, iv, 1, 1927).

[3]See *ante*, p. 71.

Poetry, in its original culture-making capacity, is born in and as play—sacred play, no doubt, but always, even in its sanctity, verging on gay abandon, mirth and jollity. There is as yet no question of the satisfaction of aesthetic impulse. This is still dormant in the experience of the ritual act as such, whence poetry arises in the form of hymns or odes created in a frenzy of ritual elation. But not only in this way; for the poetic faculty also comes to flower in social diversions and in the intense rivalries of clans, families and tribes. Nothing fertilized it more than the celebration of the new seasons, especially the spring, when young people of both sexes met in mirth and liberty.

Poetry in this form—as a product of the age-old game of attraction and repulsion played by young men and girls in a spirit of badinage—is as fundamental as the poetry born of ceremonial. Professor de Josselin de Jong of the University of Leyden has been able to amass a rich harvest of such social-agonistic poetry still fulfilling its proper function as a cultural game, and of an extremely refined character, from his field-work on the Islands of Buru and Babar in the East Indian archipelago. I have to thank the author for his great kindness in allowing me to borrow a number of particulars from his hitherto unpublished work.[1] The inhabitants of Central Buru, also called Rana, practise a form of ceremonial antiphony known as *Inga fuka*. The men and women sit facing one another and sing little songs, some of them improvised, to the accompaniment of a drum. The songs are of a mocking or teasing nature. No less than five kinds of *Inga fuka* are distinguished. The songs are always in the form of strophe and antistrophe, thrust and counter-thrust, question and answer, a challenge and a rejoinder. Sometimes they resemble riddles. The most typical *Inga fuka* is called the "*Inga fuka* of going before and following after"; each strophe begins with those words as in the children's game of "follow my leader". What constitutes the formal poetic element is the assonance which, by repeating the same word or a variation of it, links thesis to antithesis. The purely poetic element consists in allusion, the sudden bright idea, the pun or simply in the sound of the words themselves, where sense may be completely lost. Such a form of poetry can only be described and understood in terms of play, though it obeys a nice system of prosodic rules. As to their

[1]A preliminary version has been published in the *Mededeelingen der K. Nederl. Akad. van Wetenschappen*, 1935.

content, the songs are mainly amorous innuendoes, little homilies on prudence and the virtues, and malicious sallies. Though a repertoire of traditional *Inga fukas* exists the real thing is to improvise them. Existing couplets are also improved by felicitous additions and emendations. Virtuosity is highly esteemed and there is no lack of artistic skill. In sentiment and mood the translations are reminiscent of the Malay *pantūn*, which must have had some influence on Buru literature, and also of the much further distant *haikai* of Japan.

Apart from the *Inga fuka* other forms of poetry are common in Rana, all based on the same formal principles but consisting, for instance, in lengthy altercations between the families of the bride and bridegroom during the ceremonial exchange of presents at a wedding.

De Josselin de Jong found a completely different type of poetry on the island of Wetan in the Babar Group of south-eastern Islands. Here only improvisation counts. The inhabitants of Babar sing much more than do those of Buru, both communally and alone at their work. Sitting in the tops of the coconut-palms tapping the sap, the men sing mournful or mocking songs at the expense of their companions in the neighbouring trees. Sometimes the latter type of song leads to envenomed singing-duels, which in former times might end in bloody violence and murder. All songs consist of two lines known as the "trunk" and the "top" or "crown" respectively, but the scheme of question and answer is no longer discernible. A characteristic difference between Babar and Buru poetry is that in the former the effect is obtained by a playful variation of melody rather than by punning and playing with sounds.

The Malay *pantūn* just mentioned is a quatrain with crossed rhymes, the first two lines evoking an image or stating a fact, the second two clinching them by a subtle and sometimes extremely remote allusion. The whole is rather like a *jeu d'esprit.* Up to the 16th century the word *pantūn* meant a parable or proverb and only secondarily a quatrain. The concluding line is called in Javanese *djawab*—the Arabic word for answer or solution. Evidently the *pantūn* had once been a question game before becoming a fixed poetic form. Allusion by rhymed assonance has taken the place of the solution proper.[1]

[1]Cf. Hosein Djajadiningrat, *De magische achtergrond van den Maleischen pantoen*, Batavia, 1933; J. Przyluski, *Le prologue-cadre des Mille et une nuits et le thème du Svayamvara*, Journal Asiatique, ccv, 1924, p. 126.

Undoubtedly akin to the *pantūn* is the Japanese form of poetry commonly known as the *haikai*, a little poem of but three lines successively of five, seven, and five syllables, which evokes a delicate impression of the world of plants or animals, of Nature or man, sometimes touched with a breath of lyric melancholy or nostalgia, sometimes with a fleeting allusion of humour. Two examples must suffice:

"O the many things
In my heart! Let go, let go,
Sigh with the willow!

See, the kimonos
Dry in the sun. O little sleeves
Of the child that died!"

Originally the *haikai* must have been a game of chain-rhymes begun by one player and continued by the next.[1]

The fusion of play and poetry is characteristically preserved in the traditional method of reciting the Finnish *Kalevala*. Lònroth, who collected the songs, found the curious custom still in use whereby two singers sit face to face on a bench, holding each other's hands and rocking to and fro as they compete in knowledge of the stanzas. The Icelandic sagas describe a similar form of recitation.[2]

Poetry as a social game of little or no aesthetic purport is to be found everywhere and in the greatest variety of forms. The agonistic element is seldom lacking. It is directly present in antiphonal singing, the competitive poem and the singing-contest, and is implicit in impromptu versifying for the purpose, for instance, of breaking a spell. The last-named motif has obvious affinities with the "fatal" riddle of the Sphinx.

All these forms are highly developed in the Far East. In his acute interpretation and reconstruction of Ancient Chinese texts Marcel Granet gives us a picture of the whole system of poetical contests between young men and girls that once flourished in the pastoral age. A similar system was found in living use in Annam and exactly described by the Annamite scholar Nguyen van Huyen.[3] Here the poetic "argument", thinly disguising open flirtation, is often of a very refined character, being built up on

[1] *Haikai de Bashô et de ses disciples*, traduction de K. Matsus et Steinilber-Oberlin, Paris, 1936.
[2] Cf. W. H. Vogt, *Der Kultredner*, p. 166.
[3] See *ante* p. 56.

a series of proverbs which, recurring at the end of each stanza, serve as irrefutable testimonials to the lover's cause. An identical form is found in the French *débats* of the 15th century.

Poetry and singing contests as social games range, therefore, from the amiable love-plaints of ancient China and Annam to the harsh and hateful boasting or reviling matches of pre-Islamic Arabia and the slanderous drumming-contests that take the place of a lawsuit among the Eskimos. It is obvious that we must include the *Cours d'amour* of 12th century Languedoc somewhere in this category. According to one hypothesis, long since exploded, the poetry of the Troubadours originated in the love-courts of the Provençal nobility. After this opinion had rightly been discarded it remained a controversial point of philology whether such love-courts had actually existed or were simply a literary fiction. In inclining to the latter view many scholars undoubtedly went too far. That the love-court was a poetic *playing at justice* with, however, a certain practical validity, accords well enough with the customs of Languedoc in the 12th century. What we are dealing with is the polemical and casuistic approach to love-questions, and in play-form. As we saw, the Eskimo drumming-matches were generally occasioned by the gossip and goings-on of women. In both instances the theme is the dilemmas of love, and the purpose of the "court" or contest is to keep up the current code of honour and hence the reputations of the plaintiffs or defendants. The procedure in the love-courts was to imitate the regular lawsuit as closely as possible with demonstrations by analogy, the use of precedents, etc. Several of the genres found in the poetry of the Troubadours are closely related to the amatory plea, such as the *castiamen*—rebuke, the *tenzone*—dispute, the *partimen*—antiphonal song, the *joc partit*—game of question and answer (whence the English word "jeopardy"). At the bottom of all these is neither the lawsuit proper, nor a free poetical impulse, nor even social diversion pure and simple, but the age-old struggle for honour in matters of love.

Yet other forms of poetry, particularly in the Far East, must be regarded as cultural activities played on an agonistic basis. For instance, a person may be set the task of improvising a poem so as to break a "spell" or get out of a difficult situation. The point here is not whether such a custom was ever of practical importance in ordinary everyday living, but that the human mind has again and again seen in this play-motif, which is akin to both the "fatal" riddle and the game of forfeits, a means of expressing, and perhaps solving, the tricky problems of life, and that the art of poetry, not aiming directly at an aesthetic effect, found in this playing the most fertile soil for its own development. Let us borrow a couple of instances from the work of Nguyen van Huyen:

The pupils of a certain Dr. Tan had to pass the house of a girl who lived next door to the teacher on their way to school. Whenever they passed they always said: "You are sweet, you are really a dear!" This made her quite angry, so one day she waited for them and said: "Well, if you love me, I'll give you a sentence. If any of you can give me the corresponding sentence I shall love him, otherwise you'll all have to slink past my house in shame!" She gave the sentence, and none of the pupils knew the right answer, so in future they had to make a detour round the teacher's house.[1] Here we have an epic *svayamvara* or the wooing of Brunhild in the guise of an Annamese village-school idyll.

Or again, Khanh-du, of the House of Tran, had been dismissed from his post for a grave fault and took to selling coal in Chi Linh. When the Emperor appeared in this part of the world on one of his campaigns, he met the erstwhile mandarin and commanded him to make a poem on selling coal. Khanh-du made up a poem on the spot, whereupon the Emperor, deeply moved, gave him all his titles back.[2]

The improvising of verses was an endowment hardly anybody could afford to be without in the Far East. The success of an Annamite embassy to Peking would sometimes hinge on the improvisatory talents of the ambassador. Each member of it had constantly to be prepared for all sorts of questions and know the answers to the thousand and one puzzles and conundrums that the Emperor or his mandarins saw fit to put.[3] This was diplomacy at play.

The game of question and answer in verse form also serves to store up a whole mass of useful knowledge. A girl has just accepted her swain, and together they intend to open a shop. The young man asks her to tell him the names of the medicaments, and the whole treasury of the pharmacopeia follows for answer. The art of arithmetic, the knowledge of the various commodities in business and the use of the calendar in agriculture are most succinctly passed on in this way. Sometimes the lovers examine one another in literature. We remarked above that all forms of

[1] *Op. cit.* p. 131. [2] *Ibid.* p. 132. [3] *Ibid.* p. 134.

catechism are directly related to the riddle-game. This is also the case with the examination, which has always played such an extraordinarily important part in the social life of the Far East.

Civilization is always slow to abandon the verse form as the chief means of expressing things of importance to the life of the community. Poetry everywhere precedes prose; for the utterance of solemn or holy things poetry is the only adequate vessel. Not only hymns and incantations are put into verse but lengthy treatises such as the Ancient Hindu *sūtras* and *śāstras* or the earlier products of Greek philosophy. Empedocles pours his knowledge into a poem, and Lucretius still follows him in this. The preference for verse form may have been due in part to utilitarian considerations: a bookless society finds it easier to memorise its texts in this way. But there is a deeper reason, namely, that life in archaic society is itself metrical and strophical in structure, as it were. Poetry is still the more natural mode of expression for the "higher" things. Right up to 1868 the Japanese used to compose the weightiest part of a State document in poetic form. Legal historians have paid special attention to the traces of poetry in law, at least in Germanic tradition. Every student of Germanic law knows the passage in Old Frisian Law where a clause concerning the various "needs" or needful occasions on which an orphan's inheritance has to be sold, suddenly breaks into lyrical alliterative style:

"The second need is when the year becomes dear and hot hunger passes over the land and the child is like to die of hunger. Then the mother must offer the child's patrimony for sale and buy the child cow and corn, etc. The third need is when the child is stark naked and houseless and dark fog comes and cold winter, and every man withdraws into house and home and warm hollows, and the wild beast seeks the hollow tree and the lee of the mountain where he may save his life. Then the unfledged child will weep and wail and lament his naked limbs and his want of shelter and his father who should have fostered him against hunger and the chill mists of winter, and who now lies dark and deep with four nails close covered under oak and earth".

It seems to me that we are dealing here not so much with deliberate ornamentation as with the circumstance that the formulation of law still lay in that exalted sphere of the mind where poetic wording was the natural means of expression. In its sudden flight into poetry this Old Frisian example is typical of many others; in a certain sense it is more typical than the Old Icelandic *Tryggdamal* which, in a series of alliterating strophes, establishes the fact that peace has been restored, gives notice of the payment of an indemnity, sternly prohibits new quarrels and then, with respect to the declaration that "disturbers of the peace" shall everywhere be without the law, proceeds to amplify this "everywhere" in a series of poetic images:

"Wherever men
Hunt wolves,
Christian men
Go to church,
Heathen men
Offer sacrifice,
Fire flames,
Field greens,
Child calls mother,
Mother suckles child,
Hearth-fire is tended,
Ship goes voyaging,
Shields gleam,
Sun shines,
Snow falls,
Pines grow,
Falcon flies
As the dayspring is long
(Strong wind
In both his wings),
Wherever the sky
Is lifted up,
Home husbanded,
Wind roars,
Water runs seaward,
Servants sow corn".

In contrast to our former example this is obviously a purely literary embellishment of a definite legal clause; the poem could hardly have served as a valid document in practice. All the same it too testifies to the original unity of poetry and sacred jurisdiction, which is what matters here.

All poetry is born of play: the sacred play of worship, the festive play of courtship, the martial play of the contest, the disputatious play of braggadocio, mockery and invective, the nimble play of wit and readiness. How far is the play-quality of poetry preserved when civilization grows more complicated?

Let us first of all try to unravel the threefold connection between myth, poetry, and play. In whatever form it comes down to us, myth is always poetry. Working with images and the aid of imagination, myth tells the story of things that were supposed to have happened in primitive times. It can be of the deepest and holiest significance. It may succeed in expressing relationships which could never be described in a rational way. But despite the sacred and mystic quality quite natural to it in the mythopoetic phase of civilization, despite, that is to say, the absolute sincerity with which it was accepted, the question still remains whether the myth was ever entirely serious. We can safely say, I think, that myth is serious to the degree that poetry is serious. Like everything else that transcends the bounds of logical and deliberative judgement, myth and poetry both move in the play-sphere. This is not to say a *lower* sphere, for it may well be that myth, so playing, can soar to heights of insight beyond the reach of reason.

Myth, rightly understood and not in the corrupt sense which modern propaganda has tried to force upon the word, is the appropriate vehicle for primitive man's ideas about the cosmos. In it, the line between the barely conceivable and the flatly impossible has not yet been drawn with any sharpness. For the savage, with his extremely limited powers of logical co-ordination and arrangement, practically everything is possible. Despite its absurdities and enormities, its boundless exaggeration and confusion of proportions, its carefree inconsistencies and whimsical variations, the myth does not strike him as anything impossible. For all that, however, we would still like to ask whether the savage's belief in his holiest myths is not, even from the beginning, tinged with a certain element of humour. Myth and poetry both come from the play-sphere; hence it is at least probable that the savage's belief lies partly, as his life does entirely, in this same sphere.

Living myth knows no distinction between play and seriousness. Only when myth has become mythology, that is, literature, borne along as traditional lore by a culture which has in the meantime more or less outgrown the primitive imagination, only then will the contrast between play and seriousness apply to myth—and to its detriment. There is a curious intermediate phase, which the Greeks knew, when the myth is still sacred, and consequently ought to be serious, but is well understood to speak the language of the past. We are all so familiar with the figures of Greek mythology and so predisposed to accept them into our poetic consciousness that we are apt to overlook their absolutely barbaric character. In the Eddic mythology we may perhaps have some inkling of it—unless Wagner has rendered us immune and deadened our senses; but on the whole it remains true that only a mythology without direct hold on our aesthetic sensibilities can reveal to us the full measure of its savageness. We see this clearly enough in the ancient Hindu myths and the wild phantasmagorias with which ethnologists regale us from all over the world. Yet to an unbiassed eye the figures of Greek and Germanic mythology are as lacking in consistency and good taste—let alone ethics—as the unbridled fantasies of the Hindu, the African, American or Australian aborigine. Judged by our standards (which of course are not the final ones) the Hellenic and Eddic divinities are no less tasteless, disorderly and depraved in their conduct, and there is little to choose between Hermes, Thor and a god from Central Africa. It cannot be doubted that all these mythological figures as handed down by tradition are remnants of a barbarous society no longer compatible with the spiritual level that had been reached in the meantime. Hence in the period of their literary redaction myths, in order to be held in honour as sacred lore, must either suffer a mystical interpretation at the hands of priests or be cultivated purely as literature. To the degree that belief in the literal truth of the myth diminishes, the play-element, which had been proper to it from the beginning, will re-assert itself with increasing force. As early as Homer the stage of belief is past. Nevertheless the myth, after having lost its value as an adequate token of man's understanding of the cosmos, still retains the function of expressing the divine in poetical language, which is rather more than an aesthetic function, in fact, a liturgical one. When Plato or Aristotle want to give us the core of their philosophy and express it in the pithiest way they choose the myth-form: with Plato it is the myth of the soul, with Aristotle the myth of the love that all things have for the unmoved mover of the world.

The play-note so characteristic of the genuine myth is heard nowhere more distinctly than in the opening pages of the younger Edda, the *Gylfaginning* and the *Skáldskaparmál*. Here we are dealing with mythical matter that had passed completely into the literary stage and become a literature which, although officially repudiated on account of its heathen character, was still held in honour as part of the cultural heritage and continued to be read for that reason.[1] The transcribers of it were Christians, and clerics or divines at that. To my ears at least, there is an unmistakable note of jesting and humour in their retelling of these mythical happenings. It is not the tone of the Christian, consciously superior to the heathenishness his faith has vanquished and therefore inclined to mock it a little, still less is it the tone of the convert execrating the past as a time of diabolical darkness; it is rather one of half-belief, midway between play and seriousness, a tone which had echoed of old in all mythical thinking and probably sounded very little different in the heyday of heathenism. The seeming incongruity between absurd mythological themes—savage fancies pure and simple, as in the stories of Hrungnir, Groa and Aurwandil—and a highly developed poetic technique is likewise quite in accord with the very nature of myth which, however crude in substance, always and everywhere seeks the loftiest form of expression. The name of the first treatise, *Gylfaginning*—i.e. the Fooling of Gylfi—is itself full of significance. It takes the old, well-known form of a cosmogonic interrogative discourse, just like Thor's dispute in the hall of Utgardaloki. G. Neckel rightly uses the term "play" for it.[2] The interrogator, Gangleri, puts the old sacred questions concerning the origins of things, of wind, of winter and summer, etc. As a rule the answers only offer some bizarre mythological figure by way of solution. The opening chapters of the *Skáldskaparmál* also fall wholly within the play-sphere: prehistoric, styleless fantasies about dim, dull, hairy giants and wicked, crafty dwarfs; rude and outlandish prodigies and marvels which are all in the end mercifully dispelled as mere illusion. No doubt this is mythology in the last stages of decrepitude—chaotic, fatuous, would-be fanciful. It would, however, be rash to regard these features as a latter-day degeneration of ideas once grand and heroic. On the contrary, lack of style is an intrinsic part of myth.

[1] De Josselin de Jong, *op. cit.*, describes a similar state of affairs in the religion of the Buru Islanders.

[2] *Thule*, xx, 24.

The formal elements of poetry are manifold: metrical and strophical patterns, rhyme, rhythm, assonance, alliteration, stress, etc., and forms like the lyric, the drama, the epic. Various as all these factors are, they are to be met with all over the world. The same is true of the motifs of poetry which, however numerous they may be in any one language, occur everywhere and at all times. These patterns, forms and motifs are so familiar to us that we take their existence for granted and seldom pause to ask what the common denominator is that makes them so and not otherwise. This denominator, which makes for the astonishing uniformity and limitation of the poetic mode in all periods of human society, might perhaps be found in the fact that the creative function we call poetry is rooted in a function even more primordial than culture itself, namely play.

Let us enumerate once more the characteristics we deemed proper to play. It is an activity which proceeds within certain limits of time and space, in a visible order, according to rules freely accepted, and outside the sphere of necessity or material utility. The play-mood is one of rapture and enthusiasm, and is sacred or festive in accordance with the occasion. A feeling of exaltation and tension accompanies the action, mirth and relaxation follow.

Now it can hardly be denied that these qualities are also proper to poetic creation. In fact, the definition we have just given of play might serve as a definition of poetry. The rhythmical or symmetrical arrangement of language, the hitting of the mark by rhyme or assonance, the deliberate disguising of the sense, the artificial and artful construction of phrases—all might be so many utterances of the play spirit. To call poetry, as Paul Valéry has done, a playing with words and language is no metaphor: it is the precise and literal truth.

The affinity between poetry and play is not external only; it is also apparent in the structure of creative imagination itself. In the turning of a poetic phrase, the development of a motif, the expression of a mood, there is always a play-element at work. Whether in myth or the lyric, drama or epic, the legends of a remote past or a modern novel, the writer's aim, conscious or unconscious, is to create a tension that will "enchant" the reader and hold him spellbound. Underlying all creative writing is some human or emotional situation potent enough to convey this tension to others. But there are none too many of these situations—that is the point. Broadly speaking, such situations rise either from conflict, or love, or both together.

Now both conflict and love imply rivalry or competition, and competition implies play. In the great majority of cases the central theme of poetry and literature generally is strife—i.e. the task that the hero has to perform, the trials he has to undergo, the obstacles he has to surmount. The very word "hero" for the chief protagonist is telling enough. The task will be extraordinarily difficult, seemingly impossible. More often than not it will be tackled as the result of a challenge, or a vow, a promise or whim of the beloved. All these motifs carry us straight back to agonistic play. Another set of tension-producing themes hinges on the hidden identity of the hero. He is incognito either because he is deliberately concealing his identity, or because he does not know it himself, or because he can change his shape at will. In other words, he is wearing a mask, he appears in disguise, he carries a secret. Once more we are close to the old and sacred game of the hidden being who will only reveal himself to the initiated.

As a form of competition proper, archaic poetry is barely distinguishable from the ancient riddle-contest. The one produces wisdom, the other words of beauty. Both are dominated by a system of play-rules which fix the range of ideas and symbols to be used, sacred or poetic as the case may be; both presuppose a circle of initiates who understand the language spoken. The validity of either depends solely on how far it conforms to the play-rules. Only he who can speak the art-language wins the title of poet. This art-language differs from ordinary speech in that it employs special terms, images, figures, etc., which not everybody will understand. The eternal gulf between being and idea can only be bridged by the rainbow of imagination. The word-bound concept is always inadequate to the torrent of life. Hence it is only the image-making or figurative word that can invest things with expression and at the same time bathe them in the luminosity of ideas: idea and thing are united in the image. But whereas the language of ordinary life—in itself a working and workmanlike instrument—is continually wearing down the image-content of words and acquiring a superficial existence of its own (logical only in appearance), poetry continues to cultivate the figurative, i.e. image-bearing, qualities of language, with deliberate intent.

What poetic language does with images is to play with them. It disposes them in style, it instils mystery into them so that every image contains the answer to an enigma.

In archaic culture the language of poets is still the most effective means of expression, with a function much wider and more vital than the satisfaction of literary aspirations. It puts ritual into words, it is the arbiter of social relationships, the vehicle of wisdom, justice and morality. All this it does without prejudice to its play-character, for the setting of archaic culture itself is the play-circle. At this stage cultural activities are performed as social games; even the most utilitarian gravitate towards one play-group or another. But as civilization increases in spiritual amplitude, the regions where the play-factor is weak or barely perceptible will develop at the cost of those where it has free play. Civilization as a whole becomes more serious—law and war, commerce, technics and science lose touch with play; and even ritual, once the field *par excellence* for its expression, seems to share the process of dissociation. Finally only poetry remains as the stronghold of living and noble play.

The playfulness of poetic language is so obvious that there is hardly any need to illustrate it with examples. In view of the enormous importance attached to the practice of poetry in archaic culture it will not surprise us to find that its technique is brought there to the highest pitch of strictness and refinement. It is based on a meticulous code of rules absolutely binding but allowing of almost infinite variation. The system is preserved and passed on as a noble science. It is no accident that we can observe this exquisite cult of poetry in very similar forms among peoples so far apart in time and space that they can have had little or no contact with the richer and more ancient civilizations which might otherwise have influenced their literature. This is true, for instance, of pre-Islamic Arabia and the Iceland of the Eddas and sagas. Leaving aside details of metre and prosody we shall content ourselves with a single example well fitted to illustrate the connection between poetry and playing at a secret language, viz. the Old Norse *kenningar*. When the poet says "speech-thorn" for "tongue", "floor of the hall of winds" for "earth", "tree-wolf" for "wind", etc., he is setting his hearers poetic riddles which are tacitly solved. Poet and audience have to know hundreds of them. Important things—gold, shall we say—bear poetic names by the dozen. One of the treatises in the younger Edda, the

Skáldskaparmál or "Speech of the Poets", gives a long list of such poetic expressions. Not the last use of the *kenning* is as a test of mythological knowledge. Each god has his multiple pseudonyms which contain an oblique reference to his adventures, his shape or his cosmic relationship. "How do you describe Heimdall?" "He may be called 'The Son of Nine Mothers' or 'The Watchman of the Gods' or 'The White Ase', 'Loki's Enemy', 'Seeker of Freya's Necklace' and many other things".[1]

The close connections between poetry and the riddle are never entirely lost. In the Icelandic *skalds* too much clarity is considered a technical fault. The Greeks also required the poet's word to be dark. Among the troubadours, in whose art the play-function is more in evidence than in any other, special merit was attributed to the *trobarclus*—the making of recondite poetry.

Modern schools of lyric which move and have their being in realms not generally accessible and are fond of wrapping the sense in an enigmatic word, are thus remaining true to the essence of their art. With their restricted circle of readers who understand or are at least acquainted with their special language, they are a closed cultural group of very ancient descent. It is questionable, however, whether the civilization that surrounds them is capable of appreciating their purpose sufficiently to nurture an art whose *raison d'être* is yet the fulfilment of a vital function.

[1]The assumption that the first beginnings of the *kenningar* are to be sought in poetry does not necessarily preclude their connection with *tabu* concepts. See Alberta A. Portengen, *De Oudgermaansche dichtertaal in haar etymologisch verband*, Leyden, 1915.

VIII

THE ELEMENTS OF MYTHOPOIESIS

As soon as the effect of a metaphor consists in describing things or events in terms of life and movement, we are on the road to personification. To represent the incorporeal and the inanimate as a person is the soul of all myth-making and nearly all poetry. Strictly speaking, however, the process does not follow the course just indicated. There is no question of first conceiving something as lifeless and bodiless and then expressing it as something that has body, parts and passions. No; the thing perceived is conceived as having life and movement in the first place, and such is the primary expression of it, which is no afterthought. Personification in this sense arises as soon as the need is felt to communicate one's perceptions to others. Conceptions are thus born as acts of the imagination.

Are we justified in calling this innate habit of mind, this tendency to create an imaginary world of living beings (or perhaps: a world of animate ideas), a playing of the mind, a mental game?

Let us take one of the most elementary forms of personification, namely, mythical speculations concerning the origin of the world and things, in which creation is imagined as the work of certain gods using the limbs of a world-giant's body. We are familiar with this conception from the Rig-veda and the younger Edda. Philology nowadays tends to regard the texts containing the story as the literary redactions of a later period. The tenth hymn of the Rig-veda gives us a mystical paraphrase of primordial myth-matter at the hands of sacrificial priests, who have interpreted it ritualistically. The primordial Being, Purusha (i.e. man) has served as matter for the cosmos.[1] All things have been formed from his body, "the animals of the air and the wilderness and the villages"; "the moon came from his spirit, the sun from his eye, from his mouth came Indra and Agni, from his breath the wind, from his navel the sky, heaven from his head, earth from his feet, and from his ears the four quarters of the horizon; thus did they

[1] *R.V.* x, 90, 8, 13–14, 11.

(the gods)[1] fashion the worlds". They burnt Purusha as an offering. The hymn is a mixture of age-old myth-fantasies and the mystical speculations of a later phase of religious culture. We may note in passing that in one verse, the eleventh, the familiar interrogative form suddenly turns up: "When they divided Purusha, into how many parts did they divide him? What was his mouth called, and his arms, and his thighs, and his feet?"

In the same way Gangleri asks in the *Snorra Edda:* "What was the beginning? How did it begin? What was there before?" Then, in a motley conglomeration of motifs, there follows a description of the origin of the world: first of all the primordial giant Ymir is born of the collision of a hot air-current and a layer of ice.[2] The gods kill him and make the earth from his flesh, the seas and lakes from his blood, the mountains from his bones, the trees from his hair, the sky from his skull, etc.

None of this has the appearance of living myth in the very first phase of its expression. What we are dealing with, at least in the example taken from the Edda, is rather traditional material that has sunk from the level of ritual to that of literature and been preserved as the venerable remains of an ancient culture for the edification of coming generations. As we have already said, the *Gylfaginning*, where all this occurs, in its whole structure, tone and tendency seems to be playing with the old mythological themes in a way that can hardly be called serious. We must ask ourselves, therefore, whether the mentality responsible for these personifications is not wedded to a certain playfulness at the outset. In other words, recapitulating what we have said about myth in general, we feel some doubt whether in fact the primitive Hindus and Scandinavians ever really believed with the full force of conviction in such figments as the creation of the world from human limbs. At any rate the reality of this belief cannot be proved. We may go so far as to say that it is extremely improbable.

Normally we are inclined to regard the personification of abstract ideas as the late product of bookish invention—as allegory, a stylistic device which the art and literature of all ages have made hackneyed. And indeed, as soon as the poetic metaphor ceases to move on the plane of genuine and original myth and no longer forms part of some sacred activity, the

[1]Cosmogonic myths are always obliged to postulate a *primum agens* before all existence.

[2]Once more let me refer the reader to the works of H. S. Bellamy—*Moons, Myths and Man, Built Before the Flood*, etc.—for a very different interpretation. Trans.

belief-value of the personification it contains becomes problematical, not to say illusory. Personification is then used quite consciously as the material of poetry, even when the ideas it helps to formulate are still counted as holy. This verdict also applies to some of the earliest instances of personification as we find them in Homer, e.g. *Ate*—Delusion, who steals into the hearts of men, followed by the *Litai*—Supplications, ugly and squinting, all daughters of Zeus. The innumerable personifications to be met with in Hesiod are equally amorphous and colourless and artificial; his *Theogonia* offers us a whole procession of abstractions as the offspring of the bad Eris: Toil, Oblivion, Hunger, the Agonies, Homicides and Murders, the Discords, Deceit, Envy, etc. Two of the children begotten by the Titan Pallas on Styx, Daughter of Ocean—namely Kratos and Bia (Might and Violence)—have their seat where Zeus abides and follow him wherever he goes.[1] Are all these figures mere allegory, pale intangibles of the mind? Perhaps not. There are reasons for supposing that these personifications of qualities belong rather to the oldest strata of religious formulation when the powers and forces by which primitive man felt surrounded had not yet assumed human shape. Before ever the mind conceives the gods anthropomorphically when seized upon by the mysterious and tremendous menacing forces of life and nature, it gives the things that oppress or exalt it vague and indefinite names, evoking rather the sensation of shadowy beings than the clear vision of human figures.[2]

It is from this prehistoric plane of mental activity that those strange figures seem to have sprung, primitive yet curiously bookish, with which Empedocles peoples the underworld: "that joyless place where Murder and Wrath and a host of other baneful gods wander in darkness on the meadows of sorrow, together with devouring Sicknesses and Rottenness and all the works of Decay".[3] "There too was the Earth-Mother and the far-glancing Sun-Maiden, bloody Strife and grave-eyed Harmony, Dame Beautiful and Dame Ugly, Dame Hasty and Dame Slow and lovely Truth and raven-tressed Shadow".[4]

The Romans, with their singularly archaic religious conscious-

[1] *Theogonia*, 227 *sq.*, 383 *sq.*

[2] Cf. Gilbert Murray, *Anthropology and the Classics*, ed. R. R. Marett, Oxford, 1908, p. 75.

[3] *Fragments*, 121; cf. Capelle, *op. cit.* p. 242.

[4] *Fragments*, 122; cf. H. Diels, *Fragmente der Vorsokratiker*, ii, p. 219.

ness, preserved this primitive faculty of personification (which is not strictly anthropomorphic) in the practice of the so-called *indigitamenta*, an official rite whereby new divinities were installed in times of violent public excitement, with a view to tranquillizing these outbursts of collective emotion by giving them fixed form as sacred entities. It was a brilliant psychological trick for resolving dangerous social tensions and exorcising them by projection and propitiation. Thus Pallor and Pavor—Paleness and Fear—had their shrines, likewise Aius Locutius, the Voice that had warned against the Gauls, and Rediculus, who had caused Hannibal to withdraw, and Domiduca who leads safely home. The Old Testament too has instances of personification in the tetrad of Mercy, Truth, Justice and Peace in Psalm 85, where they meet one another and kiss; in the Wisdom of the *Book of Wisdom*, in the Four Horsemen of the Apocalypse, etc. Marcel Mauss mentions a Goddess of Property among the Haida Indians of British Columbia, a sort of Dame Fortune; her function is to give wealth.[1]

In all these cases we are justified in asking how far this business of personification springs from—or results in—an attitude of faith. We may go further: is not all personification from beginning to end but a playing of the mind? Examples from more recent times lead us to this conclusion. St. Francis of Assisi reveres Poverty, his bride, with holy fervour and pious rapture. But if we ask in sober earnest whether St. Francis actually believed in a spiritual and celestial being whose name was Poverty, who really *was* the idea of poverty, we begin to waver. Put in cold blood like that the question is too blunt; we are forcing the emotional content of the idea. St. Francis' attitude was one of belief and unbelief mixed. The Church hardly authorized him in an explicit belief of that sort. His conception of Poverty must have vacillated between poetic imagination and dogmatic conviction, although gravitating towards the latter. The most succinct way of putting his state of mind would be to say that St. Francis was playing with the figure of poverty. The saint's whole life is full of pure play-factors and play-figures, and these are not the least attractive part of him. Similarly Henry Suso, the German mystic of the next century, in his sweet mystico-lyrical musings indulges in the same sort of game with his beloved, Eternal Wisdom. The playground of the saints and mystics is far beyond the sphere of

[1]*Essai sur le don*, p. 112.

ordinary mortals, and still further from the rational thinking that is bound to logic. Holiness and play always tend to overlap. So do poetic imagination and faith.

I have dealt elsewhere in some detail with the ideal value of allegorical figures in certain mediaeval poets, visionaries and theologians, namely, in my essay on the relation between poetry and theology in Alain de Lille.[1] It is impossible, in my view, to make any sharp distinction between poetic personification in allegory and the conception of celestial—or infernal—beings in theology. We would be doing an injustice to a poet-theologian like Alain de Lille if we described the whole poetic treasury of his *Anticlaudianus* or *De Planctu Naturae*, so rich in images, simply as a literary "game". His images are too deep for that; the profundities of his philosophical and theological thought are absolutely bound up with them. On the other hand he remains fully aware of the imaginary character of his apparatus. Even Hildegard of Bingen lays no claim to the metaphysical reality of the Virtues she sees in her visions—in fact, she goes so far as to warn against the very idea of it.[2] The relation of the images seen to the virtues themselves, she says, is one of "signifying": *designare, praetendere, declarare, significare, praefigurare.* Nevertheless in the vision they move like living beings. With Hildegard as with Alain de Lille poetic imagination, even in mystical experience, is on their own showing continually hovering between fancy and conviction, play and seriousness.

In whatever form, from the most sacred to the most literary, from the Vedic Purusha to the fetching little figurines in the *Rape of the Lock*, personification is both a play-function and a supremely important habit of mind. Even in modern civilization it has not, by any means, dwindled to a mere artifice of literature, something to be put up with and sometimes resorted to. We are very far from having outgrown it in everyday life. Which of us has not repeatedly caught himself addressing some lifeless object, say a recalcitrant collar-stud, in deadly earnest, attributing to it a perverse will, reproaching it and abusing it for its demoniacal obstinacy? If ever you did this you were personifying in the strict sense of the word. Yet you do not normally avow your belief in the collar-stud as an entity or idea. You were only falling involuntarily into the play-attitude.

[1] In German, for the Mededeelingen der Kon. Nederl. Akad. van Wetenschappen, afd. Letterkunde, lxxiv, B, No. 6, 1932, p. 82 *sq.*

[2] *Ibid.* p. 89.

If this innate tendency of the mind, which invests the objects of ordinary life with personality, is in fact rooted in play then we are confronted with a very serious issue. We can only touch on it here. The play attitude must have been present before human culture or human speech existed, hence the ground on which personification and imagination work was a datum from the remotest past onward. Now, anthropology and comparative religion tell us that personification of gods and spirits in beast-form is one of the most important elements in archaic religious life. Theriomorphic imagination is at the bottom of the whole complex of totemism. The two halves of a tribe not only call themselves, they actually *are*, kangaroos or tortoises. An identical mode of thinking is contained in the idea of the *versipellis*, known the world over, meaning the man who can change his skin and temporarily take on the form of an animal—the werewolf, for instance. It is also implicit in the numerous metamorphoses of Zeus for the benefit of Leda, Europa, Semele, Danae, etc., and in the amalgamations of man and beast in the Egyptian pantheon. There can be no doubt that for the savage and also for archaic man in Egypt or Greece this sacred representation of man as an animal was perfectly "serious". No more than the child does he distinguish very clearly between the two species. And yet when he dons his terrifying beast-mask and appears as an animal, he is proving that he knows "better" after all. The only interpretation with which we, who are no longer altogether savage, can possibly recreate his state of mind for ourselves is to assume that the play-sphere as we observe it in the child still embraces the savage's whole life, from his holiest emotions to his most trivial and childish amusements. Would it therefore be overbold to suggest that the theriomorphic factor in ritual, mythology and religion can best be understood in terms of the play attitude?

There is another and yet deeper question arising out of our discussion of personification and allegory, and it is this we had in mind when we spoke above of a "very serious issue". Are we quite sure that present-day philosophy and psychology have wholly abandoned the allegorical mode of expression? It often seems to me that they have not and never can. Age-old allegorical thinking still creeps into their terminology, and personification thrives in the names they give to psychic impulses and states of mind. Psychoanalytic literature is riddled with it. But we may well ask whether abstract speech can ever get on without them.

Not only the elements of myth but those of poetry too are best understood as play-functions. Why does man subordinate words to measure, cadence and rhythm? If we answer: for the sake of beauty or from deep emotion, we are only getting out of our depth. But if we answer: men make poetry because they feel a need for social play, we are getting nearer the mark. The rhythmical word is born of that need; poetry enjoys a vital function and has full value in the playing of a community, and it loses both these to the degree that social games lose their ritual or festive character. Such elements as the rhyme and the distich derive from and only have meaning in those timeless, ever-recurring patterns of play: beat and counter-beat, rise and fall, question and answer, in short, rhythm. Their origin is inextricably bound up with the principles of song and dance which in their turn are comprehended in the immemorial function of play. All the qualities of poetry which come to be recognized as specific of it, i.e. beauty, sacredness, magic, are originally embraced in the primary play-quality.

We distinguish three great varieties of poetry after the immortal Greek models, namely the lyric, the epic, and the drama. Of these the lyric remains closest to the play-sphere they all started from. The lyric must be understood here in a very wide sense, so as to include not only the lyrical *genre* as such but all moods expressive of rapture. In the scale of poetic speech lyrical expression is the farthest removed from logic and comes closest to music and the dance. The lyric is the language of mystic contemplation, oracles and magic. Here the poet experiences most strongly the sensation of being inspired from without; here he is closest to supreme wisdom but also to inanity. The utter surrender of reason and logic is characteristic of the language of priests and oracles among savage peoples; very often it passes into sheer gibberish. Emile Faguet speaks somewhere of "le grain de sottise nécessaire au lyrique moderne". But it is not the modern lyrical poet alone who needs it; the whole *genre* must of necessity move outside the limitations of the intellect. One of the basic features of lyrical imagination is the tendency to maniacal exaggeration. Poetry must be exorbitant. The cosmogonic and mystical fantasies of the Rig-veda and the lofty genius of Shakespeare meet in the most daring images, for Shakespeare had passed through the whole tradition of classicism and yet retained the full impetus of the archaic *vates*.

The desire to make an idea as enormous and stupefying as possible is not peculiar to the lyric; it is a typical play-function and is common both in child-life and in certain mental diseases. Somewhere in the Shaw-Terry correspondence there is a story of a small boy rushing in from the garden shouting: "Mummy, mummy, I've found a carrot as big—as big as God!" Elsewhere a patient tells a psychiatrist that they are coming to fetch him in a carriage. "No ordinary carriage, I dare say?" "Of course not—a golden carriage". "How is it drawn?" "By forty million diamond stags!" Similar preposterous qualities and quantities are usual in Buddhist legend. This megalomaniac tendency has always been observable among editors of myths and of the lives of the saints. Hindu tradition shows the great ascetic Cyavana at his *tapas* exercises sitting in an ant-heap entirely hidden except for his eyes, which shine out of it like fiery coals. Visvamitra stands on the tips of his toes for a thousand years. Such playing with the marvellous in number or degree underlies a great many giant or dwarf stories, from the earliest myths to Gulliver. In the *Snorra Edda* Thor and his companions find a small room leading off from an enormous bed-chamber, and in that they pass the night. Next morning it turns out that they have been sleeping in the thumb of the giant Skrymir's glove.[1]

In my view this desire to astonish by boundless exaggeration or confusion of proportions should never be taken absolutely seriously, no matter whether we find it in myths which are part of a system of belief or in pure literature or in the fantasies of children. In every case we are dealing with the same play-habit of the mind. Involuntarily we always judge archaic man's belief in the myths he creates by our own standards of science, philosophy or religious conviction. A half-joking element verging on make-believe is inseparable from true myth. Here we are up against that "thaumaturgic part of poetry" whereof Plato speaks.[2]

If poetry, in the widest sense of the Greek *poiesis*, must always fall within the play-sphere, this is not to say that its essentially ludic character is always outwardly preserved. The epic severs its connection with play as soon as it is no longer meant to be recited on some festal occasion but only to be read. Nor is the lyric understood as a play-function once its ties with music have

[1] *Gylfaginning*, c. 45, cf. The hauling in of the Midgard serpent, c. 48.
[2] *Sophistes* 268 D: τῆς ποιήσεως . . . . τὸ θαυματοποιικὸν μόριον.

gone. Only the drama, because of its intrinsically functional character, its quality of being an action, remains permanently linked to play. Language itself reflects this indissoluble bond, particularly Latin and allied languages, also the Germanic. Drama is called "play" and the performance of it "playing". It might seem anomalous, although readily understandable in the light of what we have said before, that the Greeks, the very people who created drama in its most perfect form, applied the word "play" neither to the drama itself nor its performance. But the fact that the Greeks lacked a word covering the whole range of play easily accounts for this gap in their terminology. Hellenic society was so profoundly imbued with the play-spirit that this spirit never struck the Greeks as a special thing on its own.

That tragedy and comedy both derive from play is obvious enough. Attic comedy grew out of the licentious *komos* at the feast of Dionysus. Only at a later phase did it become a consciously literary exercise and even then, in the days of Aristophanes, it bears numerous traces of its Dionysian past. In the so-called *parabasis* the chorus, divided into rows and moving backwards and forwards, faces the audience and points out the victims with taunts and derision. The phallic costume of the players, the disguising of the chorus in animal-masks are traits of remote antiquity. It is not merely from caprice that Aristophanes makes wasps, birds and frogs the subject of his comedies; the whole tradition of theriomorphic personification is at the back of it. With their public criticism and stinging mockery the "old comedies" belong absolutely to those censorious, challenging yet festive antiphonal songs we have discussed before. A similar line of development from ritual to drama in the Germanic literatures, running parallel to that of Greek comedy, has recently been reconstructed with a high degree of plausibility if not actually proved by Robert Stumpfl in his book *Die Kultspiele der Germanen als Ursprung mittelalterlichen Dramas*.

Neither is tragedy in its origins a merely literary rendering of human fate. Far from being literature designed for the stage it was originally a sacred play or a played rite. But in the course of time the "acting out" of a myth-theme grew into the regular performance, with mime and dialogue, of a sequence of events constituting a story with a plot.

Comedy and tragedy alike come under the heading of competition, which, as we have seen, is in all circumstances to be called play. The Greek dramatists composed their works competitively for the feast of Dionysus. Though the State did not organize the competition it had a hand in the running of it. There was always a large crowd of second and third rate poets competing for the laurels. Comparisons, if odious, were habitual among the audience and criticism was extremely pointed. The whole public understood all the allusions and reacted to the subtleties of style and expression, sharing the tension of the contest like a crowd at a football match. Eagerly they awaited the new chorus, for which the citizens taking part in it had rehearsed a whole year.

The actual matter of the drama was also agonistic. The comedy, for instance, debated an issue or attacked a person or a point of view, as in the case of Aristophanes deriding Socrates or Euripides. As to the mood in which the drama was performed it was one of Dionysian ecstasy and dithyrambic rapture. The player, withdrawn from the ordinary world by the mask he wore, felt himself transformed into another ego which he did not so much represent as incarnate and actualize. The audience was swept along with him into that state of mind. In Aeschylus the violence of the high-flown language, the extravagances of imagination and expression fully accord with the sacred origin of the drama. The mental sphere from which the drama springs knows no distinction between play and seriousness. With Aeschylus the experience of the most formidable seriousness is accomplished in the form of play. With Euripides the tone wavers between profound seriousness and frivolity. The true poet, says Socrates in Plato's *Symposium*, must be tragic and comic at once, and the whole of human life must be felt as a blend of tragedy and comedy.[1]

[1] *Symposium* 223 D, *Philebus* 50 B.

IX

PLAY-FORMS IN PHILOSOPHY

AT THE centre of the circle we are trying to describe with our idea of play there stands the figure of the Greek sophist. He may be regarded as an extension of the central figure in archaic cultural life who appeared before us successively as the prophet, medicine-man, seer, thaumaturge and poet and whose best designation is *vates*. The sophist has two important functions in common with the more ancient type of cultural rector: his business is to exhibit his amazing knowledge, the mysteries of his craft, and at the same time to defeat his rival in public contest. Thus the two main factors of social play in archaic society are present in him: glorious exhibitionism and agonistic aspiration. It should also be borne in mind that before the coming of the sophist proper Aeschylus uses the word "sophist" to denote the wise heroes of old like Prometheus and Palamedes, both of whom, we read, proudly enumerate all the arts they have invented for the good of mankind. In this boasting of their knowledge they resemble the later sophists, such as Hippias Polyhistor, the man of a thousand arts, the mnemotechnician, the economic autarch whose boast it is that he has made everything he wears and who turns up time and again at Olympia as the all-round genius ready to debate on any subject (prepared beforehand!) and answer any questions put to him, claiming never to have found his better.[1] All this is still very much in the manner of Yājñavalkya, the riddle-solving priest of the *Brāhmanas* who makes his opponent's head fall off.[2]

The sophist's performance is called *epideixis*—an exhibition. He has, as we hinted above, a regular repertoire and charges a fee for his disquisitions. Some of his pieces have a fixed price like the fifty-drachma lectures of Prodicus. Gorgias made so much money out of his art that he was able to dedicate a statue of himself to the god at Delphi, made of solid gold. The itinerant sophist like Protagoras booked fabulous successes. It was an event when a famous sophist visited a town. He was gaped at like a miraculous being, likened to the heroes of athletics; in

[1]Plato, *Hippias minor*, 368–9. [2]See *ante*, p. 109.

short, the profession of sophist was quite on a par with sport. The spectators applauded and laughed at every well-aimed crack. It was pure play, catching your opponent in a net of argument[1] or giving him a knock-out blow.[2] It was a point of honour to put nothing but twisters, to which every answer must be wrong.

When Protagoras calls sophistry "an ancient art" (τέχνην παλαιάν) he goes to the heart of the matter. It is indeed the ancient game of wits which, starting in the remotest cultures, vacillates between solemn ritual and mere amusement, sometimes touching the heights of wisdom, sometimes sinking to playful rivalry. Werner Jaeger speaks depreciatingly of "the modern fashion of describing Pythagoras as a sort of medicine-man", deeming so base an opinion unworthy of contradiction.[3] He forgets, however, that the medicine-man or whatever you choose to call him is, both by nature and from the historical point of view, in very truth the elder brother of all philosophers and sophists, and that they all retain traces of this ancient kinship.

The sophists themselves were perfectly well aware of the playful character of their art. Gorgias called his *Encomium on Helen* a game (παίγνιον) and his treatise *On Nature* has been termed a play-study in rhetoric.[4] Those who object to such an interpretation, as Capelle does,[5] should bear in mind that over the whole field of sophist eloquence no sharp distinction can be made between play and seriousness and that the term "play" fits the original nature of the thing most aptly. Similarly, the objection that the picture Plato gives of the sophist is a caricature or parody, is only partly true. We should not forget that all the frivolous and insincere traits exemplified in the sophist are essential elements in his make-up, recalling his remote origins. He belongs by nature to the tribe of nomads; vagrancy and parasitism are his birthright.

Nevertheless these same sophists were responsible for the milieu which gave rise to the Hellenic idea of education and culture. Greek knowledge and Greek science were not products of the school as we understand it. That is to say, they were not the by-products of an educational system designed to train the citizen for useful and profitable occupations. For the Greek, the treasures of the mind were the fruit of his leisure—σχολή—and for the free man any time that was not claimed by State service, war or

[1] *Euthydemus* 303 A. [2] πληγείς, *ibid.* 303 B.E. [3] *Paideia*, i, p. 160.
[4] H. Gomperz, *Sophistik und Rhetorik*, Leipzig, 1912, pp. 17, 33.
[5] *Vorsokratiker*, p. 344.

ritual counted as free time, so that he had ample leisure indeed.[1] The word "school" has a curious history behind it. Meaning originally "leisure" it has now acquired precisely the opposite sense of systematic work and training, as civilization restricted the free disposal of the young man's time more and more and herded larger and larger classes of the young to a daily life of severe application from childhood onwards.

Sophistry, technically regarded as a form of expression, has all the associations with primitive play as we found them in the sophist's predecessor, the *vates*. The sophism proper is closely related to the riddle. It is a fencer's trick. The Greek word πρόβλημα, in its original concrete sense, meant either something you place before yourself as a defence—a shield, for instance—or something you throw down at another's feet for him to take up—a gage. Both meanings taken in the abstract hold good for the art of the sophist.[2] His questions and arguments are so many "problemata" in precisely this sense. Games, or what we might call *jeux d'esprit*, designed to catch people out by trick-questions, held an important place in Greek conversation. The various types had been systematized under technical names and comprised the *sorites*, *apophaskon*, *outis*, *pseudomenos*, *antistrephon*, etc. One of Aristotle's disciples, Clearchus, wrote a Theory of the Riddle, particularly of the kind called *griphos*: a joke question-game played for rewards or forfeits. "What is the same everywhere and nowhere?" Answer: "Time". "What I am you are not. I'm a man, therefore you're not a man". Diogenes is supposed to have said: "If you want it to be true you'd better begin with me".[3] Chrysippus wrote a whole treatise on certain sophisms. All these catch-questions rest on the condition that your opponent shall tacitly accept the logical validity of the game without raising objections and spoiling everything like Diogenes. The propositions could be stylistically adorned with rhymes, refrains or other artifices.

The transition from this "fooling" to the pompous perorations of the sophist and the Socratic dialogue is always fluid. The sophism is akin both to the common riddle and the sacred, cosmogonic enigma. Euthydemos in the Platonic dialogue of that name is sometimes playing with purely childish tricks of grammar and logic, and sometimes verging on the profundities of

[1] Cf. R. W. Livingstone, *Greek Ideals and Modern Life*, p. 64.
[2] Cf. *Sophistes* 261 B.
[3] Prantl, *Geschichte der Logik*, i, p. 492.

cosmology and epistemology.[1] The profound utterances of early Greek philosophy, such as the Elean conclusion that there is neither "genesis nor motion nor plurality", come in the form of a game of question and answer. Even so abstract a deduction as that which leads to the impossibility of framing a judgement of general validity was made from a simple *sorites* or chain-question. "When you shake out a sack of corn, which grain makes the noise? The first?" "No". "The second?" "No". "The third, etc.?" "No". "Therefore. . . ."

The Greeks themselves always realized how much they were playing in these matters. In *Euthydemos* Plato makes Socrates disdain the artifices of sophistry as a fooling with doctrine. "This stuff", he says, "teaches you nothing about the nature of things; you only learn how to fool people with subtleties and equivocations. It is no better than tripping somebody up or taking his chair away as he is about to sit down". "When you say that you want to make a sage of this boy", he goes on, "are you fooling or are you serious?"[2] Theaetetus in the *Sophist* has to admit to the Stranger from Elea that the sophist belongs to the sort of people "who give themselves up to play" (τῶν τῆς παιδιᾶς μετεχόντων).[3] Parmenides, pressed to pronounce upon the problem of existence, calls this task "playing a difficult game" (πραγματειώδη παιδιὰν παίζειν),[4] and then launches forth into the profoundest ontological questions, keeping all the time to the game of question and answer. "The One can have no parts, is unlimited, hence formless; it is nowhere, it is motionless, timeless, unknowable". Then the thread is reversed, and again later, and yet again.[5] The argument goes back and forth like a shuttle and, in its flyings, epistemology takes on the appearance of a noble game. It is not only the sophists that play—Socrates and Plato do likewise.[6]

According to Aristotle, Zeno of Elea was the first to write a dialogue in the interrogative form peculiar to the philosophers of Megara and the sophists. It had a technique calculated to catch their opponents. Plato is supposed to have followed Sophron in particular when composing his dialogues. Now this Sophron was a writer of farces—μῖμος—and Aristotle bluntly calls the dialogue a form of *mimos*, which itself is an offshoot of comedy. So that we

[1] *Euthydemos* 293 C; *Cratylus* 386 D.
[2] *Euthydemos* 287 B, 283 B.
[3] *Sophistes* 235 A.
[4] *Parmenides* 137 B.
[5] *Ibid.* 142 B, 155 E, 165 E.
[6] Cf. Prantl, *op. cit.* i, p. 9.

need not be surprised to find even Socrates and Plato reckoned among the jugglers and thaumaturges just like the sophists.[1] If these things do not suffice to reveal the play-element in philosophy there is ample evidence of it in the Platonic dialogues themselves. The dialogue is an art-form, a fiction; for obviously real conversation, however polished it may have been with the Greeks, could never have had the gloss of the literary dialogue. In Plato's hands it is a light, airy thing, quite artificial. The setting of *Parmenides*, which is almost that of a short story, is sufficient proof of this, also the beginning of *Cratylus* and the easy, informal tone of both these and many other dialogues. A certain similarity to the *mimos* is unmistakable here. In the *Sophist* the first principles of the older philosophy are touched on in a very *scherzo* manner, and the myth of Epimetheus and Prometheus in the *Protagoras* is told with positive humour.[2]

"For the appearance and names of these gods," says Socrates in *Cratylus*, "there is a humorous as well as a serious explanation, for the gods are fond of a joke"—φιλοπαίσμονες γὰρ καὶ οἱ θεοί. Elsewhere in the same dialogue Plato has him say: "You'd know at once if I'd heard Prodicus' fifty-drachma lecture, but as it was I only heard his one-drachma one!"[3] And again he says, in the same tone of obvious satire as he juggles with absurd etymologies: "Now watch out for my special trick which I have for everything I can't solve!"[4] Finally, "I have long been amazed at my own wisdom and do not believe it". But what is one to say when the *Protagoras* ends by reversing the points of view, or when it is doubtful whether the funeral speech in the *Menexenos* is meant seriously or not?

Plato's speakers themselves regard their philosophic preoccupations as a pleasant pastime. Youth loves to dispute, age to be honoured.[5] "That", says Callicles in *Gorgias*, "is the long and short of it, as you will understand if you now leave philosophy and turn to greater things. For philosophy is a comely thing if you pursue it with moderation in youth, but pernicious for a man who loses himself in it for longer than is seemly".[6]

Thus the very thinkers who laid the imperishable foundations of philosophy and science regarded their labours as a youthful

[1] Aristotle, *Poetica* 1447 B; H. Reich, *Der Mimus*, Berlin, 1903, p. 354.
[2] *Sophistes* 242 CD; cf. *Cratylus* 440, 406 C.
[3] *Ibid.* 384 B. [4] *Ibid.* 409 D. [5] *Parmenides* 128 E.
[6] *Gorgias* 484 C; cf. *Menexenos* 234 A, also L. Méridier, *Platon, Oeuvres complètes*, v, 1, Paris, 1931, p. 52.

distraction. In order to establish for all time the fundamental errors of the sophists, their logical and ethical deficiencies, Plato was not above borrowing their loose, easy manner of dialogue. For, much as he deepened philosophy, he still saw it as a noble game. If both he and Aristotle deemed the fallacious arguments and quibbles of the sophists worthy of so serious and so elaborate a refutation, it could only be because their own philosophic thought had not yet broken loose from the archaic sphere of play. But, we may ask, can philosophy ever do this?

We can sketch the successive stages of philosophy roughly as follows: it starts in the remote past from the sacred riddle-game, which is at one and the same time ritual and festival entertainment. On the religious side it gives rise to the profound philosophy and theosophy of the Upanishads, to the intuitive flashes of the pre-Socratics; on the play side it produces the sophist. The two sides are not absolutely distinct. Plato raises philosophy, as the search for truth, to heights which he alone could reach, but always in that aerial form which was and is philosophy's proper element. Simultaneously it develops at a lower level into sophistical quackery and intellectual smartness. The agonistic factor in Greece was so strong that it allowed rhetoric to expand at the cost of pure philosophy, which was put in the shade by sophistication parading as the culture of the common man. Gorgias was typical of this deterioration of culture: he turned away from true philosophy to waste his spirit in the praise and misuse of glittering words and false wit. After Aristotle the level of philosophic thinking sank; emulation carried to extremes and narrow doctrinairism won the day. A similar declension was to repeat itself in the later Middle Ages, when the age of the great scholastics who sought to understand the innermost meaning of things was followed by one in which words and formulae alone sufficed.

The play-element in all this is not easy to fix with any accuracy. Sometimes a childish pun or a shallow witticism misses profundity by but a hair's breadth. Gorgias' famous treatise *On Not-being*, in which he categorically rejects all serious knowledge in favour of a radical nihilism, is as much a play-phenomenon as his *Encomium on Helen*, which he himself expressly calls a game. The absence of any clear and conscious demarcation between play and knowledge is to be seen from the fact that the Stoics treated fatuous sophistries constructed on some grammatical pitfall and the serious disquisitions of the Megarian school in precisely the same way.[1]

For the rest, disputation and declamation reigned supreme, and were ever a theme of public competition. Public speaking was a form of exhibitionism, a pretext for showing off and swanking with words. When a Greek author wanted to set out and get a judgement on some controversial question he presented it in literary form as a dispute. Thus Thucydides puts the case for peace or war in the speeches of Archidamos and Stheneladas; other questions are dealt with by Nicias and Alcibiades, Kleon and Diodotos. Thus, too, he handles the issue of might or right in the form of a highly sophistical game of question and answer concerning the breach of neutrality committed against the island of Melos. Aristophanes, in his *Clouds*, parodies the craze for pompous public disputation in the duel between the just and unjust Logos.

One of the special favourites of the sophists was the *antilogia* or double reasoning. Apart from giving free rein to play this form allowed them to hint at the perpetual ambiguity of every judgement made by the human mind: one can put a thing like this or like that. And as a matter of fact what keeps the art of winning by words tolerably pure and legitimate, is its play-character. It is only when the sophist, by his verbal pyrotechnics, pursues an intrinsically immoral aim—like Callicles presenting his "master-morality"[2]—that he becomes a falsifier of wisdom,—unless of course it be maintained that the agonistic habit is in itself immoral and false. For the ordinary run of sophist and rhetor, however, the aim was not truth or the desire for it but the purely personal satisfaction of being right. They were animated by the primitive instinct of competition, the struggle for glory. Some of Nietzsche's biographers[3] blame him for having re-adopted the old agonistic attitude of philosophy. If indeed he did so he has led philosophy back to its antique origins.

We have no wish to go into the deep question of how far the process of reasoning is itself marked by play-rules, i.e. is only valid within a certain frame of reference where those rules are accepted as binding. May it not be that in all logic, and particularly in the syllogism, there is always a tacit understanding to

[1]Prantl, *op. cit.* p. 494.
[2]*Gorgias* 483 A–484 D.
[3]H. L. Miéville, *Nietzsche et la volonté de puissance*, Lausanne, 1934; Charles Andler, *Nietzsche: sa vie et sa pensée*, Paris, 1920, i, p. 141; iii, p. 162.

take the validity of the terms and concepts for granted as one does the pieces on a chess-board? Let others puzzle this out! Our only pretension here is to indicate, very cursorily, the indubitable play-qualities in the art of declamation and disputation which succeeded the Hellenic era. No very elaborate detail will be required, since the phenomenon always recurs in the same forms and its development in the West is largely dependent on the illustrious Greek model.

It was Quintilian who introduced the art of declamation and rhetoric into Latin life and literature. The vogue for it extended far beyond the formal schools of rhetoric in Imperial Rome. Dio Chrysostom, himself a rhetor, speaks of the street-philosophers who, like the vulgar kind of sophist, turned the heads of slaves and sailors with their hodge-podge of aphorisms, wisecracks and idle chatter not devoid of seditious propaganda. Hence Vespasian's decree banishing all philosophers from Rome. But the popular mind still continued to esteem such samples of sophism as remained in vogue. Again and again the graver spirits rose up and uttered warnings; St. Augustine admonishes against "noxious contentiousness and puerile bombast designed to catch people out".[1] Pleasantries like: "You have horns for you haven't lost any horns therefore you have them still!" echoed through the whole literature of the Schools and never seemed to lose their exquisite savour. Evidently it was too much for the average intellect to detect the logical fallacy which makes such propositions purely asinine.

The spectacle of philosophy at play during the Dark Ages is seen in the conversion of the Visigoths from Arianism to Catholicism at Toledo in the year 589, which took the form of a regular theological tourney with high prelates on both sides. A no less striking illustration of the sportive character of philosophy during this epoch is afforded by the chronicler Richer,[2] who relates an episode from the life of Gerbert, afterwards Pope Sylvester II. A certain Ortric, scholaster to the cathedral of Magdeburg, being jealous of Gerbert's fame for learning, sent one of his clerks to Rheims, charging him to listen secretly to the teaching of Gerbert so as to catch him in the enunciation of a false opinion, and to report back to the Emperor, Otto II. The spy misunderstands Gerbert and duly reports what he thinks he has heard. Next year,

[1] *De Doctrina Christiana*, ii, p. 31.
[2] *Historiarum liber* (Mon. Germ. Hist. Scriptores), iv, III, c. 55–65.

980, the Emperor contrives to unite both learned men in Ravenna, and now causes them to dispute before an illustrious audience until daylight fails and the hearers are wearied. The high point of the proceedings is when Ortric charges his opponent with having called mathematics a part of physics,[1] whereas in reality Gerbert had stated that both were equal and simultaneous.

It would be a rewarding endeavour to try to find out whether a certain play-quality was not an essential part of what is called the Carolingian Renaissance—that pompous display of erudition, poetry and pietistic sententiousness where the leading lights adorned themselves with classical or Biblical names: Alcuin as Horace, Angilbert as Homer, and the Emperor Charles himself as David. Courtly culture is particularly prone to adopt the play-form; it moves in a small and restricted circle. The awe felt in the presence of Majesty is itself enough to prescribe all sorts of rules and fictions. In Charles' "Academia Palatina" the avowed ideal was the establishment of an "Athenae Novae", but in actual fact pious aspirations were tempered by elegant entertainment. The courtiers competed in verse-making and mutual mockery. Their attempts at classic elegance by no means excluded certain very ancient traits. "What is writing?" asks Pippin, Charles' son, and Alcuin answers: "The keeper of knowledge". "What is the word?"—"The betrayer of thought". "Who begot the word?"—"The tongue". "What is the tongue?"—"The scourge of the air". "What is the air?"—"The preserver of life". "What is life?"—"The delight of the happy, the bane of the sorrowful, the expectation of death". "What is man?"—"The slave of death, the guest of one place, a traveller passing". All this strikes a familiar note: it is the old game of question and answer, the riddle-contest, the hiding of sense in a *kenning*. In short, we meet once more all the characteristics of the knowing-game as found among the ancient Hindus, the pre-Islamic Arabs, and the Scandinavians.

Towards the end of the 11th century the young countries of the West were pervaded by an all-consuming thirst for knowledge of life and everything that existed. It would ere long find institutional form in the University, one of the greatest single creations of mediaeval civilization, and in Scholasticism its highest expression. The beginnings of this great spiritual ferment were marked by the almost febrile agitation which seems inseparable

[1]Both words are used here in their mediaeval sense.

from all major renewals of culture. The agonistic element inevitably comes to the fore at such times. It manifests itself in the most varied ways at once. To beat your opponent by reason or the force of the word becomes a sport comparable with the profession of arms. The emergence of tournaments in their oldest and bloodiest form, either by groups of knights roaming the countryside bent on mutual destruction or by single champions in search of worthy adversaries (the historical forerunners of the knight-errant so beloved by a later literature), coincided in time with the evil, lamented by Peter Damiani, of professional wind-bags who wandered about prating of their art and gaining signal victories like the Greek sophists of old. In the Schools of the 12th century the most violent rivalry, going to all the lengths of vilification and slander, reigned supreme. The ecclesiastical authors give us a rapid sketch of what went on in the schools of those days: the hum of argumentation, quibbling and hair-splitting lies over all. Pupils and masters try to befool one another with "snares of words and nets of syllables", with a thousand and one stratagems and subtleties. Famous masters are pursued and lionized; people boast of having seen them or studied under them as pupils.[1] These often make a mint of money as did the sophists in Greece. Roscelinus, in his envenomed calumniation of Abelard, shows us the latter counting up, every evening, the money that his false teachings brought him and daily dissipating it in debaucheries. Abelard himself declares that he only undertook his studies in order to earn money and that he made a great deal. His abrupt transition from teaching Physics (i.e. Philosophy) to the interpretation of the Holy Scriptures was the result of a wager, his colleagues having dared him to do it by way of a *tour de force*.[2] He had long preferred the weapons of dialectic to those of war, and had passed through all the places where the eloquent art flourished until he "pitched the camp of his school" on the Hill of St. Genevieve in order to "besiege" from there the rival who held the chair at Paris.[3] This mixture of rhetoric, war and play can also be found in the scholastic competitions of the Muslim theologians.[4]

Competition is an outstanding feature of the whole develop-

[1]Hugo de Sancto Victore, *Didascalia*, Migne *P.L.* t. 176, 772 D, 803; *De Vanitate Mundi*, *ibid.* 709; John of Salisbury, *Metalogicus*, i, c. 3; *Policraticus*, v, c. 15.
[2]*Opera*, i, pp. 7, 9, 19; ii, p. 3.
[3]*Ibid.* i, p. 4.
[4]For this information I have to thank Professor C. Snouck Hurgronje.

ment of Scholasticism and the Universities. The lasting vogue for the problem of "universals" as the central theme of philosophic discussion, which led to the split between the Realists and the Nominalists, was probably agonistic at bottom and sprang from the fundamental need to form parties on a point at issue. Partisanship is inseparable from cultural growth. The point at issue may be a relatively unimportant one, though in this case it was crucial for the human mind; the controversy is still unresolved to-day. The whole functioning of the mediaeval University was profoundly agonistic and ludic. The everlasting disputations which took the place of our learned discussions in periodicals, etc., the solemn ceremonial which is still such a marked feature of University life, the grouping of scholars into *nationes*, the divisions and subdivisions, the schisms, the unbridgeable gulfs—all these are phenomena belonging to the sphere of competition and play-rules. Erasmus was fully aware of this when he complains, in a letter to his stiff-necked opponent Noel Bédier, of the narrowness of the Schools which only deal with material handed down by their predecessors and, in a controversy, ban any point of view that does not conform to their own particular tenets. "In my opinion", he says, "it is quite unnecessary to act in the Schools as you act when playing cards or dice, where any infringement of the rules spoils the game. In a learned discussion, however, there should be nothing outrageous or risky in putting forward a novel idea".[1]

All knowledge—and this naturally includes philosophy—is polemical by nature, and polemics cannot be divorced from agonistics. Epochs in which great new treasures of the mind come to light are generally epochs of violent controversy. Such was the 17th century, when Natural Science underwent a glorious efflorescence coinciding with the weakening of authority and antiquity, and the decay of faith. Everything is taking up new positions; camps and factions fill the scene. You have to be for Descartes or against him, for or against Newton, "les modernes", "les anciens", the flattening of the earth at the poles, inoculation, etc. The 18th century saw a lively intellectual commerce between the savants of different countries, though mercifully the limited techniques of the time prevented the chaotic exuberance of printed matter which is so distressing a feature of our day. The age was exquisitely suited to serious or merely trifling pen-

[1] *Erasmi opus epist.*, ed. Allen, vi, No. 1581, 621 *sq.*

combats. Together with music, the wig, frivolous Rationalism, the grace of rococo and the charm of the salon these voluminous pen-combats are an essential part of that playfulness which nobody will deny the 18th century, and for which we are often tempted to envy it.

X

PLAY-FORMS IN ART

PLAY, we found, was so innate in poetry, and every form of poetic utterance so intimately bound up with the structure of play that the bond between them was seen to be indissoluble. The same is true, and in even higher degree, of the bond between play and music. In an earlier chapter we noted that in some languages the manipulation of musical instruments is called "playing", to wit, in the Arabic language on the one hand and the Germanic and Slavonic on the other. Since this semantic understanding between East and West can hardly be ascribed to borrowing or coincidence, we have to assume some deep-rooted psychological reason for so remarkable a symbol of the affinity between music and play.

However natural this affinity seems to us it is far from easy to form a clear idea of its rationale. The most we can do is to enumerate the elements which music and play have in common. Play, we said, lies outside the reasonableness of practical life; has nothing to do with necessity or utility, duty or truth. All this is equally true of music. Furthermore, musical forms are determined by values which transcend logical ideas, which even transcend our ideas of the visible and the tangible. These musical values can only be understood in terms of the designations we use for them, specific names like rhythm and harmony which are equally applicable to play or poetry. Indeed, rhythm and harmony are factors of all three—poetry, music, and play—in an absolutely equal sense. But whereas in poetry the words themselves lift the poem, in part at least, out of pure play into the sphere of ideation and judgement, music never leaves the play-sphere. The reason why poetry has such a prominently liturgical and social function in archaic cultures lies precisely in its close connection, or rather indissoluble union, with musical recitation. All true ritual is sung, danced and played. We moderns have lost the sense for ritual and sacred play. Our civilization is worn with age and too sophisticated. But nothing helps us to regain that sense so much as musical sensibility. In feeling music we feel ritual. In the enjoyment of music, whether it is meant to express religious ideas or not, the perception of the beautiful and the sensation of holiness merge, and the distinction between play and seriousness is whelmed in that fusion.

It is important for our theme to understand just how and why the ideas of play, work and aesthetic enjoyment had quite a different relation in Greek thought from our own. The word μουσική was far wider in scope than our "music". It not only embraced singing and dancing to instrumental accompaniment but covered all the arts, artistries and skills presided over by Apollo and the *Muses*.[1] These are called the "musical" arts as distinct from the plastic or mechanical arts which lie outside the province of the Muses. In Greek thought everything "musical" was closely related to ritual, above all to the feasts where, of course, ritual had its proper function. Nowhere, perhaps, is the relationship between ritual, dancing, music and play described more lucidly than in Plato's *Laws*.[2] The gods, he says, out of pity for the race of men born to sorrow, ordained the feasts of thanksgiving as a respite from their troubles and gave them Apollo, lord of the Muses, and Dionysus to be their companions in the feast, that by this divine companionship at feast-tide order might always be restored among men. Then follows Plato's oft-quoted explanation of play, how all young creatures cannot keep either their bodies or their voices still, how they must continually be moving and making a noise for joy, leaping and skipping and dancing and uttering all manner of cries. But whereas all other creatures know not the distinction between order and disorder which is called rhythm and harmony, to us men the same gods who were given us as companions in the dance have granted the perception of rhythm and harmony, which is invariably accompanied by

[1]Many pages could be devoted to the etymology of the word "muse", which preserves its root in many languages. The Greek *mousa* is held to derive from the verb *μάειν*, to seek after, crave, covet, and the literal meaning to be "inventress", invention being inferred from seeking and desiring. *Mousa* may also have referred originally to the emotion of "fine frenzy" implied in *μάειν* and its derivatives (*μεμαώς*: excited, *μαίνεσθαι*: to rage, *μανία*: frenzy, *μάντις*: seer). All these meanings are comprised in the English verb "muse", as the cognate forms in other languages show. Desire implies brooding, meditation; meditation implies leisure, and both together give the state of "bemusement", and when bemused you are very apt to mumble and mutter. Hence *μύζειν*, to mutter; in Norwegian *mussa*, *mysja*, whisper; cf. Italian *mussare*. The Italian *musare*, to gape at, only implies an intense condition of pondering and wondering. Compare the Italian *muso*, mouth; whence *muzzle*. The leisure element in musing is given directly in the German *Musse*, idleness, and indirectly in *amusement*. Trans.

[2]*Laws*, ii, 653.

pleasure. Here, as clearly as possible, a direct connection is established between music and play. But this idea, important as it is, cannot fail to be hampered in the Greek mind by the semantic peculiarity to which we have alluded before, namely that the word for play—παιδιά—is always, on account of its etymology, fraught with the sense of child's play, the infantile, the nugatory. Hence παιδιά could hardly serve to denote the higher forms of play, it was too reminiscent of the child. Therefore the higher forms had to find expression in specific terms such as ἀγών—contest, σχολάζειν—to take one's leisure, to idle, διαγωγή—(literally "passing" but only approximately rendered by "pastime"),[1] which completely miss the essential play-element. In this way the Greek mind failed to realize the fundamental unity of all these ideas in one general concept, as in the clearly conceived Latin word *ludus* and the words for play in the younger European languages. That is why Plato and Aristotle have to go to such lengths to decide whether and how far music is more than play. The passage just quoted from Plato continues as follows:[2]

> "That which has neither utility nor truth nor likeness, nor yet, in its effects, is harmful, can best be judged by the criterion of the charm (χάρις) that is in it, and by the pleasure it affords. Such pleasure, entailing as it does no appreciable good or ill, is play—παιδιά."

We should note, however, that Plato is speaking all the time of the musical recital—music as we understand it. He goes on to say that we should seek for higher things in music than this pleasure; but let us now turn to Aristotle:[3]

> "The nature of music is not easy to determine, neither is the profit which we derive from a knowledge of it. Is it, perhaps, for the sake of play [παιδιά: which we might render here by 'amusement' or 'distraction'] and recreation that we desire music as we desire sleep and drink, which are likewise neither important in themselves nor serious (σπουδαῖα) but pleasant and potent to dispel care? Certain it is that many use music in this way and to these three—music, drink, and sleep—add dancing. Or should we say rather that music conduces to virtue in so far as, like gymnastics, it makes the body fit, breeds a certain ethos and enables us to enjoy things in the proper way? Or lastly [and this is yet a third function, according to Aristotle], may it not contribute to mental recreation (διαγωγή) and to understanding (φρόνησις)?"

This διαγωγή is a highly significant word. It means literally the "passing" or "spending" of time, but to render it by "pastime" is only admissible if one has Aristotle's attitude to work and leisure. "Nowadays", he says,[4] "most people practise music for

[1]See *infra*.
[2]*Laws*, ii, 667 E.
[3]*Politics*, viii, 1399 A.
[4]*Ibid.* 1337 B.

pleasure, but the ancients gave it a place in education (παιδεία), because Nature requires us not only to be able to work well but also to idle well (σχολάζειν δύνασθαι καλῶς)". This idleness or leisure is *the* principle of the universe, for Aristotle. It is preferable to work; indeed, it is the aim (τέλος) of all work. Such an inversion of the relations familiar to us must seem strange until we realize that in Greece the free man had no need to work for his living and thus had leisure to pursue his life's aim in noble occupations of an educative character. The question for him was how to employ his σχολή or free time. Not in playing, for then play would be the aim of life and that, for Aristotle, is impossible because παιδιά merely is child's play. Playing may serve as relaxation from work, as a sort of tonic inasmuch as it affords repose to the soul. Leisure, however, seems to contain in itself all the joy and delight of life. Now this happiness, i.e. the cessation of striving after that which one has not, is the *telos*. But all men do not find it in the same thing. It will, moreover, be best where those who enjoy are best and their aspirations the noblest. Hence it is clear that we must educate ourselves to this *diagōge* and learn certain things—not, be it noted, for the sake of work but for their own sake. For this reason our forefathers reckoned music as *paideia*—education, culture; as something neither necessary nor useful, like reading and writing, but only serving to pass one's free time.

In this exposition we find that the demarcation between play and seriousness is very different from ours and that the criteria for their evaluation are no longer our criteria. *Diagōge* imperceptibly acquires the meaning of such intellectual and aesthetic preoccupations as are becoming to free men. Children, says Aristotle,[1] are not yet capable of it, for *diagōge* is a final aim, a perfection; and the perfect is inaccessible to the imperfect. The enjoyment of music comes near to being such a final aim of action because it is sought not for the sake of future good but for itself.

This conception of music sets it midway between a noble game and "art for art's sake". We cannot, however, assert with truth that Aristotle's view dominated the Greek idea of the nature and significance of music. His view was crossed by another, simpler and more popular, according to which music had a very definite function technically, psychologically and above all morally. It belonged to the mimetic arts, and the effect of this mimēsis is to

[1] *Politics*, viii, 1339 A, 29.

arouse ethical feelings of a positive or negative kind.[1] Any melody, "mode" or attitude struck in the dance *represents* something, illustrates or portrays it, and according to whether the thing portrayed is good or bad, beautiful or ugly, the same qualification will attach to the music. Herein lies its ethical and educative value, since the experience of the *mimesis* arouses the sentiments imitated.[2] Thus the Olympian melodies rouse enthusiasm, other rhythms and melodies suggest anger, sedateness, courage, contemplation, etc. Whereas no ethical effect is associated with the sense of touch or taste, and only very feebly with that of sight, the melody of its own nature expresses an *ethos*. The various *modes* in particular are vehicles of ethical significance. The Lydian mode makes sad, the Phrygian quietens; likewise the flute excites, etc., each instrument having a different ethical function. For Plato, *mimesis* is a general term descriptive of the mental attitude of the artist.[3] The imitator—*mimetes*—that is to say the creative as well as the executive artist, knows not himself whether the thing he imitates is good or bad; *mimesis* is mere play to him, not serious work.[4] This is true even of the tragic poets, he says; they too are only *mimetikoi*—imitators. We must leave on one side the question of what this somewhat depreciatory definition of creative work really means; it is not altogether clear. The point for us is that Plato understood creativity as play.

This digression on the value accorded to music in Greece will have made it abundantly clear how, in trying to define the nature and function of music, man's thought has always gravitated towards the sphere of pure play. Even if this primary fact that the essential nature of all musical activity is play is not always explicitly stated, it is implicitly understood everywhere. In the more primitive phases of culture the various properties of music were distinguished and defined with a certain crude naiveté. People expressed the rapture caused by sacred music in terms of heavenly choirs, celestial spheres, etc. Apart from its religious function music was then praised chiefly as an edifying pastime, a delectable artifice, or simply a jolly entertainment. It was only quite late that music was appreciated and openly acknowledged as a highly personal thing, the source of some of our deepest emotional experiences, and one of life's greatest blessings. For a long time its function was purely social and ludic, and though the

[1] Plato, *Laws*, ii, 668.

[2] Aristotle, *Politics*, viii, 1340 A.

[3] *Republic*, x, 602 B.

[4] εἶναι παιδιάν τινα καὶ οὐ σπουδὴν τὴν μίμησιν.

technical ability of the executant was greatly admired the musicians themselves were looked down upon and their art was ranked among the menial occupations. Aristotle calls them low people, and vagrants they remained—on a par with jugglers, tumblers, mummers, etc.—almost up to our own time. In the 17th century a prince kept his musicians as he might keep his stables, and a court orchestra was a thoroughly domestic affair. Under Louis XIV the *musique du roi* required the office of a permanent composer. The king's "vingt-quatre violons" were stage-players at the same time. One of the musicians, Bocan, was a dancing-master too. Everybody knows that even Haydn still wore livery at the Esterházys and received his orders daily from the Prince. On the one hand the aristocratic public of those days must have been great connoisseurs, but their reverence for the majesty of art and their respect for its executants were, on the other hand, excessively small. Concert manners as we understand them to-day, with their absolute sacramental silence and magical awe of the conductor, are of very recent date. Prints of musical performances in the 18th century show the audience engaged in elegant conversation. Critical interruptions aimed at the orchestra or conductor were a regular feature of musical life in France even thirty years ago. Music was still largely a *divertissement* and what was most admired about it was virtuosity. The composer's creations were not by any means regarded as sacrosanct, as his own property to which he had inalienable rights. Executants made such lavish use of the free *cadenza* that steps had to be taken. Frederick the Great, for instance, prohibited singers from embellishing a composition to the extent of altering its nature.

In few human activities is competition more ingrained than in music, and has been so ever since the battle between Marsyas and Apollo. Wagner has immortalized these vocal battles in his *Meistersinger*. As instances from periods following that of the Meistersinger themselves we may cite the contest between Handel and Scarlatti got up by Cardinal Ottoboni in the year 1709, the chosen weapons being harpsichord and organ. In 1717 Augustus the Strong, King of Saxony and Poland, wanted to organize a contest between J. S. Bach and a certain Marchand, but the latter failed to appear. In 1726 all London society was in an uproar because of the competition between the two Italian singers Faustina and Cuzzoni: there were fisticuffs and catcalls.

Factions and cliques develop with astonishing ease in musical life. The 18th century is full of these musical coteries—Bononcini versus Handel, Gluck versus Piccini, the Parisian "Bouffons" versus the Opera. The musical squabble sometimes took on the character of a lasting and embittered feud, such as that between the Wagnerians and the Brahmsians.

Romanticism, which has stimulated our aesthetic consciousness in so many respects, has also been the chief promoter of an ever-widening appreciation of music as a thing of the deepest value in life. This appreciation has, of course, not ousted any of music's more ancient functions. The agonistic element is flourishing still. In the newspapers I found a report of an international contest that was held for the first time in Paris in the year 1937. The prize, founded by the late senator Henry de Jouvenel, was for the best rendering of Fauré's 6th Nocturne for piano.

If in everything that pertains to music we find ourselves within the play-sphere, the same is true in even higher degree of music's twin-sister, the dance. Whether we think of the sacred or magical dances of savages, or of the Greek ritual dances, or of the dancing of King David before the Ark of the Covenant, or of the dance simply as part of a festival, it is always at all periods and with all peoples pure play, the purest and most perfect form of play that exists. Not every form of dancing, it is true, shows this play-quality to the full. It is most readily discernible in choral or figure dances, but it is also there in the solo dance—wherever, in fact, the dance is a performance, an exhibition, a display of rhythmical movement as in the minuet or quadrille. The supersession of the round dance, choral and figure dances by dancing *à deux*, whether this take the form of gyrating as in the waltz or polka or the slitherings and slidings and even acrobatics of contemporary dancing, is probably to be regarded as a symptom of declining culture. There are reasons enough for such an assertion if we survey the history of the dance and the high standards of beauty and style it attained in former ages, and still attains where the dance has been revived as an art-form—e.g. the ballet. For the rest, however, it is certain that the play-quality tends to be obscured in modern forms of dancing.

The connections between playing and dancing are so close that they hardly need illustrating. It is not that dancing has something of play in it or about it, rather that it is an integral part of play: the relationship is one of direct participation, almost of essential identity. Dancing is a particular and particularly perfect form of playing.

Turning from poetry, music and dancing to the plastic arts we find the connections with play becoming less obvious. The Hellenic mind had clearly grasped the fundamental difference between the two fields of aesthetic production and perception by assigning one complex of arts and crafts to the Muses while denying this dignity to others, namely, those which we rank among the plastic arts. These, in so far as they were thought subject to divine guidance at all, came under the dominion of Hephaestus or Athena Erganē—the Athene of work. The plastic artists did not win anything like the attention and appreciation bestowed on the poets. This is not to say that the honour accorded to an artist was measured by whether he belonged to a Muse or not; for, as we have already seen, the social status of the musician was on the whole very low.

The differentiation between the plastic and the musical arts corresponds by and large to the seeming absence of the play-quality in one as compared with its pronounced presence in the other. We do not have to seek far for the main reason for this. In order to become aesthetically active the arts of the Muses, or the "music" arts, have to be performed. A work of art, though composed, practised or written down beforehand, only comes to life in the execution of it, that is, by being represented or *produced* in the literal sense of the word—brought before a public. The "music" arts are action and are enjoyed as such every time that action is repeated in the performance. This assertion is apparently contradicted by the fact that Astronomy, Epic and History each have their special Muse; but it should be remembered that the attribution of a special function to each of the nine Muses belongs to a late epoch, and that Epic and History at least (respectively the domain of Clio and Calliope) were originally and quite definitely part of the profession of the *vates* and, as such, were not designed to be read or studied but to be recited in strophes to solemn musical accompaniment. They were action just as music and dancing were, and, like them, required production. Moreover this quality of action is not lost if the enjoyment of poetry shifts from the hearing of it to the reading of it. Such action, which is the soul of all the arts presided over by the Muses, can legitimately be called play.

The case is quite different with the plastic arts. The very fact of their being bound to matter and to the limitations of form inherent in it, is enough to forbid them absolutely free play and deny them that flight into the ethereal spaces open to music and poetry. In this respect dancing is in an anomalous position. It is musical and plastic at once: musical since rhythm and movement are its chief elements, plastic because inevitably bound to matter. Its execution depends on the human body with its limited manoeuvreability, and its beauty is that of the moving body itself. Dancing is a plastic creation like sculpture, but for a moment only. In common with the music which accompanies it and is its necessary condition, it lives from its capacity for repetition.

Apart from the intrinsic contrast between the plastic and the "music" arts there is also an affective or operational contrast. The architect, the sculptor, the painter, draughtsman, ceramist and decorative artist in general all fix a certain aesthetic impulse in matter by means of diligent and painstaking labour. Their work has duration and is visible at any moment. The emotional effect or operation of their art is not, as in music, dependent on a special kind of performance by others or by the artists themselves. Once finished their work, dumb and immobile, will produce its effect so long as there are eyes to behold it. The absence of any public *action* within which the work of plastic art comes to life and is enjoyed would seem to leave no room for the play-factor. However much the plastic artist may be possessed by his creative impulse he has to work like a craftsman, serious and intent, always testing and correcting himself. His inspiration may be free and vehement when he "conceives", but in its execution it is always subjected to the skill and proficiency of the forming hand. If therefore the play-element is to all appearances lacking in the execution of a work of plastic art, in the contemplation and enjoyment of it there is no scope for it whatever. For where there is no visible action there can be no play.

Admitting that this quality of handicraft, of industry, even of strenuosity in the work of plastic art obstructs the play-factor, we find that this condition is further intensified by the very nature of the thing, which is determined to a large extent by its practical purpose—and this is in no way dependent on aesthetic impulse.

The man who is commissioned to make something is faced with a serious and responsible task: any idea of play is out of place. He has to build an edifice—a temple or dwelling—worthy of its function in ritual or fit for human use. Or he has to make a vessel, a garment, an image, each of which may have to correspond to the idea it renders symbolically or in imitation.

Hence the processes of plastic art run completely outside the sphere of play, and its exhibition is necessarily part of some rite or other, a festival, entertainment or social event. The unveiling of statues, the laying of foundation-stones, exhibitions, etc., are not, in themselves, an intrinsic part of the creative process, and are mostly phenomena of recent date. The "music" arts live and thrive in an atmosphere of common rejoicing; the plastic arts do not.

Despite this fundamental difference it is possible to find traces of the play-factor in the plastic arts. In archaic culture the work of art had its place and function very largely in ritual, as an object of sacred significance. Buildings, statues, garments, weapons beautifully ornamented could all belong to the religious world. Such objects had magic power, they were charged with symbolical value as very often they represented a mystic identity. Now ritual and play are so closely connected that it would be strange indeed if we did not find the play-qualities of ritual somewhere reflected in the making and appreciation of works of art. Not without hesitation I venture to suggest to classical scholars that a semantic link between ritual, art and play may possibly be hidden in the Greek word ἄγαλμα. *Agalma* is derived from a verbal root with a complex of meanings, central to which is the idea of exultation and jubilation, comparable to the German *frohlocken*, often used in a religious sense. On the periphery stand such meanings as "to celebrate", "to make resplendent", "to make a show of", "to rejoice", "to adorn". The primary meaning of the substantive is held to be an ornament, a show-piece, a precious object—in short, the thing of beauty that is a joy for ever. Αγάλματα νυκτός is a poetical name for the stars. Finally, at some remove from all this, *agalma* means a statue, particularly the statue of a god. I venture to suggest that the word acquired this meaning via a middle term signifying "votive gift". If the Greeks did in fact denote the image of a god, and hence the essence of sacred art, by a term expressive of joyful offering (exulting and exalting), we come quite close to that mood of sacred play which is so characteristic of archaic ritual. I would hesitate to draw more definite conclusions from this observation.

A theory designed to explain the origin of plastic art in terms of an innate "play-instinct" (*Spieltrieb*) was propounded long ago by Schiller.[1] An almost instinctive, spontaneous need to decorate things cannot, indeed, be denied; and it may conveniently be called a play-function. It is known to everybody who, pencil in hand, has ever had to attend a tedious board meeting. Heedlessly, barely conscious of what we are doing, we play with lines and planes, curves and masses, and from this abstracted doodling emerge fantastic arabesques, strange animal or human forms. We may leave it to the psychologists to attribute what unconscious "drives" they will to this supreme art of boredom and inanition. But it cannot be doubted that it is a play-function of low order akin to the child's playing in the first years of its life, when the higher structure of organized play is as yet undeveloped. As an explanation of the origin of decorative motifs in art, let alone of plastic creation as a whole, a psychic function of this kind must strike us as somewhat inadequate. It is impossible to assume that the aimless meanderings of the hand could ever produce such a thing as style. Apart from this the plastic urge is by no means content with the mere ornamentation of a surface. It operates in three directions: towards decoration, towards construction, and towards imitation. To derive art wholly from some hypothetical "play-instinct" obliges us to do the same for architecture and painting. It seems preposterous to ascribe the cave-paintings of Altamira, for instance, to mere doodling—which is what it amounts to if they are ascribed to the "play-instinct". As to architecture the hypothesis is flatly absurd, because there the aesthetic impulse is far from being the dominant one, as the constructions of bees and beavers clearly prove. Though the primary importance of play as a cultural factor is the main thesis of this book, we still maintain that the origin of art is not explained by a reference to a play-"instinct", however innate. Of course, when we contemplate certain examples from the teeming treasury of plastic form, we find it hard indeed to suppress the idea of a play of fancy, the playful creativity of mind or hand. The grotesque wildness of the dancing-masks among savage peoples, the monstrous intertwining of figures on totem-poles, the magical mazes of ornamental motifs, the caricature-like distortions of

[1] *Ueber die aesthetische Erziehung des Menschen*, 1795, 14th letter.

human and animal forms—all these are bound to suggest play as the growing-point of art. But they should do no more than suggest it.

If, however, in the process of artistic creation as a whole the play-factor is less apparent in the plastic arts than in those we have termed the "music" arts, or arts of the Muses, the picture immediately changes when we turn from the *making* of works of art to the manner in which they are received in the social milieu. Here we can see at once that, as a subject of competition, plastic skill ranks as high as almost any other human faculty. The agonistic impulse, which we found to be powerfully operative over so many fields of culture, also comes to fruition in art. The desire to challenge a rival to perform some difficult, seemingly impossible feat of artistic skill lies deep in the origins of civilization. It is the equivalent of the various contests we encountered in the field of knowledge, poetry or courage. Can we now say straight out that master-pieces or show-pieces of plastic skill, expressly commissioned, did for architecture what the sacred riddle-contest did for philosophy, or the singing and versifying matches for poetry? In other words, did plastic art develop in and through competition? Before answering we must realize that it is next to impossible to distinguish absolutely between the contest in making and the contest in excelling. Samples of strength and skill, like Odysseus' bow-shot through the holes of a dozen axe-heads, belong entirely to the play-sphere. This feat is not a work of art as we understand it, though it is definitely a work of considerable artistry. In the archaic phase of civilization and long afterwards the word "art" covers almost all forms of human dexterity, not merely the creative. It is therefore permissible to class the permanently valuable creations of mind and hand with the master-piece in the strict sense and the *tour de force* of whatever kind, and to find the play-factor in all of them. The competition for excellence still survives wherever such things as the *Prix de Rome* are awarded; here we have a specialized form of the age-old contest to prove oneself superior to all rivals in all fields. Art and technique, dexterity and creative power were, for archaic man, united in the eternal desire to excel and win. Very low down in the social scale of competition come the κελεύσματα, jesting commands which the Greek symposiarch used to give his companions in a drinking-bout, similar to the *poenitet* of later days.

The game of forfeits and the tying and untying of knots fall within the same category. In this last-named instance there is doubtless the vestige of some sacred custom hidden behind the game. When Alexander the Great cut the Gordian knot he was behaving like a spoil-sport in more than one respect—flouting both the rules of the game and of religion.

A further digression is necessary to indicate how far competition has really contributed to the development of art. Practically all the known examples of astounding skill called forth by competition belong to mythology, legend and literature rather than to the history of art itself. The mind's delight in the exorbitant, the miraculous, the preposterous could find no richer ground than in the fantastic tales told of the wonder-working artists of olden days. The great culture-heroes, so the mythologies tell us, invented all the arts and skills which are now the treasures of civilization, as a result of some contest, very often with their life at stake. The *Vedas* have a special name of their own for the *deus faber*: *tvashtar*, that is, the maker. It was he who forged the thunderbolt (*vajra*) for Indra. He waged a contest in skill with the three *rbhu* or divine artisans, who fashioned Indra's horses, the chariot of the *Asvins* (the Hindu *Dioscuri*) and the wonder-cow of Brhaspati. The Greeks had a legend of Polytechnos and his spouse Aedon, who boasted that they loved one another more than Zeus and Hera, whereupon Zeus sent them Eris—Emulation—who sowed the seeds of contest between them in all manner of artisanship. The crafty dwarfs of Nordic mythology are in the same tradition, also Wieland the Smith, whose sword is so sharp that it can cut the fleeces of wool floating on the stream; and Daedalus. This Daedalus can do everything: he builds the Labyrinth, makes statues that walk and, faced with the task of drawing a thread through the convolutions of a shell, solves it by attaching the thread to an ant. Here the technical *tour de force* is allied to the riddle; but whereas the good riddle has its solution in some unexpected and surprising sleight of mind—a sort of mental short-circuit—the former too often loses itself in the absurd, as in the above case or the tale of the rope of sand used for sewing slices of stone.[1] Viewed in correct perspective, the miracles needed to attest a Christian's claim to a place among the saints only continue this archaic line of thought. We do not have to go far in

[1] *The Story of Ahikar*, ed. F. C. Conybeare, J. Rendel Harris and Agnes Smith Lewis, Cambridge, 1913.

hagiography to see the unmistakable connection between reports of miracles and the play spirit.

If competitive artisanship is an ever-recurrent theme in myth and legend it has played a very definite part in the actual development of art and technics. The mythical contests in skill between Polytechnos and Aedon did, in fact, have their counterpart in historical reality, as in the competition of Parrhasios and his rival on the island of Samos for the best representation of the strife between Ajax and Odysseus, or that held at the Pythian feasts between Panainos and Timagoras of Chalcis. Again, Phidias, Polycletus and others entered into a contest for the most beautiful statue of an Amazon. The historicity of such matches is proved by epigrams and inscriptions; for instance, on the pedestal of a Nikē statue we read: "This was made by Panainos . . . who also made the *acrotheria* for the temple, thereby winning the prize".[1]

Everything to do with examinations and public disputations comes, in the last analysis, from the old form of testing by means of some feat or other. The mediaeval guild was as full of these technical competitions as the mediaeval university. It made no difference whether the task was given to one person or to many. The whole guild system was so deeply rooted in the ritual of paganism that the agonistic element was naturally very strong. The master-piece, through which a man attested his claim to be accepted into the corporation of master-craftsmen, seems to have come rather late as a fixed and obligatory custom, but it has its origin in immemorial forms of social rivalry. The guilds themselves are only partly the product of economics; it was not until after the 11th century, with the revival of town life, that the corporations of artisans and traders gained the ascendant and ousted the older forms of social association based on ritual. To the very end the guild system preserved many traces of archaic play in such formalities as initiation ceremonies, speeches, badges, insignia, banquets and carousals, etc. These, however, were gradually thrust aside by pedestrian economic interests.

Two examples of competition in architecture are contained in the famous sketch-book of Villard de Honnecourt, the French architect of the 13th century. "This Presbytery", runs the legend to one of the drawings, "Villard de Honnecourt and Pierre de Corbie devised in mutual disputation"—*invenerunt inter se dis-*

[1]V. Ehrenberg, *Ost und West*, p. 76.

putando. Elsewhere, putting forward an attempt to achieve *perpetuum mobile*, he says: "Maint jor se sunt maistre despute de faire torner une ruee par li seule" (many a day have masters disputed how to make a wheel turn by itself).[1]

Anybody not knowing the age-long history of competition all over the world might be inclined to think that considerations of utility and efficiency alone inspire such forms of competitive art as survive to-day. When a prize is offered for the best plan for a town hall, or a stipend for the best student in an art-school, it would seem that the desire to stimulate invention, to detect talent and to obtain the best result, is enough. Nevertheless behind all these practical objectives there always lurks the primordial play-function of the contest as such. It is impossible to decide, of course, how far the sense of usefulness has outweighed agonistic passion in certain historical instances, as when the city of Florence, in 1418, organized a competition for the cathedral dome which Brunelleschi won out of fourteen contestants. But we could hardly ascribe this glorious work to "functionalism". Two centuries earlier this same Florence had flaunted its famous "forest of towers", each a monument to the pride of some noble house and challenging others. Historians of art and war now concur in regarding these Florentine *torri* rather as "swagger-towers" (*Prunktürme*) than as intended for serious defence. The mediaeval city had ample scope for magnificence in its ideas of play.

[1] *Album de Villard de Honnecourt*, ed. H. Omont, pl. xxix, fol. 15.

XI

WESTERN CIVILIZATION *SUB SPECIE LUDI*

IT HAS not been difficult to show that a certain play-factor was extremely active all through the cultural process and that it produces many of the fundamental forms of social life. The spirit of playful competition is, as a social impulse, older than culture itself and pervades all life like a veritable ferment. Ritual grew up in sacred play; poetry was born in play and nourished on play; music and dancing were pure play. Wisdom and philosophy found expression in words and forms derived from religious contests. The rules of warfare, the conventions of noble living were built up on play-patterns. We have to conclude, therefore, that civilization is, in its earliest phases, played. It does not come *from* play like a babe detaching itself from the womb: it arises *in* and *as* play, and never leaves it.

If this view is accepted as correct—and it hardly seems possible not to accept it—the question that at once presents itself is: can we substantiate such an assertion? Does civilization in fact never leave the play-sphere? How far can we detect the play-element in later periods of culture which are more developed, refined and sophisticated than the early ages and stages we have, in the main, been dealing with hitherto? We have repeatedly capped our examples of the play-element in archaic culture with parallels from the 18th century or from our own times. Particularly the 18th century seemed to us an age full of play-elements and playfulness. Now for us this century is but the day before yesterday. How then should we have lost all spiritual affinity with so recent a past? We must end our book by asking how much of the play spirit is still alive in our own day and generation and the world at large. Let us approach this final question by a rapid glance at certain periods of Western civilization since the Roman Empire.

The culture of the Roman Empire merits attention if only on account of the contrast it presents to Hellenic culture. Roman society seems, at first sight, to have far fewer play-characteristics than the Greek. The essence of Latin antiquity can be summed up by qualities like sobriety, probity, austerity, practical thinking of an economic and juristic order, feeble imagination and tasteless superstition. The naïve, rustic forms of worship smell of the field and the hearth-fire. The atmosphere of Roman culture in the Republican Age is still that of the clan, the tribal community which, indeed, it had barely outgrown. The pronounced concern for the State bears all the features of household worship—the cult of the *genius* (indwelling spirit). Religious conceptions, such as they are, are feebly imagined and poorly expressed. The readiness to personify any and every idea that takes possession of the mind has nothing to do with a high power of abstraction; it is rather a primitive mode of thinking that comes very near to childish play.[1] Figures like Abundantia, Concordia, Pietas, Pax, Virtus, etc., are not the crystallizations of highly developed social thinking; they are the crude and materialistic ideals of a primitive community seeking to safeguard its interests by means of business relations with the higher powers. The innumerable feasts, therefore, take an important place in this system of religious insurance. It is no accident that these rites always kept the name of *ludi* with the Romans—for that is precisely what they were, games. The strong play-element in Roman civilization is implicit in its markedly ritualistic structure, only here playing did not take on the lively colouring, the teeming imagination it displayed in Greek or Chinese civilization.

Rome grew to a World Empire and a World Emporium. To it there fell the legacy of the Old World that had gone before, the inheritance of Egypt and Hellenism and half the Orient. Its culture was fed on the overflow of a dozen other cultures. Government and law, road-building and the art of war reached a state of perfection such as the world had never seen; its literature and art grafted themselves successfully on to the Greek stem. For all that, however, the foundations of this majestic political edifice remained archaic. The State's *raison d'être* was still founded on the old nexus of ritualism. As soon as the political careerist had possessed himself of supreme power, his person and the idea of his authority were immediately transposed into ritual. He became Augustus, the bearer of divine power, the incarnation of godhead, the saviour, the restorer, the bringer of peace and prosperity, the dispenser of ease and abundance and guarantor of it. All the anxious wishes of a primitive tribe for material welfare and

[1]See *ante*, pp. 136 ff.

preservation of life were projected on to the ruler, who was henceforth reckoned the epiphany of deity. These are archaic ideas in splendid new attire. The culture-bringing hero of savage life is resuscitated in the identification of the Roman Princeps with Hercules or Apollo.

The society which possessed, and propagated, these ideas was in many respects extremely advanced. These worshippers of the Emperor's divinity were people who had passed through all the refinements of Greek philosophy, science and taste and come out into scepticism and unbelief. When Virgil and Horace glorify the newly inaugurated era with their highly cultivated poems we cannot withhold the feeling that they are playing at culture.

A State is never a utilitarian institution pure and simple. It congeals on the surface of time like frost-flowers on a window-pane, and is as unpredictable, as ephemeral and, in its pattern, as rigidly causal to all appearances as they. An impulse of culture, spawned and pushed hither and thither by disparate forces of the most various provenance, finds embodiment in that aggregation of power we call "State", which then seeks some reason for its existence, discovering it perhaps in the glory of a particular house or the excellence of a particular people. In the way in which it proclaims the principle that animates it the State will often reveal its fantastic nature, even to the point of absurd and suicidal behaviour. The Roman Empire bore all the features of this fundamental irrationality which it tried to disguise by claims to some sacred right. It was spongy and sterile in its social and economic structure. The whole system of supply, government and education was concentrated in the towns, not in the interests of the community as a whole or the State as such, but to the sole benefit of a minority battening on the disenfranchized proletariat. The municipal unit, in Antiquity, had always been the nucleus, the ideal centre of all social life and culture, and continued to be so without any rational account of it being taken by the ruling and cultured classes. Hence the Emperors never ceased to build towns, hundreds of them, to the very edge of the desert, and not a voice was raised to enquire whether these centres could ever develop into natural organisms or become the organs of a sound national life. Contemplating the eloquent remains of all this grand city-building we have to ask ourselves whether the function of these cities as cultural centres was ever in any way related to their pompous splendour. To judge by the achievements of

Rome in its later days these outposts, however magnificently planned and built, can never have been important arteries for the circulation of goods and services, nor could much of what was best in the culture of antiquity have remained alive in them. Temples for a religion in decay, petrified in traditional forms and riddled with superstition, halls and basilicas for a Civil Service and a judiciary which, because of political and economic upheavals, were slowly degenerating and being suffocated under a system of State slavery, extortion, graft and nepotism, circuses and amphitheatres for bloody and barbarous games, a dissolute stage, baths for a cult of the body more enervating than invigorating—none of this makes for a solid and lasting civilization. Most of it served merely for show, amusement and futile glory. The Roman Empire was a façade, eaten from within. The wealth of liberal-handed donors whose flaunting inscriptions evoke visions of fabulous greatness and opulence, was in reality built on very weak foundations, ready to crumble at the first heavy blow. The food-supply was never tolerably secure, and the State itself sapped the organism of its health and wealth.

A meretricious glitter lies over the whole of this civilization. Religion, art and letters always seem to be protesting with suspicious emphasis that all is well with Rome and her progeny, that abundance is assured and victory safe and sound beyond a shadow of doubt. Such is the language of the proud buildings, the columns, the triumphal arches, the altars with their frescoes and friezes, the murals and mosaics in the houses. Sacred and profane merge completely in Roman decorative art. It delights in graceful and harmless little scenes full of nymphs and genii. The little house-fired figures stand there with a certain capricious charm, but with no crispness of style, surrounded by fruit and flowers and dispensing abundance under the supervision of benevolent and somewhat homely gods. All speaks of quiet and safety, allegories are gracious and shallow, and the whole betrays the would-be playfulness of an unquiet mind troubled by the dangers of a menacing reality but seeking refuge in the idyllic. The play-element is very prominent here, but it has no organic connection with the structure of society and is no longer fecund of true culture. Only a civilization on the wane produces an art like this.

The policy of the Emperors too is rooted in this constant need loudly to proclaim the well-being of the Empire and all the peoples inhabiting it. Only to a very small extent are the objects of this policy at all rational—but has it ever been otherwise? The conquest of new territories is, of course, meant to ensure prosperity and safety by obtaining new areas of supply and pushing the boundaries of Empire further and further afield, away from the vulnerable heart. Maintenance of the Pax Augusta is in itself a definite and reasonable aim. But the utilitarian motive is subordinated to a religious ideal. Triumphal processions, laurels and martial glory are not means to an end, they are a sacred task imposed on the Emperor by Heaven.[1] The *triumphus* is far more than a solemn celebration of military success; it is a rite through which the State recuperates from the strains of war and re-experiences its well-being. In so far as the basis of all policy is the winning and keeping of prestige this primitive agonistic ideal pervades the whole colossal structure of the Roman Empire. All nations give it out that the wars they have waged or endured have been so many glorious struggles for existence. As regards the Gallic and Punic Wars the Republic would have had some justification for such a claim. So would the Empire, when the barbarians set in on all sides. But the question is always whether the first impulse in war-making is not largely agonistic, i.e. envy of and lust for power and glory rather than hunger or defence.

The play-element in the Roman State is nowhere more clearly expressed than in the cry for *panem et circenses*. A modern ear is inclined to detect in this cry little more than the demand of the unemployed proletariat for the dole and free cinema tickets. But it had a deeper significance. Roman society could not live without games. They were as necessary to its existence as bread—for they were holy games and the people's right to them was a holy right. Their basic function lay not merely in celebrating such prosperity as the community had already won for itself, but in fortifying it and ensuring future prosperity by means of ritual. The great and bloody Roman games were a survival of the archaic play-factor in depotentialized form. Few of the brutalized mob of spectators felt anything of the religious quality inherent in these performances, and the Emperor's liberality on such occasions had sunk to mere alms-giving on a gigantic scale to a miserable proletariat. All the more significant, therefore, of the importance attached to the play-function in Roman culture is the fact that not one of the innumerable new cities, literally

[1]Cf. M. Rostovtzeff, *Social and Economic History of the Roman Empire*, Oxford, 1926.

built on sand, omitted to erect an amphitheatre, destined to endure through the ages very often as the only trace of a very short-lived municipal glory. The bull-fight in Spanish culture is a direct continuation of the Roman *ludi*, although preceded by forms more akin to the mediaeval tournament than the *corrida* is to-day, which bears a family resemblance to the gladiatorial combats of ancient time.

The distribution of largesse to the urban populace was not the monopoly of the Emperor. During the first centuries of the Empire thousands of citizens from all quarters competed in the founding and donating of halls, baths, theatres, in the mass distribution of food, in the institution or equipping of new games, all of which was recorded for posterity in boastful inscriptions. What was the moving spirit behind all this frenzied activity? Are we to look on this munificence in the light of Christian charity, as a precursor of it? Nothing could be further from the truth. The object of this liberality and the forms it took speak quite another language. Can we attribute it, then, to *public spirit* in the modern sense? Without a doubt the ancient delight in giving was more akin to public spirit than to Christian charity. Still, the real nature of this passion for splendid donations would be more adequately summed up by calling it the *potlatch* spirit. Munificence for the sake of honour and glory, for the sake of outdoing your neighbour and beating him—that is what we can discern in all this, and therein the age-old ritual-agonistic background of Roman civilization comes to light.

The play-element also appears very clearly in Roman literature and art. High-flown panegyrics and hollow rhetoric are the mark of the one; superficial decoration thinly disguising the massive under-structure, murals dallying with an inane *genre* or degenerating into flabby elegance dominate the other. It is features like these that stamp the last phase of Rome's ancient greatness with inveterate frivolity. Life has become a game of culture; the ritual form persists, but the religious spirit has flown. All the deeper spiritual impulses withdraw from this culture of the surface and strike new root in the mystery religions. Finally, when Christianity cut Roman civilization off from its ritual basis, it withered rapidly.

One curious proof of the tenacity of the play-factor in Roman antiquity yet remains to be indicated, namely, the survival of the *ludi*-principle in the Hippodrome of Byzantium. In the Christian era the mania for horse-racing had been completely severed from its ritual origins, but racing still continued to be the focus of social life. Popular passions, once assuaged by bloody combats of men and beasts, had to be content with horse-racing, which was now a purely profane pleasure, unconsecrated but still capable of drawing the whole public interest into its orbit. The circus in the most literal sense of the word became the centre not only of racing but of political and even religious faction. The Racing Societies, known by the four colours of the charioteers, were not merely the organizers of contests but recognized political institutions. The parties were called *demes*, their leaders *demarchs*. A general returning in triumph from a victorious campaign celebrated his *triumphus* in the Hippodrome; there the Emperor showed himself to the people, there—sometimes—justice was administered. This *mélange* of holiday-making and public life had little to do with the archaic unity of play and ritual, once so vital for the growth of culture. It was but the after-play of civilization in decline.

I have dealt elsewhere[1] and at such length with the play-element in the Middle Ages that a few words must suffice here. Mediaeval life was brimful of play: the joyous and unbuttoned play of the people, full of pagan elements that had lost their sacred significance and been transformed into jesting and buffoonery, or the solemn and pompous play of chivalry, the sophisticated play of courtly love, etc. Few of these forms now had any real culture-creating function, except for the ideal of courtly love which led to the "dolce stil nuovo" and to Dante's *Vita Nuova*. For the Middle Ages had inherited its great culture-forms in poetry, ritual, learning, philosophy, politics and warfare from classical antiquity, and they were fixed forms. Mediaeval culture was crude and poor in many respects, but we cannot call it primitive. Its business was to work over traditional material, whether Christian or classical, and assimilate it afresh. Only where it was not rooted in antiquity, not fed by the ecclesiastical or Graeco-Roman spirit, was there room for the play-factor to "play" and create something entirely new. That was the case wherever mediaeval civilization built directly on its Celto-Germanic past or on even earlier autochthonous layers. The system of chivalry was built in this way (although mediaeval scholars might find examples of it in the Trojan or other classical

[1] *The Waning of the Middle Ages.*

heroes) and a good deal of feudalism. The initiation and dubbing of knights, the enfeoffing of a tenure, tournaments, heraldry, chivalric orders, vows—all these things hark back beyond the classical to a purely archaic past, and in all of them the play-factor is powerfully operative and a really creative force. Closer analysis would show it at work in other fields as well, for instance in law and the administration of justice with its constant use of symbols, prescribed gestures, rigid formulas, the issue of a cause often hanging on the exact pronunciation of a word or syllable. The legal proceedings against animals, wholly beyond the comprehension of the modern mind, are a case in point. In fine, the influence of the play-spirit was extraordinarily great in the Middle Ages, not on the inward structure of its institutions, which was largely classical in origin, but on the ceremonial with which that structure was expressed and embellished.

Let us now cast a quick glance at the Renaissance and the Age of Humanism. If ever an élite, fully conscious of its own merits, sought to segregate itself from the vulgar herd and live life as a game of artistic perfection, that élite was the circle of choice Renaissance spirits. We must emphasize yet again that play does not exclude seriousness. The spirit of the Renaissance was very far from being frivolous. The game of living in imitation of Antiquity was pursued in holy earnest. Devotion to the ideals of the past in the matter of plastic creation and intellectual discovery was of a violence, depth and purity surpassing anything we can imagine. We can scarcely conceive of minds more serious than Leonardo and Michelangelo. And yet the whole mental attitude of the Renaissance was one of play. This striving, at once sophisticated and spontaneous, for beauty and nobility of form is an instance of culture at play. The splendours of the Renaissance are nothing but a gorgeous and solemn masquerade in the accoutrements of an idealized past. The mythological figures, allegories and emblems, fetched from God knows where and all loaded with a weight of historical and astrological significance, move like the pieces on a chess-board. The fanciful decorations in Renaissance architecture and the graphic arts, with their lavish use of classical motifs, are much more consciously playful than is the case with the mediaeval illuminator, suddenly inserting a drollery into his manuscript. There are two play-idealizations *par excellence*, two "Golden Ages of Play" as we might call them: the pastoral life and the chivalrous life. The Renaissance roused both from their slumber to a new life in literature and public festivity. We would be hard put to it to name a poet who embodies the play-spirit more purely than Ariosto, and in him the whole tone and tenor of the Renaissance are expressed. Where has poetry ever been so unconstrained, so absolutely at play? Delicately, elusively he hovers between the mock-heroic and the pathetic, in a sphere far removed from reality but peopled with gay and delightfully vivid figures, all of them lapped in the inexhaustible, glorious mirth of his voice which bears witness to the identity of play and poetry.

The word "Humanism" arouses visions less colourful, more serious, if you like, than does the Renaissance. Nevertheless what we have said of the playfulness of the Renaissance will be found to hold good of Humanism as well. To an even greater extent it was confined to a circle of initiates and people "in the know". The Humanists cultivated an ideal of life formulated strictly in accordance with an imagined antiquity. They even contrived to express their Christian faith in classicistic Latin, which lent it more than a touch of paganism. The importance of these pagan tendencies has often been exaggerated. But it is certain that the Christianity of the Humanists was tinged with a certain artifice, a certain artificiality even, something not altogether serious. They spoke with an accent, and the accent was not that of Christ. Calvin and Luther could not abide the tone in which the Humanist Erasmus spoke of holy things. Erasmus! his whole being seems to radiate the play-spirit. It shines forth not only in the *Colloquies* and the *Laus Stultitiae* but in the *Adagia*, that astonishing collection of aphorisms from Greek and Latin literature commented on with light irony and adorable jocosity. His innumerable letters and sometimes his weightiest theological treatises are pervaded by that blithe wit he can never completely do without.

Whoever surveys the host of Renaissance poets from the "grands rhetoriqueurs" like Jean Molinet and Jean Lemaire de Belges to full-blown Renaissance products like Sannazaro or Guarino, the creators of the new pastorals so much in vogue, cannot fail to be struck by the essentially ludic character of their genius. Nothing could be more playful than Rabelais—he is the play-spirit incarnate. The *Amadis de Gaule* cycle reduces heroic adventure to pure farce, while Cervantes remains the supreme magician of tears and laughter. In Marguerite of Navarre's

Heptameron we have a strange amalgam of coprophilia and platonism. Even the school of Humanist jurists, in their endeavours to make the law stylish and aesthetic, evince the almighty play-spirit of the times.

It has become the fashion, when speaking of the 17th century, to extend the term "Baroque" far beyond the scope of its original application. Instead of simply denoting a tolerably definite style of architecture and sculpture, "the Baroque" has come to cover a vast complex of more or less vague ideas about the essence of 17th-century civilization. The fashion started in German scholarship some forty years ago and spread to the public at large mainly through Spengler's *Decline of the West.* Now painting, poetry, literature, even politics and theology, in short, every field of skill and learning in the 17th century, have to measure up to some preconceived idea of "the Baroque". Some apply the term to the beginning of the epoch, when men delighted in colourful and exuberant imagination; others to a later period of sombre stateliness and solemn dignity. But, taken by and large, it evokes visions of conscious exaggeration, of something imposing, overawing, colossal, avowedly unreal. Baroque forms are, in the fullest sense of the word, art-forms. Even where they serve to limn the sacred and religious, a deliberately aesthetic factor obtrudes itself so much that posterity finds it hard to believe that the treatment of the theme could possibly have sprung from sincere religious emotion.

The general tendency to *overdo* things, so characteristic of the Baroque, finds its readiest explanation in the play-content of the creative impulse. Fully to enjoy the work of Rubens, Bernini or that Dutch prince of poets, Joost van den Vondel, we must be prepared at the outset to take their utterances *cum grano salis.* This is probably true of most art and poetry, it may be objected; if so, it affords yet another proof of our main contention—the fundamental importance of play. For all that, the Baroque manifests the play-element to an altogether striking degree. We should never enquire how far the artist himself feels or intends his work to be perfectly serious, firstly because it is impossible for anybody else to plumb his feelings and intentions to the bottom, secondly because the artist's own subjective feelings are largely irrelevant. The work of art is a thing *sui generis.* Thus with Hugo Grotius, for instance. Hugo Grotius was of an exceptionally serious nature, gifted with little humour and animated by a boundless love of truth. He dedicated his masterpiece, the imperishable monument to his spirit, *De jure belli et pacis*, to the King of France, Louis XIII. The accompanying dedication is an example of the most high-falutin' Baroque extravagance on the theme of the King's universally recognized and inestimable justice, which eclipses the grandeurs of Ancient Rome, etc. His pen bows and scrapes, the enormous compliments loom larger and larger. We know Grotius, and we know the feeble and unreliable personality of Louis XIII. We cannot refrain from asking ourselves: Was Grotius in earnest, or was he lying? The answer, of course, is that he was playing the dedicatory instrument in the style proper to the age.

There is hardly another century so stamped with the style of the times as the seventeenth. This general moulding of life, mind and outward appearance to the pattern of what we must, for want of a better word, call "the Baroque" is most strikingly typified in the costume of the age. It should be noted first of all that this characteristic style is found in the men's dress rather than the women's, and particularly in the full court-dress. Men's fashions show a wide margin of variation throughout the century. They tend to deviate further and further from the simple, the natural, and the practical until, about 1665, the high-point of deformation is reached. The doublet has become so short that it comes almost up to the arm-pits; three-quarters of the shirt bulges out between doublet and hose, and the latter have become preposterously short and wide to the point of no longer being recognizable. The *rhingrave* mentioned by Molière and others had all the appearance of a little petticoat or apron and was generally interpreted as such, until some twenty years ago a genuine specimen of this article was found in an English wardrobe and proved to be a pair of breeches after all. This fantastic outfit was sewn all over with ribbands and bows and lace, even round the knees; and yet, ludicrous as it was, it managed to preserve a high degree of elegance and dignity, thanks chiefly to the cloak, the hat and the periwig.

The periwig constitutes a chapter by itself not only in the history of dress but in the history of civilization. There is no single article that illustrates more aptly the playfulness of the cultural impulse than the periwig as worn in the 17th and 18th centuries.

In a way it is a sign of an imperfect appreciation of history to call the 18th century the age of the wig, for in reality it was far more characteristic of the seventeenth and altogether more curious then. How ironical it is that the highly serious age of Descartes, Pascal and Spinoza, the age of Rembrandt and Milton, of the planting of colonies overseas, of hardy seafarers, of adventurous traders, of blossoming science and the great moralists, should also have been the age of that comical object, the wig! In the 'twenties we can follow, from paintings, the transition from close-cropped heads to long chevelures, and soon after the middle of the century the wig becomes the obligatory head-gear for anybody who wishes to pass for a gentleman, a noble, a councillor, lawyer, soldier, ecclesiastic or merchant. Even admirals wear it perched on top of their gala-dress. In the 'sixties it reaches its most sumptuous and bizarre form in the so-called *allonge* or full-bottomed wig. As an example of the *chic* run mad, nothing more exaggerated, more stupendous or, if you like, more ridiculous could possibly be imagined. But it is not enough to abuse or deride it; the long-lasting vogue for the wig deserves closer attention. The starting-point, of course, is the fact that the long chevelures worn in the 'thirties and 'forties demanded of most men more than nature could produce. The wig began as a substitute for unsatisfactory richness of locks, consequently an imitation of nature. But as soon as the wearing of wigs had passed into common fashion it rapidly lost all pretence of counterfeiting a natural chevelure and became a true element of style. So almost from the beginning we are dealing with a work of art. The wig framed the face in the manner of a picture-frame—indeed, the framing of pictures was roughly contemporaneous with the wig-fashion in dress. It served to isolate the face, give it a fallaciously noble air, raise it, as it were, to a higher power. It is thus the acme of Baroque. In the *allonge* type the dimensions have become quite hyperbolical, yet the whole fashion retains an elegance, an unforced grandeur bordering on majesty and perfectly suited to express the style of young Louis XIV and his epoch. Here, we must admit, all aesthetics notwithstanding, an effect of genuine beauty is obtained: the *allonge* wig is applied art. But we should not forget, when contemplating the portraits of the period, that the illusion of beauty they give us is incomparably greater than it can ever have been for contemporaries who saw the living—the all too living—models of this art. The pictures and prints are extremely flattering inasmuch as they leave unexpressed the squalid underside—the disgusting unwashedness of the age.

The remarkable thing about the wig-fashion is not merely that, unnatural, cumbrous and insanitary as it was, it lasted a full century and a half, which in itself shows that it is something more than a freak of fancy, but that it moves progressively away from the natural hair-growth and becomes more and more stylized. This stylization occurs in three ways: through powder, curls, and laces. After the turn of the century the wig is only worn powdered—black, brown or blond wigs are abolished in favour of the uniform white or grey. What the cultural or psychological reasons for this powdering habit may be, are wrapped in mystery; but it is certain that the medium of portraiture is highly flattering to it. Then, about the middle of the 18th century, the wig is swept up into a regular panache of high-combed hair in front with rows of tight little curls over the ears and tied at the back with laces. Every pretence of imitating nature is abandoned; the wig has become the complete ornament.

Two points remain to be mentioned in passing. Women wore wigs only when occasion demanded, but on the whole their coiffure followed the masculine fashions until, towards the end of the 18th century, it reached the limit of extravagance and artificiality. The other point is that the reign of the wig was never absolute, even though the lower classes aped the fashion with wigs of yarn or some other material. But while the tragic roles of classical drama were played in wigs after the fashion of the day, as early as the eighteen-hundreds we not infrequently see portraits of young men with natural long hair, particularly in England. This denotes, I think, an undercurrent running in the reverse direction, towards the free and easy, the deliberately nonchalant, which set in with Watteau and ran all through the 18th century as a protest against stiffness and artificiality and a vindication of all that was natural and innocent. It is the germ of Rousseauism and Romanticism that we are uncovering here. To follow this tendency in other cultural fields would be an attractive and important task, and many connections with play would certainly come to light. But an investigation of this sort would lead us too far. Suffice it that our long digression on the wig may serve to show the whole phenomenon as one of the most remarkable instances of the play-factor in culture.

The French Revolution sounded the death-knell of the wig,

without, however, bringing it to an abrupt stop. The subsequent history of hair and beards is a mine of curious knowledge, hardly worked at all so far; but that, too, we must leave to one side.

If we have discerned a lively element of play in the period we call the Baroque we must concede it *a fortiori* to the ensuing period of Rococo. This term, too, has suffered from a general widening and loosening of its scope, not so much, perhaps, in English, which is less given to nebulous abstractions than certain continental languages. But even if taken to mean simply an art-style proper, the word Rococo has so many associations with play and playfulness that it might almost be a definition of it. Moreover, in the very idea of "style" in art, is there not a tacit admission of a certain play-element? Is not the birth of a style itself a playing of the mind in its search for new forms? A style lives from the same things as does play, from rhythm, harmony, regular change and repetition, stress and cadence. Style and fashion are more consanguineous than orthodox aesthetics are ready to admit. In fashion the aesthetic impulse is adulterated with all sorts of extraneous emotions—the desire to please, vanity, pride; in style it is crystallized in pure form. Style and fashion, however, and hence art and play, have seldom blended so intimately as in Rococo, except perhaps in Japanese culture. Whether we think of a piece of Meissen porcelain or the pastoral idyll—refined to a degree of tenderness and delicacy unknown since Virgil—or a picture by Watteau or Lancret, or an 18th-century interior, or the naïve craze for the exotic which introduced Turks, Indians and Chinese into literature amid flutters of sentimental excitement,—the impression of play never leaves us for a moment.

But this play-quality in 18th-century civilization goes deeper. Statecraft had never been so avowedly a game as in that age of secret cabals, intrigues and political filibustering which produced figures like Alberoni, Ripperda and Theodore Neuhoff, King of Corsica. Ministers and princes, as irresponsible as they were omnipotent and unhampered by any troublesome international tribunals, were free to gamble any time they liked with their countries' destinies, a smile on their lips and with an exquisitely polite flourish, as though they were making a move on a chess-board. It was fortunate indeed for Europe that the effect of their short-sighted policies was limited by other factors, such as the slowness of communications and relatively inferior instruments of destruction. But the results of this playing at politics were deplorable enough, in all conscience.

On the cultural side we find the spirit of ambitious emulation everywhere, manifesting itself in clubs, secret societies, literary salons, artistic coteries, brotherhoods, circles and conventicles. Every conceivable interest or occupation becomes a focus for voluntary association. Natural history collections and curios are all the rage. This is not to say that these impulses were worthless; on the contrary, it was precisely the whole-hearted abandon to play, the *élan* of it, that made them immensely fruitful for culture. The play-spirit also imbued the literary and scientific controversies which formed so large a part of the higher occupations and amusements of the international élite that waged them. The distinguished reading public for whom Fontenelle wrote his *Entretiens sur la pluralité des mondes* was perpetually dissolving and re-grouping about some controversial point or other. The whole of 18th-century literature seems to consist of lay and play figures: abstractions, pallid allegories, vapid moralizings. That masterpiece of capricious wit, Pope's *Rape of the Lock*, could only have been penned when it was.

Our own times have been very slow in recognizing the high level of 18th-century art. The 19th century had lost all feeling for its play-qualities and simply did not see the underlying seriousness. In the elegant convolutions and luxuriance of the Rococo the Victorians saw nothing of the musical ornamentation that hid the straight line, only feebleness and unnaturalness. They failed to understand that beneath all this finery the spirit of the age was seeking a way back to Nature, but a way with style. It chose to ignore the fact that in the masterpieces of architecture which this century produced in great abundance, ornamentation never attacked the severe and sober lines of the buildings, hence these preserved all the noble dignity of their harmonious proportions. Few periods of art have managed to balance play and seriousness as gracefully as the Rococo, and in few periods are the plastic and the musical so beautifully attuned.

Music, as we have hinted before, is the highest and purest expression of the *facultas ludendi*. It does not seem over-bold to attribute the supreme importance of 18th-century music to the perfect balance of its play-content and its aesthetic content. As a purely acoustic phenomenon music had been refined and enriched in many ways. Old instruments had been improved, new ones invented, with the result that the orchestra could achieve a greater volume of sound and a wider range of modulation. Women's voices played a larger part in musical performances. The more instrumental music gained on music designed for the voice alone, the looser became its connection with words and the stronger its position as an independent art. The increasing secularization of life also contributed to this. The practice of music for its own sake came to be a regular avocation, although, since it was composed largely to order for liturgical or festive purposes, it did not enjoy anything like the publicity it enjoys to-day.

From all this the play-content of music in the 18th century, its function as a social game, will be abundantly clear. But how far is its aesthetic content playful? In reply we would elaborate our earlier argument that musical forms are in themselves play-forms. Like play, music is based on the voluntary acceptance and strict application of a system of conventional rules—time, tone, melody, harmony, etc. This is true even where all the rules we are familiar with have been abandoned. The conventionality of musical values is obvious to anybody who knows how enormously music differs in different parts of the world. No uniform acoustic principle connects Javanese or Chinese music and Western music, or mediaeval and modern music. Every civilization has its own musical conventions, and the ear only tolerates, as a rule, the acoustic forms to which it is accustomed. In this inner diversity of music, therefore, we have renewed proof that it is essentially a game, a contract valid within circumscribed limits, serving no useful purpose but yielding pleasure, relaxation, and an elevation of spirit. The need for strenuous training, the precise canon of what is and what is not allowed, the claim made by every music to be the one and only valid norm of beauty—all these traits are typical of its play-quality. And it is precisely its play-quality that makes its laws more rigorous than those of any other art. Any breach of the rules spoils the game.

Archaic man was well aware that music was a sacred force capable of rousing the emotions, and a game. Only much later was it appreciated as a significant addition to life and an expression of life, in short, an art in our sense of the word. Even the 18th century, for all its musical fecundity, had but a very defective appreciation of the emotional function of music, as Rousseau's trivial interpretation of it in terms of sounds imitated from Nature makes clear. The late advent of anything like a psychology of music may elucidate what we meant by a certain balance between the play-content and the aesthetic content of music in the 18th century. It contained in itself the whole weight of its own emotionality, unconsciously, almost artlessly. Even Bach and Mozart could hardly have been aware that they were pursuing anything more than the noblest of pastimes—*diagoge* in the Aristotelian sense, pure recreation. And was it not just this sublime naiveté that enabled them to soar to the heights of perfection?

It might seem only logical to deny the period that followed the Rococo any vestige of the play-quality. The age of the new Classicism and of emergent Romanticism evokes visions of brooding, melancholy figures, impenetrable gloom, and tearful seriousness, all of which would seem to exclude the very possibility of play. But on closer inspection the exact opposite appears to be the case. If ever a style and a *Zeitgeist* were born in play it was in the middle of the 18th century. As to the new Classicism, the European spirit, constantly reverting to Antiquity as the great source of ideals, has always sought and found in the classics just what suited it at a particular time. Pompeii rose seasonably from its grave to enrich with new motifs an age that inclined to cool, lapidary grace and marmoreal smoothness. The Classicism of Adam, Wedgwood and Flaxman was born of the 18th century's light and playful touch.

Romanticism has as many faces as it has voices. Regarded as a movement or current that arose about 1750, we might describe it as a tendency to retrovert all emotional and aesthetic life to an idealized past where everything is blurred, structureless, charged with mystery and terror. The delineation of such an ideal space for thought is itself a play-process. There is more to it than that, however. We can actually observe Romanticism being born in play, as a literary and historical fact. Its birth-certificate is provided by the letters of Horace Walpole. Perusing them, one becomes increasingly aware that this remarkable man, the father of Romanticism if ever it had one, still remained extremely classicist in his views and convictions. For him, who did more than anybody else to give it form and substance, Romanticism was only a hobby. He wrote his *Castle of Otranto*, that first and awkward specimen of the thriller in mediaeval setting, half from caprice, half from "spleen". The antique bric-à-brac with which he crammed Strawberry Hill to the garrets and which he called "Gothic", was neither art nor sacred relics in his eyes, merely "curiosities". Personally he surrendered not at all to his so-called Gothicism; he regarded it as trifling, a bagatelle, and despised it in others. He was only dallying with moods and fancies.

Simultaneously with the craze for Gothicism, Sentimentalism won a place in European life and literature. The reign of this tremulous condition which lasted for a quarter of a century or longer in a world whose thoughts and deeds were very far removed from the sensibilities of lachrymose heroines, can best be compared with the ideal of courtly love in the 12th and 13th centuries. In both cases the entire upper class was edified by an artificial and eccentric ideal of life and love. The élite in the 18th century was, of course, much larger than in the feudal-aristocratic world ranging from Bertran de Born to Dante. In Sentimentalism we have one of the first literary coteries where the aristocrat has been conspicuously ousted by the bourgeois. It had packed among its intellectual luggage all the social and educational ideals of the age. Even so, the resemblances are striking. All personal emotions from the cradle to the grave are worked up into an art-form of some kind. Everything centres on love and marriage. Perhaps in no other epoch has connubial bliss been the subject of so much fervent idealization, with unrequited love and love cut short by death as good runners-up. But, unlike the Troubadours, the Romantics adulterated their ideal with all sorts of conditions drawn from "real" life: questions of education, much in the news just then, the relations between parents and children, palpitations at sick-beds, pathetic descriptions of mourning, death and decay—all these were the daily pabulum of the reading public.

How far were they "in earnest"? Which professed the time-style more sincerely and experienced it more profoundly: the Humanists of an earlier century or the Romantics and "sensitives" of the eighteenth and nineteenth? It would seem undeniable that the former were more convinced of the classical ideal as a valid norm than the devotees of the Gothic were of their hazy, dreamified Past. When Goethe wrote his *Totentanz* with skeletons dancing in a moonlit churchyard, he was playing and nothing more. All the same Sentimentalism goes, I think, deeper. A Dutch patrician of the 17th century getting himself rigged out in what he imagines to be "antique" dress in order to sit or stand for his portrait, knew very well that he was masquerading in the guise of a Roman senator. There was no question of his actually living up to the model of civic virtue his draperies proclaimed. But though Goethe was undoubtedly playing in his *Totentanz*, the readers of Julie and Werther did seriously try to live according to the sentimentalist ideal, and often succeeded horribly well. In other words, Sentimentalism was more of a genuine *imitatio* than the Ciceronian or Platonist pose of the Humanists and their successors in the Baroque. The fact that an emancipated spirit like Diderot could, in all seriousness, rave about the lush emotionalism of Greuze's *Father's Curse*, or that Goethe and even Napoleon swore by Ossian, would seem to prove our contention.

And yet, and yet—the effort to adapt life and thought to the sentimental code cannot have gone as deep as this would lead us to suppose. The ideal was constantly belied on all sides by the brute facts of individual life and contemporary history. As distinct from the purely literary cultivation of sensibility, it was perhaps only in languishing scenes of family life and in the contemplation of Nature—particularly in her stormier moods—that sentimentalism had free play.

The nearer we come to our own times the more difficult it is to assess objectively the value of our cultural impulses. More and more doubts arise as to whether our occupations are pursued in play or in earnest, and with the doubts comes the uneasy feeling of hypocrisy, as though the only thing we can be certain of is make-believe. But we should remember that this precarious balance between seriousness and pretence is an unmistakable and integral part of culture as such, and that the play-factor lies at the heart of all ritual and religion. So that we must always fall back on this lasting ambiguity, which only becomes really troublesome in cultural phenomena of a non-ritualistic kind. There is nothing to prevent us from interpreting a cultural phenomenon that takes itself with marked seriousness, therefore, as play. But insofar as Romanticism and kindred movements are divorced from ritual we shall inevitably, in our assessment of them, be assailed by the most vexing ambiguities.

The 19th century seems to leave little room for play. Tendencies running directly counter to all that we mean by play have become increasingly dominant. Even in the 18th century utilitarianism, prosaic efficiency and the bourgeois ideal of social welfare—all fatal to the Baroque—had bitten deep into society. These tendencies were exacerbated by the Industrial Revolution and its conquests in the field of technology. Work and production became the ideal, and then the idol, of the age. All Europe donned the boiler-suit. Henceforth the dominants of civilization were to be social consciousness, educational aspirations, and scientific judgement. With the enormous development of industrial power, advancing from the steam-engine to electricity, the illusion gains ground that progress consists in the exploitation of solar energy. As a result of this luxation of our intellects the shameful misconception of Marxism could be put about and even believed, that economic forces and material interests determine the course of the world. This grotesque over-estimation of the economic factor was conditioned by our worship of technological progress, which was itself the fruit of rationalism and utilitarianism after they had killed the mysteries and acquitted man of guilt and sin. But they had forgotten to free him of folly and myopia, and he seemed only fit to mould the world after the pattern of his own banality.

Thus the 19th century seen from its worst side. But the great currents of its thought, however looked at, were all inimical to the play-factor in social life. Neither liberalism nor socialism offered it any nourishment. Experimental and analytical science, philosophy, reformism, Church and State, economics were all pursued in deadly earnest in the 19th century. Even art and letters, once the "first fine careless rapture" of Romanticism had exhausted itself, seemed to give up their age-old association with play as something not quite respectable. Realism, Naturalism, Impressionism and the rest of that dull catalogue of literary and pictorial coteries were all emptier of the play-spirit than any of the earlier styles had ever been. Never had an age taken itself with more portentous seriousness. Culture ceased to be "played". Outward forms were no longer intended to give the appearance, the fiction, if you like, of a higher, ideal mode of life. There is no more striking symptom of the decline of the play-factor than the disappearance of everything imaginative, fanciful, fantastic from men's dress after the French Revolution. Long trousers, hitherto the typical garb of peasants, fishermen and sailors in many countries—as the figures in the *Commedia dell' Arte* show—suddenly became the fashion for gentlemen, together with a certain wildness of hair which expressed the pathos of the

Revolution. Dishevelment also seized women's hair-styles, as we can see from Schadow's portrait of Queen Louise of Prussia. Rage though they might, for a while, in the excesses of the "Incroyables" and the "Merveilleuses", and in the military costumes of the Napoleonic era (showy, romantic and unpractical), the more fantastic fashions were doomed to come to an end with it. From then on men's dress became increasingly colourless and formless and subject to fewer and fewer changes. The elegant gentleman of former days, resplendent in the gala dress befitting his dignity, is now a serious citizen. Sartorially speaking, he no longer plays the hero, the warrior or grandee. With his top-hat he crowns himself, as it were, with the symbol of his sobriety. Only in the slightest of dissipations and extravagances does the play-element in men's dress assert itself, in imperceptible variations like tight-fitting trousers, stock-collars, jaw-scrapers, as compared with the leaps and bounds of old. After these the last traces of the decorative fade out, to leave at best a shadow of bygone stateliness in evening-dress. Gay colours vanish completely, and rich fabrics are replaced by some bleak and serviceable cloth of Scottish make. The tail-coat, once the essential item in a gentleman's wardrobe, ends a career of many centuries by becoming the garb of waiters, ousted for good and all by the jacket. Except for sportswear the variations have now virtually ceased. If you chose to appear nowadays in the costume of 1890, you would at most make the impression of patronising a rather odd tailor.

This levelling down and democratization of men's fashions is far from unimportant. The whole transformation of mind and society since the French Revolution is expressed in it.

Women's dress, or rather ladies' dress (for it is the upper classes that represent civilization in this matter) has not, of course, followed the general denaturing and dulling of men's fashions. The aesthetic factor and sex-appeal are so primary here that they put the evolution of women's clothes on a different level. Consequently the fact that the latter have developed along different lines is not in itself remarkable. The remarkable thing is rather that, despite all the satire heaped upon the extravagances and follies of ladies' dress ever since the Middle Ages, it has, over this whole period, suffered far fewer transformations and given rise to far fewer excesses than men's. One has only to think of the period between 1500 and 1700: violent, repeated changes in the male costume and a tolerable degree of stability in the female. This is what, up to a point, one would expect: the codes of decency and the consequent avoidance of fashions too loose, or too short, or too low, precluded gross modifications in the basic structure of female attire: a skirt reaching to the feet, and a bodice. Only towards the turn of the 18th century do ladies' fashions really begin to "play". While towering coiffures sprout up in the Rococo period, the spirit of Romanticism breathes in the quasi-negligée, the languishing looks, the streaming hair, the bare arms and the revelation of ankles and more. Oddly enough, the *décolleté* was in full swing centuries before bare arms, as we know from the fulminations of mediaeval moralists. From the Directoire period on, women's fashions stride ahead of men's both in the frequency and the extent of their changes. Previous centuries had known nothing—unless we go back to archaic times—like the crinolines of the 1860's and the bustles that followed. Then, with the new century, the current of fashion sets the other way and carries women's dress back to a simplicity and naturalness unknown since 1300.

XII

THE PLAY-ELEMENT IN CONTEMPORARY CIVILIZATION

LET us not waste time arguing about what is meant by "contemporary". It goes without saying that any time we speak of has already become an historical past, a past that seems to crumble away at the hinder end the further we recede from it. Phenomena which a younger generation is constantly relegating to "former days" are, for their elders, part of "our own day", not merely because their elders have a personal recollection of them but because their culture still participates in them. This different time-sense is not so much dependent on the generation to which one happens to belong as on the knowledge one has of things old and new. A mind historically focussed will embody in its idea of what is "modern" and "contemporary" a far larger section of the past than a mind living in the myopia of the moment. "Contemporary civilization" in our sense, therefore, goes deep into the 19th century.

The question to which we address ourselves is this: To what extent does the civilization we live in still develop in play-forms? How far does the play-spirit dominate the lives of those who share that civilization? The 19th century, we observed, had lost many of the play-elements so characteristic of former ages. Has this leeway been made up or has it increased?

It might seem at first sight that certain phenomena in modern social life have more than compensated for the loss of play-forms. Sport and athletics, as social functions, have steadily increased in scope and conquered ever fresh fields both nationally and internationally.

Contests in skill, strength and perseverance have, as we have shown, always occupied an important place in every culture either in connection with ritual or simply for fun and festivity. Feudal society was only really interested in the tournament; the rest was just popular recreation and nothing more. Now the tournament, with its highly dramatic staging and aristocratic embellishments, can hardly be called a sport. It fulfilled one of the functions of the theatre. Only a numerically small upper class took active part in it. This one-sidedness of mediaeval sporting life was due in large measure to the influence of the Church. The Christian ideal left but little room for the organized practice of sport and the cultivation of bodily exercise, except insofar as the latter contributed to gentle education. Similarly, the Renaissance affords fairly numerous examples of body-training cultivated for the sake of perfection, but only on the part of individuals, never groups or classes. If anything, the emphasis laid by the Humanists on learning and erudition tended to perpetuate the old under-estimation of the body, likewise the moral zeal and severe intellectuality of the Reformation and Counter-Reformation. The recognition of games and bodily exercises as important cultural values was withheld right up to the end of the 18th century.

The basic forms of sportive competition are, of course, constant through the ages. In some the trial of strength and speed is the whole essence of the contest, as in running and skating matches, chariot and horse races, weight-lifting, swimming, diving, marksmanship, etc.[1] Though human beings have indulged in such activities since the dawn of time, these only take on the character of organized games to a very slight degree. Yet nobody, bearing in mind the agonistic principle which animates them, would hesitate to call them games in the sense of play—which, as we have seen, can be very serious indeed. There are, however, other forms of contest which develop of their own accord into "sports". These are the ball-games.

What we are concerned with here is the transition from occasional amusement to the system of organized clubs and matches. Dutch pictures of the 17th century show us burghers and peasants intent upon their game of *kolf*; but, so far as I know, nothing is heard of games being organized in clubs or played as matches. It is obvious that a fixed organization of this kind will most readily occur when two groups play against one another. The great ball-games in particular require the existence of permanent teams, and herein lies the starting-point of modern sport. The process arises quite spontaneously in the meeting of village against village, school against school, one part of a town against the rest, etc. That the process started in 19th-century England is understand-

[1]A happy variation of the natatorial contest is found in *Beowulf*, where the aim is to hold your opponent under water until he is drowned.

able up to a point, though how far the specifically Anglo-Saxon bent of mind can be deemed an efficient cause is less certain. But it cannot be doubted that the structure of English social life had much to do with it. Local self-government encouraged the spirit of association and solidarity. The absence of obligatory military training favoured the occasion for, and the need of, physical exercise. The peculiar form of education tended to work in the same direction, and finally the geography of the country and the nature of the terrain, on the whole flat and, in the ubiquitous commons, offering the most perfect playing-fields that could be desired, were of the greatest importance. Thus England became the cradle and focus of modern sporting life.

Ever since the last quarter of the 19th century games, in the guise of sport,[1] have been taken more and more seriously. The rules have become increasingly strict and elaborate. Records are established at a higher, or faster, or longer level than was ever conceivable before. Everybody knows the delightful prints from the first half of the 19th century, showing the cricketers in top-hats. This speaks for itself.

Now, with the increasing systematization and regimentation of sport, something of the pure play-quality is inevitably lost. We see this very clearly in the official distinction between amateurs and professionals (or "gentlemen and players" as used pointedly to be said). It means that the play-group marks out those for whom playing is no longer play, ranking them inferior to the true players in standing but superior in capacity. The spirit of the professional is no longer the true play-spirit; it is lacking in spontaneity and carelessness.[2] This affects the amateur too, who begins to suffer from an inferiority complex. Between them they push sport further and further away from the play-sphere proper until it becomes a thing *sui generis*: neither play nor earnest. In modern social life sport occupies a place alongside and apart from the cultural process. The great competitions in archaic cultures had always formed part of the sacred festivals and were indispensable as health and happiness-bringing activities. This ritual tie has now been completely severed; sport has become profane, "unholy"

[1] It is probably significant that we no longer speak of "games" but of "sport". Our author may not have been sufficiently familiar with the development of "sport" in the last ten or twenty years, here and in America, to stress the all-important point that sport has become a business, or, to put it bluntly, a commercial racket. Trans.

[2] Note G. K. Chesterton's dictum: If a thing is worth doing at all it is worth doing badly! Trans.

in every way and has no organic connection whatever with the structure of society, least of all when prescribed by the government. The ability of modern social techniques to stage mass demonstrations with the maximum of outward show in the field of athletics does not alter the fact that neither the Olympiads nor the organized sports of American Universities nor the loudly trumpeted international contests have, in the smallest degree, raised sport to the level of a culture-creating activity. However important it may be for the players or spectators, it remains sterile. The old play-factor has undergone almost complete atrophy.

This view will probably run counter to the popular feeling of to-day, according to which sport is the apotheosis of the play-element in our civilization. Nevertheless popular feeling is wrong. By way of emphasizing the fatal shift towards over-seriousness we would point out that it has also infected the non-athletic games where calculation is everything, such as chess and some card-games.

A great many board-games have been known since the earliest times, some even in primitive society, which attached great importance to them largely on account of their chanceful character. Whether they are games of chance or skill they all contain an element of seriousness. The merry play-mood has little scope here, particularly where chance is at a minimum as in chess, draughts, backgammon, halma, etc. Even so all these games remain within the definition of play as given in our first chapter. Only recently has publicity seized on them and annexed them to athletics by means of public championships, world tournaments, registered records and press reportage in a literary style of its own, highly ridiculous to the innocent outsider.

Card-games differ from board-games in that they never succeed in eliminating chance completely. To the extent that chance predominates they fall into the category of gambling and, as such, are little suited to club life and public competition. The more intellectual card-games, on the other hand, leave plenty of room for associative tendencies. It is in this field that the shift towards seriousness and over-seriousness is so striking. From the days of *ombre* and *quadrille* to whist and bridge, card-games have undergone a process of increasing refinement, but only with bridge have the modern social techniques made themselves master of the game. The paraphernalia of handbooks and systems and professional training has made bridge a deadly earnest business. A recent newspaper article estimated the yearly winnings of the Culbertson couple at more than two hundred thousand dollars. An enormous amount of mental energy is expended in this universal craze for bridge with no more tangible result than the exchange of relatively unimportant sums of money. Society as a whole is neither benefited nor damaged by this futile activity. It seems difficult to speak of it as an elevating recreation in the sense of Aristotle's *diagoge*. Proficiency at bridge is a sterile excellence, sharpening the mental faculties very one-sidedly without enriching the soul in any way, fixing and consuming a quantity of intellectual energy that might have been better applied. The most we can say, I think, is that it might have been applied worse. The status of bridge in modern society would indicate, to all appearances, an immense increase in the play-element to-day. But appearances are deceptive. Really to play, a man must play like a child. Can we assert that this is so in the case of such an ingenious game as bridge? If not, the virtue has gone out of the game.

The attempt to assess the play-content in the confusion of modern life is bound to lead us to contradictory conclusions. In the case of sport we have an activity nominally known as play but raised to such a pitch of technical organization and scientific thoroughness that the real play-spirit is threatened with extinction. Over against this tendency to over-seriousness, however, there are other phenomena pointing in the opposite direction. Certain activities whose whole *raison d'être* lies in the field of material interest, and which had nothing of play about them in their initial stages, develop what we can only call play-forms as a secondary characteristic. Sport and athletics showed us play stiffening into seriousness but still being felt as play; now we come to serious business degenerating into play but still being called serious. The two phenomena are linked by the strong agonistic habit which still holds universal sway, though in other forms than before.

The impetus given to this agonistic principle which seems to be carrying the world back in the direction of play derives, in the main, from external factors independent of culture proper—in a word, communications, which have made intercourse of every sort so extraordinarily easy for mankind as a whole. Technology, publicity and propaganda everywhere promote the competitive spirit and afford means of satisfying it on an unprecedented scale. Commercial competition does not, of course, belong to the immemorial sacred play-forms. It only appears when trade begins to create fields of activity within which each must try to surpass and outwit his neighbour. Commercial rivalry soon makes limiting rules imperative, namely the trading customs. It remained primitive in essence until quite late, only becoming really intensive with the advent of modern communications, propaganda and statistics. Naturally a certain play-element had entered into business competition at an early stage. Statistics stimulated it with an idea that had originally arisen in sporting life, the idea, namely, of trading records. A record, as the word shows, was once simply a memorandum, a note which the inn-keeper scrawled on the walls of his inn to say that such and such a rider or traveller had been the first to arrive after covering so and so many miles. The statistics of trade and production could not fail to introduce a sporting element into economic life. In consequence, there is now a sporting side to almost every triumph of commerce or technology: the highest turnover, the biggest tonnage, the fastest crossing, the greatest altitude, etc. Here a purely ludic element has, for once, got the better of utilitarian considerations, since the experts inform us that smaller units—less monstrous steamers and aircraft, etc.—are more efficient in the long run. Business becomes play. This process goes so far that some of the great business concerns deliberately instil the play-spirit into their workers so as to step up production. The trend is now reversed: play becomes business. A captain of industry, on whom the Rotterdam Academy of Commerce had conferred an honorary degree, spoke as follows:

> "Ever since I first entered the business it has been a race between the technicians and the sales department. One tried to produce so much that the sales department would never be able to sell it, while the other tried to sell so much that the technicians would never be able to keep pace. This race has always continued: sometimes one is ahead, sometimes the other. Neither my brother nor myself has regarded the business as a task, but always as a game, the spirit of which it has been our constant endeavour to implant into the younger staff."

These words must, of course, be taken with a grain of salt. Nevertheless there are numerous instances of big concerns forming their own Sports Societies and even engaging workers with a view not so much to their professional capacities as to their fitness for the football eleven. Once more the wheel turns.

It is less simple to fix the play-element in contemporary art than in contemporary trade. As we tried to make clear in our tenth chapter, a certain playfulness is by no means lacking in the process of creating and "producing" a work of art. This was obvious enough in the arts of the Muses or "music" arts, where a strong play-element may be called fundamental, indeed, essential to them. In the plastic arts we found that a play-sense was bound up with all forms of decoration; in other words, that the play-function is especially operative where mind and hand move most freely. Over and above this it asserted itself in the master-piece or show-piece expressly commissioned, *the tour de force*, the wager in skill or ability. The question that now arises is whether the play-element in art has grown stronger or weaker since the end of the 18th century.

A gradual process extending over many centuries has succeeded in de-functionalizing art and making it more and more a free and independent occupation for individuals called artists. One of the landmarks of this emancipation was the victory of framed canvases over panels and murals, likewise of prints over miniatures and illuminations. A similar shift from the social to the individual took place when the Renaissance saw the main task of the architect no longer in the building of churches and palaces but of dwelling-houses; not in splendid galleries but in drawing-rooms and bed-rooms. Art became more intimate, but also more isolated; it became an affair of the individual and his taste. In the same way chamber music and songs expressly designed for the satisfaction of personal aestheticisms began to surpass the more public forms of art both in importance and often in intensity of expression.

Along with these changes in form there went another, even more profound, in the function and appreciation of art. More and more it was recognized as an independent and extremely high cultural value. Right into the 18th century art had occupied a subordinate place in the scale of such values. Art was a superior ornament in the lives of the privileged. Aesthetic enjoyment may have been as high as now, but it was interpreted in terms of religious exaltation or as a sort of curiosity whose purpose was to divert and distract. The artist was an artisan and in many cases a menial, whereas the scientist or scholar had the status at least of a member of the leisured classes.

The great shift began in the middle of the 18th century as a result of new aesthetic impulses which took both romantic and classical form, though the romantic current was the more powerful. Together they brought about an unparalleled rise in aesthetic enjoyment all the more fervent for having to act as a substitute for religion. This is one of the most important phases in the history of civilization. We must leap over the full story of this apotheosis of art and can only point out that the line of art-hierophants runs unbroken from Winckelmann to Ruskin and beyond. All the time, art-worship and connoisseurship remained the privilege of the few. Only towards the end of the 19th century did the appreciation of art, thanks largely to photographic reproduction, reach the broad mass of the simply educated. Art becomes public property, love of art *bon ton*. The idea of the artist as a superior species of being gains acceptance, and the public at large is washed by the mighty waves of snobbery. At the same time a convulsive craving for originality distorts the creative impulse. This constant striving after new and unheard-of forms impels art down the steep slope of Impressionism into the turgidities and excrescences of the 20th century. Art is far more susceptible to the deleterious influences of modern techniques of production than is science. Mechanization, advertising, sensation-mongering have a much greater hold upon art because as a rule it works directly for a market and has a free choice of all the techniques available.

None of these conditions entitles us to speak of a play-element in contemporary art. Since the 18th century art, precisely because recognized as a cultural factor, has to all appearances lost rather than gained in playfulness. But is the net result a gain or a loss? One is tempted to feel, as we felt about music, that it was a blessing for art to be largely unconscious of its high purport and the beauty it creates. When art becomes self-conscious, that is, conscious of its own grace, it is apt to lose something of its eternal child-like innocence.

From another angle, of course, we might say that the play-element in art has been fortified by the very fact that the artist is held to be above the common run of mortals. As a superior being he claims a certain amount of veneration for his due. In order to savour his superiority to the full he will require a reverential public or a circle of kindred spirits, who will pour forth the requisite veneration more understandingly than the public at large with its empty phrases. A certain esotericism is as necessary for art to-day as it was of old. Now all esoterics presuppose a convention: we, the initiates, agree to take such and such a thing thus and thus, so we will understand it, so admire it. In other words, esoterics requires a play-community which shall steep itself in its own mystery. Wherever there is a catch-word ending in *-ism* we are hot on the tracks of a play-community. The modern apparatus of publicity with its puffy art-criticism, exhibitions and lectures is calculated to heighten the play-character of art.

It is a very different thing to try to determine the play-content of modern science, for it brings us up against a fundamental difficulty. In the case of art we took play as a primary datum of experience, a generally accepted quantity; but when it comes to science we are constantly being driven back on our definition of that quantity and having to question it afresh. If we apply to science our definition of play as an activity occurring within certain limits of space, time and meaning, according to fixed rules, we might arrive at the amazing and horrifying conclusion that all the branches of science and learning are so many forms of play because each of them is isolated within its own field and bounded by the strict rules of its own methodology. But if we stick to the full terms of our definition we can see at once that, for an activity to be called play, more is needed than limitations and rules. A game is time-bound, we said; it has no contact with any reality outside itself, and its performance is its own end. Further, it is sustained by the consciousness of being a pleasurable, even mirthful, relaxation from the strains of ordinary life. None of this is applicable to science. Science is not only perpetually seeking contact with reality by its usefulness, i.e. in the sense that it is *applied*, it is perpetually trying to establish a universally valid pattern of reality, i.e. as *pure* science. Its rules, unlike those of play, are not unchallengeable for all time. They are constantly being belied by experience and undergoing modification, whereas the rules of a game cannot be altered without spoiling the game itself.

The conclusion, therefore, that all science is merely a game can be discarded as a piece of wisdom too easily come by. But it is legitimate to enquire whether a science is not liable to indulge in play within the closed precincts of its own method. Thus, for instance, the scientist's continued penchant for systems tends in the direction of play. Ancient science, lacking adequate foundation in empiricism, lost itself in a sterile systematization of all conceivable concepts and properties. Though observation and calculation act as a brake in this respect they do not altogether exclude a certain capriciousness in scientific activities. Even the most delicate experimental analysis can be, not indeed manipulated while actually in progress, but played in the interests of subsequent theory. True, the margin of play is always detected in the end, but this detection proves that it exists. Jurists have of old been reproached with similar manoeuvres. Philologists too are not altogether blameless in this respect, seeing that ever since the Old Testament and the Vedas they have delighted in perilous etymologies, a favourite game to this day for those whose curiosity outstrips their knowledge. And is it so certain that the new schools of psychology are not being led astray by the frivolous and facile use of Freudian terminology at the hands of competents and incompetents alike?

Apart from the possibility of the scientific worker or amateur juggling with his own method he may also be seduced into the paths of play by the competitive impulse proper. Though competition in science is less directly conditioned by economic factors than in art, the logical development of civilization which we call science is more inextricably bound up with dialectics than is the aesthetic. In an earlier chapter we discussed the origins of science and philosophy and found that they lay in the agonistic sphere. Science, as some one has not unjustly said, is polemical. But it is a bad sign when the urge to forestall the other fellow in discovery or to annihilate him with a demonstration, looms too large in the work done. The genuine seeker after truth sets little store by triumphing over a rival.

By way of tentative conclusion we might say that modern science, so long as it adheres to the strict demands of accuracy and veracity, is far less liable to fall into play as we have defined it, than was the case in earlier times and right up to the Renaissance, when scientific thought and method showed unmistakable play-characteristics.

These few observations on the play-factor in modern art and science must suffice here, though much has been left unsaid. We are hastening to an end, and it only remains to consider the play-element in contemporary social life at large and especially in politics. But let us be on our guard against two misunderstandings from the start. Firstly, certain play-forms may be used consciously or unconsciously to cover up some social or political design. In this case we are not dealing with the eternal play-element that has been the theme of this book, but with false play. Secondly, and quite independently of this, it is always possible to come upon phenomena which, to a superficial eye, have all the appearance of play and might be taken for permanent play-tendencies, but are, in point of fact, nothing of the sort. Modern social life is being dominated to an ever-increasing extent by a quality that has something in common with play and yields the illusion of a strongly developed play-factor. This quality I have ventured to call by the name of Puerilism,[1] as being the most appropriate appellation for that blend of adolescence and barbarity which has been rampant all over the world for the last two or three decades.

It would seem as if the mentality and conduct of the adolescent now reigned supreme over large areas of civilized life which had formerly been the province of responsible adults. The habits I have in mind are, in themselves, as old as the world; the difference lies in the place they now occupy in our civilization and the brutality with which they manifest themselves. Of these habits that of gregariousness is perhaps the strongest and most alarming. It results in puerilism of the lowest order: yells or other signs of greeting, the wearing of badges and sundry items of political haberdashery, walking in marching order or at a special pace and the whole rigmarole of collective voodoo and mumbo-jumbo. Closely akin to this, if at a slightly deeper psychological level, is the insatiable thirst for trivial recreation and crude sensationalism, the delight in mass-meetings, mass-demonstrations, parades, etc. The club is a very ancient institution, but it is a disaster when whole nations turn into clubs, for these, besides promoting the precious qualities of friendship and loyalty, are also hotbeds of sectarianism, intolerance, suspicion, superciliousness and quick to defend any illusion that flatters self-love or group-consciousness. We have seen great nations losing every shred of honour, all sense of humour, the very idea of decency and fair play. This is not the place to investigate the causes, growth and extent of this world-wide bastardization of culture; the entry of half-educated masses into the international traffic of the mind, the relaxation of morals and the hypertrophy of technics undoubtedly play a large part.

[1]Cf. *In the Shadow of To-morrow*, Heinemann, 1936, ch. 16.

One example of official puerilism must suffice here. It is, as we know from history, a sign of revolutionary enthusiasm when governments play at nine-pins with names, the venerable names of cities, persons, institutions, the calendar, etc. *Pravda*[1] reported that as a result of their arrears in grain deliveries three *kolkhozy* in the district of Kursk, already christened Budenny, Krupskaya and the equivalent of Red Cornfield, has been re-christened Sluggard, Saboteur and Do-Nothing by the local soviet. Though this *trop de zèle* received an official rebuff from the Central Committee and the offensive soubriquets were withdrawn, the puerilistic attitude could not have been more clearly expressed.

Very different is the great innovation of the late Lord Baden-Powell. His aim was to organize the social force of boyhood as such and turn it to good account. This is not puerilism, for it rests on a deep understanding of the mind and aptitudes of the immature; also the Scout Movement expressly styles itself a game. Here, if anywhere, we have an example of a game that comes as close to the culture-creating play of archaic times as our age allows. But when Boy-Scoutism in degraded form seeps through into politics we may well ask whether the puerilism that flourishes in present-day society is a play-function or not. At first sight the answer appears to be a definite yes, and such has been my interpretation of the phenomenon in other studies.[2] I have now come to a different conclusion. According to our definition of play, puerilism is to be distinguished from playfulness. A child playing is not puerile in the pejorative sense we mean here. And if our modern puerilism were genuine play we ought to see civilization returning to the great archaic forms of recreation where ritual, style and dignity are in perfect unison. The spectacle of a society rapidly goose-stepping into helotry is, for some, the dawn of the millennium. We believe them to be in error.

More and more the sad conclusion forces itself upon us that the play-element in culture has been on the wane ever since the 18th century, when it was in full flower. Civilization to-day is no longer played, and even where it still seems to play it is false play—I had almost said, it plays false, so that it becomes increasingly difficult to tell where play ends and non-play begins. This is particularly true of politics. Not very long ago political life in

[1] January 9th, 1935.

[2] *Over de grenzen van spel en ernst in de cultuur*, p. 25, and *In the Shadow of To-morrow*, ch. 16.

parliamentary democratic form was full of unmistakable play-features. One of my pupils has recently worked up my observations on this subject into a thesis on parliamentary eloquence in France and England, showing how, ever since the end of the 18th century, debates in the House of Commons have been conducted very largely according to the rules of a game and in the true play-spirit. Personal rivalries are always at work, keeping up a continual match between the players whose object is to checkmate one another, but without prejudice to the interests of the country which they serve with all seriousness. The mood and manners of parliamentary democracy were, until recently, those of fair play both in England and in the countries that had adopted the English model with some felicity. The spirit of fellowship would allow the bitterest opponents a friendly chat even after the most virulent debate. It was in this style that the "Gentleman's Agreement" arose. Unhappily certain parties to it were not always aware of the duties implicit in the word gentleman. There can be no doubt that it is just this play-element that keeps parliamentary life healthy, at least in Great Britain, despite the abuse that has lately been heaped upon it. The elasticity of human relationships underlying the political machinery permits it to "play", thus easing tensions which would otherwise be unendurable or dangerous—for it is the decay of humour that kills. We need hardly add that this play-factor is present in the whole apparatus of elections.

In American politics it is even more evident. Long before the two-party system had reduced itself to two gigantic teams whose political differences were hardly discernible to an outsider, electioneering in America had developed into a kind of national sport. The presidential election of 1840 set the pace for all subsequent elections. The party then calling itself Whig had an excellent candidate, General Harrison of 1812 fame, but no platform. Fortune gave them something infinitely better, a symbol on which they rode to triumph: the log cabin which was the old warrior's modest abode during his retirement. Nomination by majority vote, i.e. by the loudest clamour, was inaugurated in the election of 1860 which brought Lincoln to power. The emotionality of American politics lies deep in the origins of the American nation itself: Americans have ever remained true to the rough and tumble of pioneer life. There is a great deal that is endearing in American politics, something naïve and spontaneous for which we look in vain in the dragoonings and drillings, or worse, of the contemporary European scene.

Though there may be abundant traces of play in domestic politics there would seem, at first sight, to be little opportunity for it in the field of international relationships. The fact, however, that these have touched the nadir of violence and precariousness does not in itself exclude the possibility of play. As we have seen from numerous examples, play can be cruel and bloody and, in addition, can often be false play. Any law-abiding community or community of States will have characteristics linking it in one way or another to a play-community. International law between States is maintained by the mutual recognition of certain principles which, in effect, operate like play-rules despite the fact that they may be founded in metaphysics. Were it otherwise there would be no need to lay down the *pacta sunt servanda* principle, which explicitly recognizes that the integrity of the system rests on a general willingness to keep to the rules. The moment that one or the other party withdraws from this tacit agreement the whole system of international law must, if only temporarily, collapse unless the remaining parties are strong enough to outlaw the "spoilsport".

The maintenance of international law has, at all stages, depended very largely on principles lying outside the strict domain of law, such as honour, decency, and good form. It is not altogether in vain that the European rules of warfare developed out of the code of honour proper to chivalry. International law tacitly assumed that a beaten Power would behave like a gentleman and a good loser, which unhappily it seldom did. It was a point of international decorum to declare your war officially before entering upon it, though the aggressor often neglected to comply with this awkward convention and began by seizing some outlying colony or the like. But it is true to say that until quite recently war was conceived as a noble game—the sport of kings—and that the absolutely binding character of its rules rested on, and still retained, some of the formal play-elements we found in full flower in archaic warfare.

A cant phrase in current German political literature speaks of the change from peace to war as "das Eintreten des Ernstfalles"—roughly, "the serious development of an emergency". In strictly military parlance, of course, the term is correct. Compared with the sham fighting of manoeuvres and drilling and training, real war is undoubtedly what seriousness is to play. But German political theorists mean something more. The term "Ernstfall" avows quite openly that foreign policy has not attained its full degree of seriousness, has not achieved its object or proved its efficiency, until the stage of actual hostilities is reached. The true relation between States is one of war. All diplomatic intercourse, insofar as it moves in the paths of negotiation and agreement, is only a prelude to war or an interlude between two wars. This horrible creed is accepted and indeed professed by many. It is only logical that its adherents, who regard war and the preparations for it as the sole form of serious politics, should deny that war has any connection with the contest and hence with play. The agonistic factor, they tell us, may have been operative in the primitive stages of civilization, it was all very well then, but war nowadays is far above the competitiveness of mere savages. It is based on the "friend-foe principle". All "real" relationships between nations and States, so they say, are dominated by this ineluctable principle.[1] Any "other" group is always either your friend or your enemy. Enemy, of course, is not to be understood as *inimicus* or ἐχθρός, i.e. a person you hate, let alone a wicked person, but purely and simply as *hostis* or πολέμιος, i.e. the stranger or foreigner who is in your group's way. The theory refuses to regard the enemy even as a rival or adversary. He is merely in your way and is thus to be made away with. If ever anything in history has corresponded to this gross over-simplification of the idea of enmity, which reduces it to an almost mechanical relationship, it is precisely that primitive antagonism between phratries, clans or tribes where, as we saw, the play-element was hypertrophied and distorted. Civilization is supposed to have carried us beyond this stage. I know of no sadder or deeper fall from human reason than Schmitt's barbarous and pathetic delusion about the friend-foe principle. His inhuman cerebrations do not even hold water as a piece of formal logic. For it is not war that is serious, but peace. War and everything to do with it remains fast in the daemonic and magical bonds of play. Only by transcending that pitiable friend-foe relationship will mankind enter into the dignity of man's estate. Schmitt's brand of "seriousness" merely takes us back to the savage level.

Here the bewildering antithesis of play and seriousness presents

[1] Carl Schmitt, *Der Begriff des Politischen*, Hamburg, 1933.

itself once more. We have gradually become convinced that civilization is rooted in noble play and that, if it is to unfold in full dignity and style, it cannot afford to neglect the play-element. The observance of play-rules is nowhere more imperative than in the relations between countries and States. Once they are broken, society falls into barbarism and chaos. On the other hand we cannot deny that modern warfare has lapsed into the old agonistic attitude of playing at war for the sake of prestige and glory.

Now this is our difficulty: modern warfare has, on the face of it, lost all contact with play. States of the highest cultural pretensions withdraw from the comity of nations and shamelessly announce that "pacta non sunt servanda". By so doing they break the play-rules inherent in any system of international law. To that extent their playing at war, as we have called it, for the sake of prestige is not true play; it, so to speak, plays the play-concept of war false. In contemporary politics, based as they are on the utmost preparedness if not actual preparation for war, there would seem to be hardly any trace of the old play-attitude. The code of honour is flouted, the rules of the game are set aside, international law is broken, and all the ancient associations of war with ritual and religion are gone. Nevertheless the methods by which war-policies are conducted and war-preparations carried out still show abundant traces of the agonistic attitude as found in primitive society. Politics are and have always been something of a game of chance; we have only to think of the challenges, the provocations, the threats and denunciations to realize that war and the policies leading up to it are always, in the nature of things, a gamble, as Neville Chamberlain said in the first days of September 1939. Despite appearances to the contrary, therefore, war has not freed itself from the magic circle of play.

Does this mean that war is still a game, even for the aggressed, the persecuted, those who fight for their rights and their liberty? Here our gnawing doubt whether war is really play or earnest finds unequivocal answer. It is the *moral* content of an action that makes it serious. When the combat has an ethical value it ceases to be play. The way out of this vexing dilemma is only closed to those who deny the objective value and validity of ethical standards. Carl Schmitt's acceptance of the formula that war is the "serious development of an emergency" is therefore correct—but in a very different sense from that which he intended. His point of view is that of the aggressor who is not bound by ethical considerations. The fact remains that politics and war are deeply rooted in the primitive soil of culture played in and as contest. Only through an ethos that transcends the friend-foe relationship and recognizes a higher goal than the gratification of the self, the group or the nation will a political society pass beyond the "play" of war to true seriousness.

So that by a devious route we have reached the following conclusion: real civilization cannot exist in the absence of a certain play-element, for civilization presupposes limitation and mastery of the self, the ability not to confuse its own tendencies with the ultimate and highest goal, but to understand that it is enclosed within certain bounds freely accepted. Civilization will, in a sense, always be played according to certain rules, and true civilization will always demand fair play. Fair play is nothing less than good faith expressed in play terms. Hence the cheat or the spoil-sport shatters civilization itself. To be a sound culture-creating force this play-element must be pure. It must not consist in the darkening or debasing of standards set up by reason, faith or humanity. It must not be a false seeming, a masking of political purposes behind the illusion of genuine play-forms. True play knows no propaganda; its aim is in itself, and its familiar spirit is happy inspiration.

In treating of our theme so far we have tried to keep to a play-concept which starts from the positive and generally recognized characteristics of play. We took play in its immediate everyday sense and tried to avoid the philosophical short-circuit that would assert all human action to be play. Now, at the end of our argument, this point of view awaits us and demands to be taken into account.

"Child's play was what he called all human opinions", says late Greek tradition of Heraclitus.[1] As a pendant to this lapidary saying let us quote at greater length the profound words of Plato which we introduced into our first chapter: "Though human affairs are not worthy of great seriousness it is yet necessary to be serious; happiness is another thing. . . . I say that a man must be serious with the serious, and not the other way about. God alone is worthy of supreme seriousness, but man is made God's

[1] *Fragments*, 70.

plaything, and that is the best part of him. Therefore every man and woman should live life accordingly, and play the noblest games, and be of another mind from what they are at present. For they deem war a serious thing, though in war there is neither play nor culture worthy the name, which are the things *we* deem most serious. Hence all must live in peace as well as they possibly can. What, then, is the right way of living? Life must be lived as play, playing certain games, making sacrifices, singing and dancing, and then a man will be able to propitiate the gods, and defend himself against his enemies, and win in the contest". Thus "men will live according to Nature since in most respects they are puppets, yet having a small part in truth". To which Plato's companion rejoins: "You make humanity wholly bad for us, friend, if you say that". And Plato answers: "Forgive me. It was with my eyes on God and moved by Him that I spoke so. If you like, then, humanity is not wholly bad, but worthy of some consideration."[1]

The human mind can only disengage itself from the magic circle of play by turning towards the ultimate. Logical thinking does not go far enough. Surveying all the treasures of the mind and all the splendours of its achievements we shall still find, at the bottom of every serious judgement, something problematical left. In our heart of hearts we know that none of our pronouncements is absolutely conclusive. At that point, where our judgement begins to waver, the feeling that the world is serious after all wavers with it. Instead of the old saw: "All is vanity", the more positive conclusion forces itself upon us that "all is play". A cheap metaphor, no doubt, mere impotence of the mind; yet it is the wisdom Plato arrived at when he called man the plaything of the gods. In singular imagery the thought comes back again in the *Book of Proverbs*, where Wisdom says: "The Lord possessed me in the beginning of his ways, before he made any thing from the beginning. I was set up from eternity, and of old before the earth was made . . . I was with him forming all things: and was delighted every day, playing before him at all times; playing in the world. And my delights were to be with the children of men."[2]

[1] *Laws*, 803–4; cf. also 685. Plato's words echo sombrely in Luther's mouth when he says: "All creatures are God's masks and mummeries" (Erlanger Ausgabe, xi, p. 115).

[2] viii, 22-3, 30-1. This is the Douay translation, based on the Vulgate. The text of the English A.V. and R.V. does not bring out the idea of "play".

Whenever we are seized with vertigo at the ceaseless shuttlings and spinnings in our mind of the thought: What is play? What is serious? we shall find the fixed, unmoving point that logic denies us, once more in the sphere of ethics. Play, we began by saying, lies outside morals. In itself it is neither good nor bad. But if we have to decide whether an action to which our will impels us is a serious duty or is licit as play, our moral conscience will at once provide the touchstone. As soon as truth and justice, compassion and forgiveness have part in our resolve to act, our anxious question loses all meaning. One drop of pity is enough to lift our doing beyond intellectual distinctions. Springing as it does from a belief in justice and divine grace, conscience, which is moral awareness, will always whelm the question that eludes and deludes us to the end, in a lasting silence.

INDEX

Abelard, 155
Abner, 41
Abyssinia, 84, 88
Achilles, Shield of, 79–80
Actualization by representation, 14
Adat, 78
Adolescence, in modern culture, 205
Aeschylus, 145, 146
Aesthetics, play and, 7, 10
Agalma, 167
Agon, 30–1, 48
'Agonal" man, 71, 72
Alain de Lille, 140
Alberoni, 186
Alboin, 69
Allegorical thinking, modern, 141
Allonge, 184
Amadis de Gaule, 181
Amateurs and professionals, 197
American politics, 207
Anaximander, 117
Animals, personification of, 141
,, , play of, 1
Annam, 56, 83, 124, 126
Antilogia, 152
Antithesis in play, 47
Arabia, 59, 66–8
Arabic, words for "play" in, 35, 42
Aramaic, words for "play" in, 35
Archilochus, 68, 87
Architecture, 168
Ariosto, 181
Aristophanes, 144, 145, 152
Aristotle, 64, 130, 149, 160–1, 163
Art, appreciation, extension of, 201–2
,, , modern, play-element in, 201–3
Ases, 52, 57, 69, 81
Athletics, 51
Augustine, St., 153
Augustus, Emperor of Rome, 174–5
Augustus the Strong, 163

Babar, 123
Bach, J. S., 163
Bacon, Francis, 119
Baden-Powell, Lord, 206
Badr, Battle of, 92
Ballet, 164
Ball-games, 196
Baroque period, play-element in, 182–6
Battle, and play, 40–1
,, , fixed time and place for, 98–9
Beauty, 7
Beowulf, 70, 121
Bernini, 182
Betting, 53
Biological function of play, 1–2
Birds, play-activities of, 47
Blackfoot, words for "play" in, 33, 43
Blackstone, 94
Board-games, 198
Boas, F., 59
Bocan, 163
Bolkestein, Prof., 30–1, 33
Bragging matches, 65
Brāhmanas, 108, 112
Breda, siege of, 98
Bridge, 198–9
Brunner, H., 93
Bull-fighting, 178
Burckhardt, Jacob, 71–2, 73, 74
Buru, 122
Bushido, 34, 102
Buytendijk, Prof., 43
Byzantium, games at, 178–9

Capelle, 147
Card-games, 198–9
Carolingian Renaissance, 154
Catch-questions, Greek, 148; *see also* Riddle
Cervantes, 181
Chalcas and Mopsos, 109
Chalcis, war with Eretria, 96
Chamberlain, Neville, 210
Charlemagne, 70, 154
Charles V, 53, 93

Charles of Anjou, 99
Charles the Bold, 98
Cheating, 52
Chiang Kai-shek, 99
Child and savage, comparison, 24
China, 14, 54–6, 65, 66
,, , war in ancient, 97–8
Chinese, words for "play" in, 32
Chivalry, 96, 179–80
Christianity, and Humanists, 181
Chrysippus, 148
Circle, magic, 57
City-building, Roman, 175–6
Civilities, exchange of, in war, 98
Clearchus, 115, 148
Cleopatra, 62
Club, the, 12, 205
Combat des Trente, 89
Combat, single, 91 ff.
Comedy, Greek, 144–5
Comic, the, 6
Commerce, competition in, 200
Communities for play, 12
Competition, 11
,, , and plastic art, 169–72
,, , in drama, 144–5
,, , *see also Agon*
"Contest" and "play", Greek distinction, 30–1
,, ,, ,, , relation, 40–1, 48 ff.
Contest, in ancient China, 55
,, , musical, 163
,, , seasonal, 55–6
Cora Indians, 22
Costume, Baroque, 183
,, , 19th-century, 192–4
Cours d'amour, 125
Courtesy match, 66
Creation myths, 136–7
Crécy, battle of, 99
Culture, play-element of, 46
,, , modern, bastardisation of, 205
Cuzzoni, 163

Daedalus, 170
Danaids, 83
Dance, 164–5, 166
Dante, 179
Davy, 61, 76
de Jong, de Josselin, 122, 123
de Jouvenel, Henri, 164
Deussen, Paul, 106
de Vries, 69
Diagoge, 160–1
Dialogue, forms, 113
,, , *see also* Plato
Dice-playing, 57
Diderot, 191
Dike, 80, 94
Dilemma, 112
Dio Chrysostom, 153
Diogenes, 148
Dionysia, and drama, 144–5
Disfida di Barletta, 89
Disinterestedness of play, 9
Display, 13
Disputations, theological, 112, 114
Doodling, 168
Drama, 5, 14, 144–5
Dress, *see* Costume
Dressing up, 13
Drinking contests, 73
Dromenon, 14
Drumming-match, 85
Dualism, of social communities, 53
,, , sexual, 54
Duel, judicial, 93
,, , private, 94
Dutch, words for "play" in, *see* Germanic languages
Duyvendak, Prof., 32

"Earnest", as opposite of "play", 44
Economic factor in history, 192
Eddas, 69, 83, 109–10, 113, 120, 130, 131, 134–5, 137, 143
Egyptian religion, 26
Ehrenberg, Victor, 72, 74–5, 82
Electioneering, 207
Eloquence, Parliamentary, 207
Empedocles, 116, 117–18, 127, 138
Enemy, the, 209
England, as cradle of modern sport, 197

English, words for "play" in, *see* Germanic languages
Erasmus, 6, 156, 181
Erotic use of word "play", 43
Eskimo, 85–6, 125
Esotericism and art, 202–3
Essence of play, 2
Euripides, 145
Euthydemos, 148
Exaggeration, 143
Exercise, bodily, and culture, 196
Exoticism, and moderns, 26

Faguet, Emile, 142
Fashions, in dress, 193–4
Fate, 79
Faustina, 163
Festivals, 21 f.
Feudalism, and aristocratic contest, 102
Florence, 172
Folly, 6
Fontenelle, 187
Francis, St., and Poverty, 139
Fraud, 52
Frederick the Great, 163
Frederick II, Emperor, 114–15
Freedom, 7–8
Freya, 52
Friend-foe principle, 209
Frobenius, L., 15 ff., 20, 24, 46
Fun, element in play, 3
„ , and sacred rites, 22
Function of play, definitions, 2, 28

Gaber, 70
Gage, 50–1
Gaimar, Geoffroi, 70
Games, Hellenic, 49, 73
„ , organised, 196
„ , Roman, 177–8
Gelp, 70
"Gentlemen's Agreement", 217
Gerbert, 153–4
Germanic languages, words for "play" in, 36 ff., 43
Gierke, Otto, 82
Gift ritual, 62 ff.
Goethe, 78, 190–1
Gorgias, 146, 147, 151
Gothicism, 190
Granet, Marcel, 54–5, 59, 97, 124
Greece, artistic prize-contests, 171
„ , education in, 147
„ , legal contests in, 87
„ , slanging-matches in, 68
„ , war in, 96–7
Greek, words for "play" in, 29–31
„ culture, agonistic principle in, 63 ff., 71 ff.
Greeks, and myth, 130
Gregariousness, 205
Grimm, 42
Grotius, Hugo, 182–3
Guardini, Romano, 19
Guarino, 181
Guilds, mediaeval, 171
Gunther, 52
Gylfaginning, 131, 137
Gypsies, and potlatch, 61

Haberfeldtreiben, 86
Haikai, 124
Hampe, K., 115
Handel, 163
Harald Gormsson, 70
Harrison, Jane, 81
Hauptmann trial, 87
Haydn, 163
Hebrew, words for "play" in, 35
Held, G. J., 57–8, 61
Heraclitus, 116, 117, 211
Heralds, 71, 121
Heretics, 12
Herodotus, 96
Hesiod, 87, 117, 138
Heyne, M , 37
Hildegard of Bingen, 140
Hippias, 146
Holidays, 21
Homer, 64, 138
Honour, 50, 63 ff.
„ , and the duel, 94
„ contests, 66 ff.
Horace, 175
Horse-racing, Byzantine, 179
Humanism, play-element in, 181–2
„ , and body-culture, 196

Iambos, 68
Ibn Sabin, 114–15
Identification, 15
Images, 4, 14
Indigitamenta, 139
Industrial Revolution, 192
Inga fuka, 122–3
Instinct, play-, 1, 16
Insurance, life, 53
International relations, 208 ff.
Ireland, legends, 69
Iurgum, 87

Jaeger, Werner, 80, 87, 117, 147
Japan, 56, 127
,, , aristocratic culture in, 102
Japanese, words for "play" in, 34–5
Jason, 52
Java, 78
Jensen, A. E., 22–4
Joab, 41
Jocus, 36
John, Duke of Brabant, 99
Jongleur, 121
Joute de jactance, 66
Judge, costume of, 77
Judicial proceedings, play-element in, 76 ff.
Jul-feast, 69
Justice, archaic and modern, 79

Kalevala, 120, 124
Kant, 38
Kauravas, 52, 57
Kenningar, 134–5
Kerényi, K., 21–2
Kouretes, 48
Kula, 62–3
Kwakiutl, 23, 58

Language, 4
,, , poetic, 132–4
Latin, words for "play" in, 35
Laughter, 6
Law, international, 100–1, 208 ff.
,, , poetry and, 127
Lawsuit, as *Agon*, 76
Leisure, Greek, 147–8, 160–1
Lemaire, Jean, 181
Limitedness of play, 9–10
Littmann, 87
Liturgy, 19
Livy, 62
Loango, 23
Locker, G. W., 60
Logic, part of play in, 153
Lots, casting of, 79
Love-courts, 125
Love-play, 43
Loyalty, 104
Luck, 56
Ludus, the word, 35–6
Lusus, 29 *n.*
Lyric poetry, 142

Mahābhārata, 52, 57, 59, 83, 112
Malinowski, B., 23, 62, 66
Mamalekala, 59
Marett, R. R., 23
Marguerite de Navarre, 181
Marriage choice, and contest, 83
Marxism, 192
Masks, 26
Maunier, R., 61
Mauss, Marcel, 59, 61, 139
Meaux, 65
Melanesia, 59, 62
Menander, 112–13
Metaphor, 4, 136
Michael Scotus, 114
Middle Ages, play-element in, 179–80
Milindapañha, 112–13
Mimesis, 162
Mind, place of, in play, 3–4
Miracles, 170–1
Molinet, Jean, 181
Montaigne, 94
Mu'āqara, 59, 66–7
Muller, F., 98
Munificence, Roman, 178
Muses, 159 and *n.*, 165
Music, play-element in, 158 ff.
,, , eighteenth century, 187–8
Musical art, in Greece, 159–62
Musical instruments, "playing", 42

Musician, social status of, 163
Mycale, Battle of, 96
Mysteries, Greek, 26
Myth, 4–5
„ and poetry, 129 ff., 136 ff.

Nāgasena, 112–13
Names, puerilistic attitude to, 206
Neckel, G., 131
Neuhoff, Theodore, 186
Nguyen van Huyen, 56, 83, 124, 126
Nibelungenlied, 83
Nietzsche, 152
19th century, play-element in, 191–4
Nobility, and virtue, 64 ff.

Object of play, 50
Old Testament, personification in, 139
Olympic Games, 49
Opposite of play, words for, 44
Oracles, 79
Ordeal, 81–2, 91
Order, and play, 10
Ortega y Gasset, J., 55 *n.*
Ortric, 153–4
Ottoboni, Card., 163

Palamedes, 146
Panem et circenses, 177
Pantūns, 123
Parabasis, 144
Parliament, eloquence in, 207
Parrhasios, 171
Paulus Diaconus, 69
Pechuel-Loesche, 23
Pelops, 52
Penelope, 83
Periwig, 183–6
Persia, Shah of, 49
Personification, 136 ff.
„ , Roman, 174
Peter Damiani, 155
Philip of Burgundy, 62
Philology, 204
Philosophers, Greek, 115 ff.
Philosophy, development from riddle-game, 146 ff.
Phratria, 53
Pindar, 73
Places, sacred, 19–20
„ „ , lawcourts as, 77
Plastic arts, and play, 165 ff.
„ „ , and competition, 169–72
Plato, 18–19, 27, 37, 48, 87, 130, 143, 145, 147, 149–51, 159, 160, 162, 211–12
"Play", the word and its equivalents, 28 ff.
Play, an independent concept, 6
„ , non-moral character, 6
„ , definition, 2, 28
Play-ground, 10, 14
„ , *see also* Places, sacred
Play-language, Japanese, 34
Plutarch, 49 *n.*
Poetry, relation to play, 119 ff.
Poets, as possessors of knowledge, 120
„ , Renaissance, 181
Politics, modern, and play, 206 ff.
Polytechnos, 170
Pope, Alexander, 187
Potlatch, 58 ff., 82
Poverty, St. Francis and, 139
Pretending, 8, 22
Pretium, 51
Prize, 50–1
"Problems", 148
Prodicus, 146
Production, and art, 165
Prometheus, 146
Protagoras, 146, 147
Proverbs, Book of, 212
Prunktürme, 172
Psychoanalysis, 24, 141
Psychology, 204
Puerilism, 205–6
Pythagoras, 147

Question contests, 111 ff., 126
Quintilian, 153

Rabelais, 181
"Rags", 13
Rahder, Prof., 34
Ramayana, 83

Rana, 122–3
Rape of the Lock, 140, 187
"Real life", play and, 8
Records, 200
Renaissance, play-element at, 180–2
Repetition, 10
Representation, 13, 15, 161
Rhythm, 142, 159
Richelieu, 94
Richer, 153
Riddles, 105 ff.
,, and poetry, 133–5
Rig-veda, *see* Vedas
Ripperda, 186
Ritual, 5, 15, 17 ff.
,, and music, 158–9
,, and plastic arts, 167
,, , in Roman culture, 174–5
Rococo period, play-element in, 186–9
Roman culture, and agonistic principle, 74
,, ,, , play-elements of, 173 ff.
Romance languages, words for "play" in, 36, 42
Romans, and personification, 138–9
Romantic period, play-element in, 189–91
Rome, legal contests in, 87
Romulus and Remus, 65
Roscelinus, 155
Rousseau, 188
Rubens, 182
Rules of game, 11
Ruskin, 103
Rutilius Rufus, 88

Sacred performances, 14
Sages, question-contests of, 112
Salamis, Battle of, 96
Sannazaro, 181
Sanskrit, words for "play" in, 31–2, 43
Satire, 68
Saxo Grammaticus, 121
Scarlatti, 163
Schiller, 168
Schmitt, Carl, 209, 210
Scholasticism, 154, 156
Schröder, R., 93
Science, play-content of, 203–4
Scouting, 206
Secrecy, 12
Seizure, 16–17
Sensationalism, 205
Sentimentalism, 190–1
Seriousness and play, 5–6, 8
,, , and sacred rites, 22–3
,, , words for concept of, 44–5
Sexual act, and play, 43
Sexual display, in animals, 9
Shakespeare, 142
Shou-sin, 66
Significance of play, 1
Skáldskaparmál, 131, 135
Slanging-matches, 68 ff.
,, ,, and litigation, 84
Social life, modern, and play, 205
Society, play and, 46
Socrates, *see* Plato
Solitary and social play, 47
Sophisms, 148
Sophists, 87, 146 ff.
Sophron, 149
Spengler, 182
Spoil-sport, the, 11
Sports, modern, 196 ff.
Stakes, 50
State, the Roman, 175
Stoicism, 88, 151
Stock Exchange, 52
Stumpfl, R., 144
"Style", 186
Success, 49–50
Suso, Henry, 139
Sylvester II, *see* Gerbert

Tacitus, 57
Tension, 10–11, 47
Themistocles, 96
Theriomorphism, 141
Theseus, 52
Thucydides, 152
Thulr, 121

Tibet, 56
Tlinkit, 59, 60
Tolstoy, 57
Tongking, 56
Toradja, 108
Totemism, 53, 141
Tournament, 195–6
Trade, play-element in, 200
Tradition, play and, 10
Tragedy, Greek, 144–5
Trial by battle, 93
Triumphus, 177, 179
Trobriand Islands, 62, 66
Troubadours, 125
Tryggdamal, 128

Uhlenbeck, Prof., 33
Uncertainty, 47
Unity, mystic, 25
Universals, problem of, 156
University, mediaeval, 154, 156
Upanishads, 26, 107

Valéry, Paul, 11, 132
Van den Vondel, Joost, 182
Vates, 120, 146, 165
Vedas, 15, 26, 105–7, 136–7, 170
Versipellis, 141
Vico, Giambattista, 119
Victory, as representation of salvation, 56
„ , in war, 92
Villard de Honnecourt, 171
Virgil, 175
Virtue, 63
Visigoths, conversion of, 153
Voluntary character of play, 7

Wager-element, in litigation, 83–4
Wagner, 130, 163
Walpole, Horace, 189–90
War, agonistic aspect, 90, 95 ff.
„ , modern, 209
„ , motives, 90
„ , play-element in, 89 ff.
„ , Ruskin on, 103
„ , words for, 91 *n.*
Watteau, 185
Wedding, 83
Wensinck, Prof., 35
Wetan, 123
Wieland the Smith, 170
Wig, 183–6
„ , judge's, 77
Will, Divine, and fate, 79
William Rufus, 70
"Winning", 50
„ , and divine justice, 81–2
Winter festival, ancient Chinese, 54–5
Words used for "play" idea, 29

Yam stores, 66
Yanaka, 109
Yasnas, 114
Yin and *yang*, 54, 117

Zend-avesta, 113–14
Zeno of Elea, 115, 149
Zeus, 81
„ , metamorphoses of, 141